ASTROLOGY
AND THE AUTHENTIC SELF

ASTROLOGY

AND THE

AUTHENTIC SELF

*Integrating Traditional and
Modern Astrology to Uncover
the Essence of the Birth Chart*

DEMETRA GEORGE

IBIS PRESS
Lake Worth, FL

Published in 2008 by Ibis Press
An imprint of Nicolas-Hays, Inc.
P. O. Box 540206
Lake Worth, FL 33454-0206
www.ibispress.net

Distributed to the trade by
Red Wheel/Weiser, LLC
65 Parker St. • Ste. 7
Newburyport, MA 01950
www.redwheelweiser.com

ISBN 978-089254-149-2
Ebook ISBN 978-089254-563-6

Library of Congress Cataloging-in-Publication Data

George, Demetra, 1946-
 Astrology and the authentic self : integrating traditional and modern
astrology to uncover the essence of the birth chart / by Demetra George.
    p. cm.
Includes bibliographical references.
ISBN 978-0-89254-149-2 (alk. paper)
1. Astrology. 2. Horoscopes. 3. Self-realization. I. Title.
BF1711.G46 2008
133.5--dc22   2008040217.

Book design and production by Studio 31.
www.studio31.com

Printed in the United States of America (MG)

TABLE OF CONTENTS

ACKNOWLEDGMENTS

For all my students, clients, and friends who have taught me astrology through the telling of your life stories: Sunnyridge Mining Claim family; ongoing classes on the Oregon Coast, Motherpeace School, Eugene and Portland communities, Kepler College, Online College of Astrology, Arizona Institute of Astrology, Astrosynthesis, Zoe Ministries, pilgrims to Greece; and countless faces from astrological societies and schools on three continents, in dozens of countries, and in many states. Special thanks to Kenneth Johnson, Mark Marek, Scott Silverman, and Loren Sears who have given me feedback and encouragement in the development of this book, and to Bruce Schennum.

Appreciation to Donald Weiser, Yvonne Paglia, Laurel Trufant, and James Wasserman for their support and assistance in helping bring this book to publication.

And with gratitude for my teachers who have passed their knowledge on to me: the Oceanside Rosicrucian Fellowship, Dane Rudhyar, Virginia Dayan, Marc Robertson, Diana Stone, Joanne Wickenburg, Zipporah Dobyns, Maritha Pottenger, Tony Joseph, Robert Zoller, Alan White, Robert Schmidt, Lee Lehman, Brian Clark, David Calderwood, Malcolm Wilson, Dennis Harness, Tsering Everest, Chagdud Tulku, and Douglas Bloch who taught me how to write.

This book is dedicated to my grandson, Cedar Davis Frankfort.

Prologue:

Essence of Heartdrops

*A*strology *and the Authentic Self* is a guide to uncovering the essential meaning of the birth chart. It is written for practicing astrologers who want to give insights to clients about the kinds of activities their charts support that will help them live meaningful and purposeful lives. Personal worthiness arises from doing what we do well, and astrology provides a means to discover and affirm that individual potential. This discussion integrates the basic doctrines of traditional astrology, which provide a clear and analytical assessment of what is possible for individuals to realize in their lives, with the archetypal approach of modern astrology that aims for a healing of the psyche.

This book is for my students—those I have already encountered in my thirty-five years of teaching astrology and those I have yet to encounter through this work. All of your faces are before me as I write, and it is to you that I address these words. I hope to give you the essence of my heartdrops—a distillation of my insights into the most basic and fundamental principles involved in reading a chart for a client. My ultimate motivation in writing is to benefit others by pointing the way to understanding the essential meaning of their lives.

Astrology and the Authentic Self is not an exhaustive treatment of every doctrine in astrology, nor is it meant to be a complete teaching on the doctrines I discuss. Rather, it is a template for reaching directly into the heart of a chart, extracting that which is most essential about the life, and saying something meaningful within the context of a one-hour consultation. Our work as consulting astrologers is to read a chart and then convey, in the limited time allowed by the reading, the essence of the most important things of all that can possibly be said about it. We have to make every word count.

My intention is to suggest an utterly simple, clear, logical method for discerning the purpose of a life as indicated in the astrological birth chart. My model employs the methods and criteria of traditional astrology to provide a solid structural foundation for the insights of modern psychological approaches, which aim at healing the psyche.

Throughout the book, the key question is how to synthesize what you know as an astrologer with what you say as a counselor. As an astrologer, it is imperative that you make sound judgments concerning the topics and events that are likely to be realized in a client's life, as well as the motifs that are unlikely to unfold based on the astrological indications. The techniques of traditional astrology can help you in this analysis. But as a counselor, it is not appropriate for you to communicate information that may bring your clients to a state of despair and disappointment. Your job is to steer clients skillfully away from the activities whose outcomes are unlikely and instead guide them toward actions that can be realized as part of their life purpose, supported by the chart indicators. As a counselor, you don the mantle of healer.

The philosophical premise that underlies and informs all the practical techniques described in this book is that we live in a conscious cosmos that is permeated with a creative intelligence and an intrinsic order. Every life has a purpose within the larger whole. Astrology is one means by which to discern this purpose. The natal chart is constructed to facilitate the living out of that purpose, which is often the most natural and instinctive response of an individual and which brings a sense of meaning to everyday life. The natal chart describes the conditions of the karma or fate into which we are born, but it is our response to our fate that shapes our destiny. And in exceptional circumstances, grace does exist.

Introduction:

A Blueprint for the
Essential Meaning of the Birth Chart

Some people come to astrologers to obtain specific information about a particular question or topic; others come out of casual curiosity. But many come because they feel lost, confused, frightened, or alienated. They come because they are searching for something that will give meaning to their lives. They come with the hope that the astrologer can point them in the right direction.

The questions implicit in this quest reach to the heart of the inquiry concerning the nature of the cosmos and the place of human beings within it. Does each fleeting individual life have a transcendent purpose that is experienced as a personal calling? Is this calling part of a larger plan that speaks to the organic unity of the cosmos? If this personal calling is recognized, can it allow us to feel that our lives are authentic expressions of our real inner selves? And can it shape and inform all the ordinary activities in the progression of events from birth to death in a manner that imparts a sense of unique destiny and purposeful intentionality?

This book operates from the premise that we each have a purpose to our lives, that this purpose in some way enhances the well-being of others in the world, and that it is of value to each of us to recognize and express this purpose. Astrology can provide insights that illuminate this personal meaning. Although astrology can clearly describe your character, fate, and fortune, in its highest expression, it is a window into your soul that helps you live a life that expresses your authentic self for the greater good.

In *The Soul's Code*, James Hillman talks about, ". . . calling, about fate, about character, about innate image. Together they make up the 'acorn theory,' which holds that each person bears a uniqueness that asks to be lived and that is already present before it can be lived."

He argues that we each have a pattern that leads us toward a certain purpose and destiny and that this pattern exists from the moment of birth.[1] We will explore how astrology is one way by which to reveal this destiny.

Over 2000 years ago, the Greek philosopher Plato wrote in his cosmological treatise, the *Timaeus,* that the world was a living creature endowed with soul and intelligence.[2] It is only in such a world that astrology as a tool for self-realization is feasible. In a universe that is conscious and alive, everything emanates from the mind of the cosmos. The celestial bodies, as points of light, are the visible manifestations of that higher consciousness and, as such, act as intermediaries between the heavens and the Earth. They move and are moved by resonance in accordance with the emanations that pour forth from the divine mind. The configurations of the celestial bodies at the moment of birth reflect the pattern of thought that initiates the span of a human life and marks the goal toward which that life moves. The end result is implicit in the beginning moment, as the oak tree is in the acorn. To the extent that you recognize and express this innate purpose, despite the mixture of happiness and suffering that characterizes what it entails to be human, you acknowledge and fulfill the reason for your existence.

A question that clients frequently ask is: Based on my chart, what should I be doing with my life? The clarification of our innate authentic nature is the primary inquiry of this book.

In a contemporary astrology—with ten planets, four major and 12,000 minor asteroids, countless fixed stars, numerous minor aspects and patterns, hundreds of Arabic parts, a dizzying array of computer-driven options for timing techniques, a dozen different house systems, three competing zodiacs, and conflicting rulership systems—your challenge is to cut straight through the complexity and multiplicity to the heart of the matter and derive the essential meaning of the chart with simplicity and elegance. Your goal is to establish the basic framework of the life with a clear, lucid, well-defined structure, but one that allows for the creativity of self-expression, and then incorporate the multitude of other astrological factors that give texture, color, scent, sound, and taste to a personality born into time and acting with intention.

It is important to distinguish between three different kinds of natal-chart interpretation.

- A basic overview, which involves an assessment of the major themes of the chart, the interpretations of each planet, the areas of concentration of the natal energies, and the parts of the chart that are being activated at a specific time.
- A thorough delineation, which entails a synthesis of all the major and minor details, as well as various timing factors.
- A delineation given as an oral reading, within an hour or an hour and a half, that covers the most important points, as well as questions asked by the client. This is ultimately the work of a practicing astrologer.

A thorough understanding of a nativity can entail many pages of writing or many hours of spoken words; but in your actual interaction with a client, you can only convey a small fraction of what the chart indicates. Within the context of a consultation, you have only a short time in which to make a genuine connection between a chart and its owner. How do you reconcile all that you perceive as the necessary informing background of the chart with what you can actually communicate in a limited period of time?

This book sets forth a model of how to give one-hour consultations that include an analysis of both the natal chart and the current timing activations. What distinguishes this model from other teachings that discuss synthesis and delineation is that it makes the main focus of the reading more than simply a description of character or prognostications about the future, although it will contain elements of both these perspectives. The challenge for you as an astrologer is not to demonstrate your skill at making accurate statements and predictions, but rather to create a space in which clients can see clearly into their own authentic natures. This is the essential meaning of the birth chart.

Before you can receive the divine spark of inspiration and the gifts of illumination that astrology has to offer, you must have a solid structural foundation, tightly constructed and well anchored in what the Greeks called *techne*—the technical aspects of the craft. Without it, although you may give accurate and helpful readings, you will not be an astrologer. The Greek word *thema* (Θέμα) means "that which is placed or laid down." One of its cognates, *themeliakos*, translates as "a foundation or a building site." These words were used by Hellenistic astrologers to refer to a birth chart, as when they spoke of the *thema mundi*, the birth chart of the world. In the following pages, we will explore how to interpret the astrological code given at our birth as instructions for building a structure that can give shape and meaning to our lives.

It helps to have a plan. You must learn how to distinguish between what is significant and what is not, identify major themes quickly and easily, synthesize the chart in all its complexity, distill the chart down to what is essential, and finally communicate its meaning to your client in language that is accessible and in a tone that is both truthful and empowering. The model presented here will help you make order out of chaos and simplicity out of complexity using a systematic approach to assembling the various components of the birth chart. The question that directs our investigation is what kinds of activities the chart supports for the living of a meaningful life with purposeful intention.

Here is the blueprint for how we shall proceed.

THE BLUEPRINT

In Part I, Laying the Foundation, we'll review the fundamentals of astrological grammar. We will practice making simple one-sentence statements that integrate the meaning of a planet occupying a sign and a house, and ruling one or two other houses. Then I will introduce the teachings of traditional astrology that evaluate the condition of a planet. We will consider the perspective that, based on a planet's sign, house, and aspects, not all planets are equal in their capacity to bring about the matters they signify and to lead to positive outcomes for the individual. Thus, some people will be able to bring about certain topics in their lives and not have success with others. These kinds of situations call up a counselor's greatest skills in holding a healing environment for the possibility of unrealized hopes and dreams.

In Part II, Establishing the Framework, we'll discuss the core of the model. The ancient astrologers called the Sun, Moon, and Ascendant "the places of life." Traditionally, these three points were among the five candidates (along with the Lot of Fortune and the pre-natal lunation) for the determination of the length of life. As such, they can be said to represent the places in the chart that contain the vital essence of the life force whose outflow is directed toward the essential life purpose.

I propose that the positions and conditions of the Ascendant and its ruler, the Sun, and the Moon establish the basic framework of the chart in which the essential meaning of the life purpose can be discerned. The whole of the life's meaning is encapsulated in these four factors, in conjunction with the web of interrelationships of other planets and asteroids configured to these points. The procedure is very simple, as it focuses on the evaluation of just four primary factors. However, the rules for evaluating these factors are comprehensive and detailed.

In this model, the Sun signifies the intention of the soul and the content of the life purpose; the Moon represents the body that gives the soul life, the senses by which we perceive the world, and the practical means by which we actualize our purpose; the Ascendant and its ruler point to what motivates the soul to action and what topic steers the life on its course. By the end of Part II, you will be able to delineate and express the main theme of a chart by considering only the positions of the Sun, the Moon, and the Ascendant and its ruler.

In Part III, Building the Structure, you'll see how, once the main theme of a chart is established, all the other factors provide added detail to this central motif. The derivatives of the solar and lunar lights are the Lot of Fortune, the lunation phases, the lunar nodes, and eclipses that provide the secondary levels of meaning. Within this context, the other configurations formed by the planets (classical and modern), asteroids, fixed stars, and other sensitive points flesh out the structure by filling in the details and showing how aspect patterns tie the motifs together. This enables judgments about the topics of relationship, career, health, finances, etc.

This model gives you a hierarchy of timing techniques you can use to time the unfolding and realization of the life potential. It does not relegate discussion of timing to the end of the reading, but instead weaves it throughout the session when applicable to each component being examined. Part III concludes with a chapter that lays out the sequence and timing of a one-hour consultation, and gives suggestions about when to discuss and integrate the various factors that comprise the reading.

In Part IV, The Person Who Lives in the Chart, we'll discuss how to interact with a real live client—complete with real live issues— who enters your consulting room and is living out the meaning of his or her chart. How do you treat clients with respect and sensitivity given that your beliefs and values may differ from theirs? And how do you deal with the specter of a client's personal suffering staring you in the face? We will explore how to use myth to raise issues and draw parallels that otherwise might be too painful or humiliating to address, yet may fester within. We will look at ways to frame the wounded-healer archetype as a model for compassion and selfless service to others. The ancient astrologer was a mediator between heaven and Earth who provided a sacred container through which the wisdom of the divine realm was distributed to human beings, helping them to move forward with their decisions and lives.

We'll close with a discussion of how to move from the role of astrologer to the role of counselor. How do you bridge the gap between what you know about the chart through a deep and careful study of the various astrological factors, and what you actually say to a client who has come to you for guidance, often in a state of crisis? You must have a solid objective judgment of what a chart actually indicates before you begin to formulate what will be most helpful to your client. How can you be truthful, yet convey hope rather than despair? How do you acknowledge the truth of karma or fate, yet give redemptive meaning to suffering? In short, how can a vision of your clients' authentic selves inspire them to live out their life purposes and, in the process, facilitate personal healing that radiates outward to benefit others?

Now that you know the plan, let's take a look at the language you will use as you carry it out.

PART I
LAYING THE FOUNDATION

CHAPTER ONE

THE GRAMMAR OF ASTROLOGY

THE MAJOR COMPONENTS of the astrological language are planets, signs, houses, and aspects. To successfully delineate a chart, you must have a solid understanding of the meanings of these symbols and the capacity to combine and synthesize their significations. Because this knowledge is so important, we'll look first at how to combine the individual meanings of a planet occupying a sign and a house into a meaningful sentence. Then we'll consider how the expression of that planet is modified by its relationship to another planet.

If you already understand these principles, skim through this chapter and go on to chapter 2. If this is altogether new material for you, first familiarize yourself with the meanings of the basic symbols and the process of synthesizing the keywords of the astrological alphabet. There are many excellent books on this aspect of astrological interpretation. *Astrology for Yourself* by Douglas Bloch and Demetra George will give you hands-on practice creating these sentences and other delineations using a programmed text format and your own chart.

Learning to read a chart is like learning to read. Your first step in learning to read was to learn the letters of the alphabet; in astrology, you must memorize the glyphs of the planets and signs. If you have not mastered that, you won't make much progress when you look at a chart. Take time to become familiar with writing and recognizing these glyphs before going any further in this lesson. Make yourself a set of flash cards, carry them around in your pocket, and get those images firmly imprinted in your mind. In first grade, you probably had a composition book in which you wrote out the letters of the alphabet—line after line of repetitions. Do the same for the astrological glyphs. Refine your penmanship—even though we are in the computer age in which no one actually writes long-hand anymore. You'll gain a certain level of understanding of the meanings of the symbols by simply writing the glyphs repeatedly.

Once you learned to write the letters of alphabet, you began to associate them with their sounds and began to recognize words. In astrology, this corresponds to learning the individual significations of each planet, sign, and house. If you look at a planet in a particular sign and house and have no recollection of even one keyword for any one of the symbols, you cannot go any further in your studies. On the back of your flashcards, write out a few basic meanings for each planet, sign, and house. Go over them until those meanings come instantaneously to mind. As an educator, I am an advocate of a certain amount of rote learning and memorization. It is the quickest way to develop proficiency in some contexts.

Each of the three major components of the astrological language—signs, planets, and houses—has basic keywords associated with it. And each is located in a specific place in the astrological chart. These keywords combine to create astrological sentences that follow the conventions of grammatical structure. And these sentences, which express the significations of a planet in a sign and house, form meaningful statements when combined in the proper sequence.

The Structure of the Birth Chart

We will be using a sample chart of a man named Bill throughout the remainder of this book to illustrate the principles of interpretation set forth (see pages 22–23). An astrological birth chart, called a nativity by ancient astrologers, is a map of the positions of the planets as they surround a person at the exact time and place of birth. The person stands symbolically in the center of the circle. This astrological map is a representation of the three-dimensional celestial sphere that has been flattened to a two-dimensional plane, just as our geographical maps are flattened to depict a round Earth.

The horizontal line connecting the Ascendant and the Descendant is called the line of the horizon. It represents the place where the sky meets Earth at the moment of birth. The planets that are above the horizon are the planets that are visible in the sky when a person is born; the planets beneath the horizon are those that were on the other side of the Earth, and therefore not visible at the time of birth.

Zodiacal Signs

The first component of astrological interpretation is the zodiacal sign. There are twelve signs in the zodiac:

♈	Aries	♎	Libra
♉	Taurus	♏	Scorpio
♊	Gemini	♐	Sagittarius
♋	Cancer	♑	Capricorn
♌	Leo	♒	Aquarius
♍	Virgo	♓	Pisces

Most people are familiar with these signs as the various Sun signs, based upon the date and month of birth. However, each person is more than just his or her Sun sign. If you look at the outer wheel of the sample chart, you can see the symbols for each of the other signs as well. Everyone has all twelve signs somewhere in their chart.

From the perspective of modern astrology, the twelve signs represent the twelve universal psychological needs:

- ♈ Aries—the need to be independent and develop self-awareness
- ♉ Taurus—the need to be resourceful and get productive results
- ♊ Gemini—the need to communicate and make mental contact with others
- ♋ Cancer—the need to give and receive emotional warmth and security

November 17, 1939
8:30 am MST +7:00
Seneca, NE
42°N02`36" 100°W49`57"

Geocentric
Tropical
Whole Signs
True Node

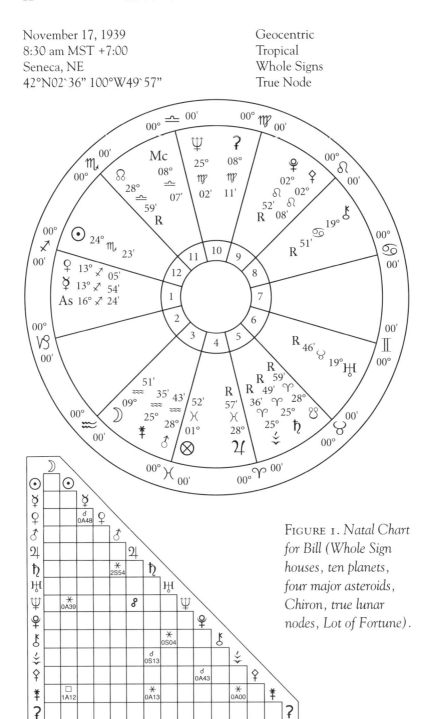

FIGURE 1. *Natal Chart for Bill (Whole Sign houses, ten planets, four major asteroids, Chiron, true lunar nodes, Lot of Fortune).*

Planet	Name	Sign	House
☽	Moon	♒	3
☉	Sun	♏	12
☿	Mercury	♐	1
♀	Venus	♐	1
♂	Mars	♒	3
♃	Jupiter	♓	4
♄	Saturn	♈	5
♅	Uranus	♉	6
♆	Neptune	♍	10
♇	Pluto	♌	9
⚷	Chiron	♋	8
⚶	Vesta	♈	5
⚴	Pallas	♌	9
⚵	Juno	♒	3
?	Ceres	♍	10
☊	North Node	♎	11
☋	South Node	♈	5
Asc.	Ascendent	♐	1
Mc	Midheaven	♎	11
⊗	Part of Fortune	♓	4

Sign	Name
♈	Aries
♉	Taurus
♊	Gemini
♋	Cancer
♌	Leo
♍	Virgo
♎	Libra
♏	Scorpio
♐	Sagittarius
♑	Capricorn
♒	Aquarius
♓	Pisces

Major Aspects

☌ Conjunction—0°00'
☍ Opposition—180°00'
△ Trine—120°00'
□ Square—90°00'
✶ Sextile—60°00'

- ♌ Leo—the need for creative expression and appreciation by others
- ♍ Virgo—the need to analyze, discriminate, and function efficiently
- ♎ Libra—the need to relate to others and create harmony and balance
- ♏ Scorpio—the need for deep involvements and intense transformations
- ♐ Sagittarius—the need to explore and expand mental and actual horizons
- ♑ Capricorn—the need for structure, organization, and discipline
- ♒ Aquarius—the need to innovate, be original, and create social change
- ♓ Pisces—the need to commit to a dream or ideal

Look at the sample chart, and you will see that all twelve signs are depicted around the outer wheel. Since everyone has all twelve signs somewhere in their chart, everyone also has all twelve of the needs somewhere in their lives.

The Wheel of Houses

There are twelve houses, just as there are twelve signs. They are named by their position (first house, second house, etc.) and are always in the same location in every chart. The houses represent twelve divisions or sectors of the zodiacal wheel, and they are usually, but not always, numbered in sequence.

If you stand in the northern hemisphere and look south, east is on your left. Stop reading for a moment and orient yourself in this manner. Now look at the sample natal chart and see it as a clock face. The first house is at nine o'clock. The Ascendant degree represents the place of sunrise on the eastern horizon. The sign that was coming up over the eastern horizon at the time of birth is called the rising sign of the chart and the exact degree of that sign is called the Ascendant, often abbreviated as Asc. or As. The Ascendant is determined by the exact time of birth, and is one of the most sensitive and important points in the chart. No matter what your Sun sign is, you can have any of the twelve signs as your rising sign because of the Earth's twenty-four-hour rotation on its axis. Approximately every two hours, a new sign rises over the horizon.

In the sample chart, the sign Sagittarius is the sign rising over the eastern horizon at the birth moment and it corresponds to the first house. The Ascendant (As.) is located at 16 degrees Sagittarius 24 minutes.

The Sun rises in the east and ascends toward the south. If you look at the upper portion of the sample chart you will see the symbol "MC."[1] This represents the Midheaven, the Sun's highest elevation in the sky around noon, depending on the latitude and the season. Then the Sun begins to descend and, when it reaches the western horizon, it sets. This point in the chart is marked by the Descendant, often abbreviated as Desc. The Descendant is not always depicted on the chart, depending upon the chart software used. Finally, the Sun sinks below the horizon and, around midnight, reaches what is called the IC (*Imum Coelii*). These four points—the Ascendant, Midheaven, Descendant, and IC—are orientated to the four directions and referred to as the four angles. They represent places of great strength within the chart.

Bill has Sagittarius rising on the Ascendant, Libra culminating at the Midheaven, Gemini setting on the Descendant, and Aries at the IC. Most chart printouts will have symbols for the Ascendant and Midheaven, but not the Descendant, which is always the same degree in the sign opposite the Ascendant (As.), or the IC, which is always the same degree in the sign opposite the Midheaven (MC).

Find the symbol for Bill's Sun again. Do you see that the Sun in the twelfth house has already risen above the horizon? Now look at Bill's time of birth—8:30 a.m., around an hour or so after dawn in the fall season of November.

Try this again with your own chart. Do you see how the placement of the Sun corresponds to the time of day at which you were born?

The four quarters are subdivided to create the twelve houses of the chart. There are various ways to divide this space, from which are derived different house systems like those of Placidus, Porphyry, Koch, and others. We will use the Whole Sign house system here. In the Whole Sign house system, the entirety of your rising sign, regardless of its degree, occupies the first house. Also note that, in the Whole Sign house system, the degrees of the MC and IC are not necessarily the beginnings of the tenth and fourth houses, as they are in quadrant house systems. We will discuss this more in the next chapter.

In Bill's chart, his rising sign is Sagittarius, so all of the degrees of Sagittarius occupy his whole first house. The sign that follows Sagittarius is Capricorn, and all of the degrees of Capricorn occupy his whole second house, all of the degrees of Aquarius occupy his third house, and so on.

The houses represent the various fields of life activities. As a whole, they represent all the different experiences that we encounter from birth to death. Each house has a number of different related significations, but the basic keywords for each house are as follows:

- First house—body, appearance, character
- Second house—personal money, possessions, livelihood
- Third house—siblings, relatives, short-distance travel, communications
- Fourth house—parents, home, land
- Fifth house—children, romance and pleasurable pursuits, creative arts
- Sixth house—health, injuries, job, daily routine and regimen, servants
- Seventh house—marriage and business partnerships
- Eighth house—death and benefits gained from death (inheritances), money received from others
- Ninth house—long-distance travel, higher education, religion, belief system
- Tenth house—profession, reputation, actions
- Eleventh house—friends, associates, group affiliations

- Twelfth house—sorrows, afflictions, enemies, karma, what is hidden, transcendence

Now you are ready to combine the meaning of a sign and a house. Remember, the signs represent the basic universal psychological needs and the houses represent the areas of life activities. A particular sign occupying a particular house points to the specific area of life activities in which a person experiences a particular need. We all have all twelve of the signs/needs somewhere in our lives, and this is where we are all similar. However, because of the time of day we were born—and therefore our rising sign and the sequence of signs in our houses—those needs come out in different areas of life activities for each of us. This is where we are all different.

> Bill has Gemini occupying his seventh house. Gemini is the need to communicate, and the seventh house represents one-to-one relationships—especially the "significant other." Bill has the need to talk, discuss, share information, and make mental connections with his partners in order to feel fulfilled in the relationship.
>
> Where do you have Gemini in your chart? What is the area of life in which you have a particular need to communicate?

Planets

The third factor in the astrological language is the planets. Look at the glyphs that appear within the various houses. These are the symbols of the planets, and each planet is notated with the exact degree and minute of the sign that it occupies. In the sample chart, the ☉ Sun is depicted by a circle with the dot in the center. It is placed in the twelfth house, and located at 24 degrees of Scorpio 23 minutes— or ☉ ♏ 24° 23'.

From the perspective of modern astrology, the planets represent the basic psychological functions or faculties common to all people. They can also be said to correspond to all the different parts of our personalities, each with its own persona and agenda telling us to do

or be something different. In the same way that the Sun is the center
of the solar system and all the planets revolve around it, the Sun in
the chart is the center or heart of our being and ultimately each of
the other planetary functions must be integrated with it before we
can make a decision or take an action.

The psychological functions of the planets are:

- ⊙ Sun—basic identity, will, and conscious purpose
- ☽ Moon—emotions, feelings, habitual responses
- ☿ Mercury—capacity to think, speak, learn, and reason
- ♀ Venus—capacity to attract what is loved and valued
- ♂ Mars—capacity to act and be assertive based on desire
- ♃ Jupiter—search for meaning, truth, and ethical values
- ♄ Saturn—capacity to create order, form, and discipline
- ♅ Uranus—unique individuality and urge for liberation
- ♆ Neptune—capacity to transcend the finite self through union
  with a larger whole
- ♇ Pluto—capacity to transform and renew

In addition to the planets, there are many asteroids and other minor
bodies that we will discuss later. The most frequently used of these
minor planets are Ceres, Pallas, Juno, Vesta, and Chiron. Some of
their symbols may appear in your chart printout.

- ? Ceres
- ⚴ Pallas
- ⚵ Juno
- ⚶ Vesta
- ⚷ Chiron

In the modern psychological model, the planets represent various
functions of the personality or various forces operating in the human
psyche. Each part of the personality operates in a certain manner
that is described by the sign in which it is placed, and it operates in
a different field of activities that is designated by its house position.
In a sense, the planet is the Who, the sign is the How, and the house
is the Where.

If the Sun is the symbol of your identity and purpose, and it is in the sign of Aries, you will operate primarily in an independent manner; if it is in Taurus, in a resourceful manner; in Gemini, in a communicative manner. If that Aries Sun is in your second house, you will be geared toward achieving financial independence; if it is located in your seventh house, you will seek independence in relationships; if it is located in your tenth house, you will seek independence in your profession. The simple sentence that expresses the Sun in Aries in the second house might read: Your basic purpose is to develop independence in generating the resources you need to secure your livelihood.

You must take the interpretation of a planet one step further by integrating the meaning of the house that it rules. Thus, in our example, you must also look to the house that the Sun rules, which will be the house that is occupied by Leo. (In chapter 2, we will discuss planetary rulership of signs.) If Leo occupies your ninth house (higher education), it will be through your educational endeavors that your financial independence is realized. Or if Leo occupies your eleventh house, friends and group affiliations will play a central role in how you earn your money. In this example, with Aries in your second house, Leo occupies your sixth house, and the topic of health and daily regimen may be an important factor in your money-making activities.

Bill's Sun is in Scorpio in the twelfth house. Combining the meanings for Scorpio and the twelfth house with the Sun, we can say that part of Bill's basic Sun purpose is for intense involvements and deep transformations in his quest for transcendence or penetration of the mysteries of life. We can also posit that, through experiences of suffering, alienation, and loss, he will be brought to his higher purpose in life. Because Leo occupies the ninth house, his explorations in higher education and spirituality play a central role in the realization of his life purpose.

Aspects

The last major component of astrological interpretation is the aspects. Aspects refer to the arc of separation or angular distance between the planets. When planets are located at a certain distance from one another, they are connected in some intrinsic manner that is either harmonious or challenging. Different astrologers use different orbs (ranges of degrees from exactitude) for measuring aspects. Aspects describe the ways in which planets can influence one another and modify each other's expression.

Sometimes you will see aspects depicted in the center of the chart wheel as lines connecting the various planets, with the glyphs for the aspects inserted upon the lines. At other times, you may see an aspect grid on one of the bottom corners of the chart printout, listing the planets horizontally and vertically, with the glyph of the aspect that connects them.

Planets, as the various functions of the psyche, can interact in harmonious, neutral, or antagonistic ways with other planets, just as we get along with some people, are neutral toward some, and have ongoing conflict with others. This condition of sympathies and antipathies exists within each of us as well. Traditional astrology recognizes five different aspects—the conjunction, the sextile, the square, the trine, and the opposition. These five aspects depict the ease or difficulty with which the planets interact.

- ☌ Conjunctions occur when planets occupy the same sign or are in close proximity in adjacent signs. The conjunction represents an intermingling of the natures of the two planets.
- ✶ Sextiles occur when planets are approximately 60 degrees apart. The sextile indicates that there is a mildly harmonious and sympathetic relationship between the planets involved.
- □ Squares occur when planets are approximately 90 degrees apart. The square points to a tense or challenging interaction between the planets involved.
- △ Trines occur when planets are approximately 120 degrees apart. The trine indicates that there is an extremely harmonious and sympathetic relationship between the planets involved.

- ☍ Oppositions occur when planets are approximately 180 degrees apart. The opposition suggests that there is an adversarial and antagonistic relationship between the planets involved.

The modern semi-sextile ⚹ (planets approximately 30 degrees apart) and the modern quincunx/inconjunct ⚻ (planets approximately 150 degrees apart), while used today, were not considered aspects by ancient astrologers.

Different astrologers use different sets of orbs (ranges) in order to define the exact distances at which planets may be connected in all of the above relationships. The orbs most commonly used by modern astrologers are:

- Conjunction—10 degrees on either side of exactitude at 0 degrees
- Sextile—6 degrees on either side of exactitude at 60 degrees
- Square—8 degrees on either side of exactitude at 90 degrees
- Trine—8 degrees on either side of exactitude at 120 degrees
- Opposition—10 degrees on either side of exactitude at 180 degrees

The interpretation of aspects on the simplest level requires a complex sentence that is formed by two individual sentences linked by a verb. In the language of astrology, this consists of one sentence for each planet in its own sign and house, joined by a verb that describes the nature of the relationship.

If your second-house Sun in Aries is also square to your Moon in Cancer in your fifth house, the complex sentence might read: Your basic purpose to develop independence in generating the resources you need to secure your livelihood creates ongoing tension with your emotional need to dedicate yourself to nurturing your children.[2]

The doctrine concerning aspects and orbs has gone through many changes since its inception in the Hellenistic astrology of the first few centuries C.E., and we will trace this progression in a later chapter.

> A simple interpretation of the Sun in Scorpio in the twelfth house square to Mars in Aquarius in the third house in Bill's chart might read: Bill's basic purpose (Sun) for intense involvements and deep transformations (Scorpio) in the quest for transcendence (twelfth house) is at cross-purposes (square) with his desire to assertively fight (Mars) for just and humanitarian motivations (Aquarius) through the use of media, speech, and modes of communications (third house).

A planet often has more than one aspect to another planet, and the development of its various interactions generates a paragraph. Paragraphs are also created by the evaluation of a planet's condition and by taking into account the house it rules and its dispositor, the planet that rules the sign in which a planet is located. These additional factors modify its meaning and expression in a particular chart in complex and subtle ways. And the timing with which certain planetary patterns become activated during the course of a life generates even more paragraphs.

However, just as you can write a whole collection of paragraphs, but still not have a coherent paper, you can generate a whole collection of astrological sentences without creating a synthesis of the chart as a whole. What you need is a unifying theme that links all of the individual statements into a coherent analysis. In Part II, we'll look at simple methods of astrological delineation that can help you discern the unity of a chart from a multiplicity of factors and variations.

The art of astrology entails more than just the creation of these simple and complex sentences describing how and where each planet expresses itself in accordance with its sign, house, and aspects. It also entails a realization that planets vary in their capacity to accomplish the matters they represent, depending on their sign, house, and aspects. This is called the determination of a planet's condition. While this was the fundamental starting point for traditional astrology, it has not been widely discussed in contemporary astrological literature. In the next chapter, you will learn how to evaluate the relative strength and weakness of each planet.

STUDY GUIDELINES

- Obtain the birth data of someone you know well and set up a chart you can use as a practice chart. Choose someone who is open to the idea and willing to discuss his or her chart with you and give you feedback.
- To test your readiness to continue, write out the following simple sentences about the chart you have chosen.
- Create twelve sentences that blend the meaning of each sign with the house it occupies.
- Create ten sentences, one for each planet, that synthesize the meaning of the planet with the sign and house it occupies, as well as the house or houses it rules.
- Determine three different aspects between different sets of planets. Create three sentences, one for each aspect, that factor the sign and house for each planet involved and the nature of the relationship between them, as determined by the aspect that links them. For now, use the orbs and manner of determining aspects with which you are familiar. The purpose of this exercise is to assess your interpretive skills.
- If you are not thoroughly familiar with the basic meaning of the individual components of the astrological alphabet and how to create simple sentences using those terms, work through *Astrology For Yourself* (Bloch and George) before going on to the next chapter. Or try some of the other practical guides for beginning astrologers that are given in the bibliography.

CHAPTER TWO

DETERMINING PLANETARY CONDITION

One of the cornerstones of traditional astrology is the importance of assessing the condition of a planet before making any kind of interpretation of its meaning—either in the natal chart or by any timing technique. The classical texts of Hellenistic, Medieval, Renaissance, and Indian (Vedic) astrologers are filled with voluminous teachings on the subject of planetary condition, with elaborate rules, formulas, and details aimed at gaining a thorough understanding of both the effectiveness of each planet to bring about the matters it signifies and its capacity to provide the circumstances for positive outcomes in life.

For the first 2000 years of the Western astrological tradition, the doctrines concerning planetary condition were an integral component of chart analysis. It is only with the beginning of the 20th century that they have fallen out of use. Now, in the first decade of the 21st, these first principles of astrological analysis are being reintroduced into the community as a result of the translation of ancient Greek and Latin astrological texts into English. Here, we'll look at ways these fundamental teachings can be utilized by modern practitioners. This simplified analysis of planetary condition will become an integral part of how you delineate a chart, and will prepare you for further studies in traditional astrology if you want to pursue them.[1]

The preliminary analysis of each planet is based on an understanding that not all planets are equal in their capacity to bring about positive outcomes for the individual—good health, prosperity, happiness, opportunities, success, and well-being, as opposed to poor health, poverty, suffering, and failure. The notion that some planets are better than others in any particular chart due to their condition stands in stark contrast to the modern psychological model in which every planet is equal in its capacity to bring about the matters it represents—albeit in different ways.

In the following discussion concerning the determination of planetary condition, we will set aside two accepted doctrines of modern astrology: the twelve-letter alphabet and the modern rulership system. The twelve-letter alphabet proposes that planets, signs, and houses are fundamentally the same and interchangeable. This book assumes planets, signs, and houses each have distinct meanings and cannot be interchanged. The modern rulership system designates Uranus, Neptune, and Pluto as rulers of the signs Aquarius, Pisces, and Scorpio, respectively. This book uses the traditional assignments whereby Saturn, Jupiter, and Mars rule these signs. The outer planets and the asteroids are not used as rulers of signs.

Modern astrology is ambivalent about addressing problematic conditions indicated by chart factors. These factors are seen as lessons for further growth—if they are acknowledged at all. In Part IV, we'll look at the problem of suffering as it is depicted in the birth chart and consider ways to help clients find redemptive value in the painful experiences of their lives. However, it is important to recognize that bad things happen to people and that certain astrological factors can and do indicate these misfortunes.

In previous eras, astrologers realized that some charts or planets were weak and difficult, and that the owners of these charts or planets were less likely to manifest certain parts of their lives, and more likely to encounter unhappiness, loss, and misfortune. This may seem like an overly fatalistic view, negating the value of many self-help techniques like positive thinking, creative visualization, and therapeutic processes that develop greater self-awareness and the power of free will to co-shape our lives. However, the reality is that, for many people, despite their best efforts and excellent aspirations, life continues to be filled with loneliness, unrealized potential, suffering, and failure. From an astrological perspective, the poor condition of certain planets in the chart can indicate that these individuals may have an extremely difficult time bringing about certain matters in ways that will benefit them. A planet's condition does not predispose a person to acting in good or bad ways—moral behavior remains in the sphere of free will; what it indicates is the presentation of fortunate or difficult life events and the likely outcomes of those situations.

Vedic and Tibetan astrology offer remedial measures to offset these difficulties—the healing power of gemstones, mantras, amulets, and good actions. Prayer, meditation, and spiritual practice can also mitigate limiting belief patterns or toxic emotional habits. Western magical tradition offers ceremonial rituals and talismans that can avert negative energies and attract positive ones. And modern psychotherapy reaches into the subconscious to surface and release the memories of forgotten traumas that hold us back from the realization of our full potential. However, before you, as an astrological counselor, can guide clients into these and alternative ways of consciously shaping their futures, you must be able to recognize when something is a problem in the chart and if, in fact, anything can be done about it.

This raises a philosophical issue. For, while each life may have a purpose, not every person has the same ability or resources to fulfill that purpose. Offering counseling around this disparity and the unlikelihood of certain kinds of events such as marriage or children being supported by the chart—whether through karma, fate, God's will, bad luck, or impersonal chance—is an issue we'll address later in the book. For now, let's consider two questions we can ask about each planet:

- To what extent is a planet effective in bringing about the matters it signifies?
- To what extent will a planet's significations result in fortunate outcomes in the life of the individual?

The ways in which each planet is modified based upon its sign, house, aspects, and relationship to the Sun determine its capacity to be effective and favorable in a chart. It may seem at times that you are being overly harsh and dogmatic in assessing the condition of a planet. The reason for this is that, as an astrologer, you want to be clear about just what you are seeing and the actual strengths and weaknesses present. However, as a counselor, it is advisable to temper your statements, unless you are sure that your client wants the hard, cold truth, no matter what it is. In practice, you will use the information gained from this preliminary analysis to inform and steer clients into areas of life where their efforts are more likely to produce successful and positive outcomes. For the sake of thoroughness, I will mention what I am omitting from this discussion as well as elaborate upon what I have decided to include.

PLANETS

In this analysis, we will distinguish between the seven visible planets (Sun, Moon, Mercury, Venus, Mars, Jupiter, and Saturn), the outer planets (Uranus, Neptune, and Pluto—the dwarf planet), and the major and minor asteroids. We will use them all, but in different ways.

The seven visible planets are the rulers of signs and thus of the houses occupied by those signs. The houses have topical meanings—finances, health, marriage, children, profession—and these seven planets have the responsibility for rendering judgment and bringing about the affairs associated with each of the twelve houses. It is only to these seven visible planets that we will apply all the rules of planetary condition. We will apply some of the rules to the remaining planets where applicable.

Although we will incorporate the outer planets in our interpretation of the meaning of the chart, we will not credit them with rendering judgment or bringing about events associated with the topics designated by the houses, because we are not using them as rulers of signs. However, to the extent that they occupy a house, the outer planets influence the matters of that house; and to the extent that they are configured (aspect) to planets, they influence the actions of that planet. The outer planets also have profound effects on the life, as evidenced by transits and progressions to them and by them.

Neither the asteroids nor the other minor planets rule signs, but like the outer planets, they influence the houses they occupy. Their strongest effect is as a shaping influence over the planets that they conjoin or oppose. This is where you will most often use the mythological motifs of the deities that share the same names as the minor bodies (see chapter 9). However, like the outer planets, they are not subject to most of the rules of planetary condition.

The seven visible planets can be classified into three categories: gender, benefic or malefic nature, and sect. The gender conditions will not be included in this discussion, nor will all the details of sect rejoicing conditions, although these terms are defined in the Glossary.

The planets can be classified according to their benefic or malefic natures in recognition that there is both good and bad in the world and that there exist both favorable and unfavorable conditions that influence the life force.

The benefic planets, Venus and Jupiter, are said to produce good for the individual according to both their general significations and the particular topics they rule in any given chart in accordance with the house or houses occupied by the sign they rule.[2] The Sun and usually the Moon are also generally considered to be of a beneficial nature.

The malefic planets, Mars and Saturn, produce difficulties in the life. Mercury can be either malefic or benefic, depending on the preponderance of malefic or benefic planets with which it is configured. This is not an absolute determination, as certain factors can modify the basically beneficial nature of Venus and Jupiter and the natural malefic tendencies of Mars and Saturn. Thus the benefic and malefic planets can all get better or worse, depending on their overall condition, and thus be more or less helpful to the contribution of favorable outcomes for the topics they signify and rule.

Claudius Ptolemy attempted to explain this difference in his assignment of the qualities of hot and cold, and wet and dry, to each planet, following the principles set forth in Aristotle's natural philosophy.[3] He deemed the benefic planets, Venus and Jupiter, as having a moist and warm nature, qualities conducive to the growth of living things. He classified the malefic planets, Mars and Saturn, as having a dry and cold nature—qualities that are destructive to the life force. Think about planting a seed; warmth and moisture will enable it to grow, while excessive cold and lack of water will deter its growth. And consider how the Greeks viewed their gods. Ares (Mars) had a lust for bloodshed and battle and was hated by everyone; Aphrodite (Venus), embodiment of beauty, was loved and desired by all.

For our purposes, we will note if a planet is a natural benefic or malefic as a baseline for whether it does good or bad, and then determine to what extent that inherent good or bad is made better or worse by other factors. We will also use this classification when we look at aspects to determine if the outcome a particular planet's significations is facilitated or hindered by its configuration with Venus, Jupiter, Mars, or Saturn.

The third classification of planets, sect (literally, "faction" in Greek), was one of the first and most important considerations of ancient astrologers, although it has been lost to modern practice. Sect considerations recognize the primacy of the Sun and Moon as the two luminaries. A chart is said to be diurnal (day) if the Sun is above the horizon (as defined by the degree of the Ascendant/Descendant axis); it is said to be nocturnal (night) if the Sun is beneath the horizon. If the chart is diurnal, the Sun is the sect leader, and the planets that belong to the sect in favor are Jupiter, Saturn, and Mercury (if Mercury is a morning star, i.e., rising before the Sun). If the chart is nocturnal, the Moon is the sect leader, and the planets that belong to the sect in favor are Venus, Mars, and Mercury (if Mercury is an evening star, i.e., rising after the Sun).[4] Note that each sect is led by a luminary and contains both one benefic and one malefic planet. Mercury tips the balance in favor of one sect or the other.

The two sects, diurnal and nocturnal, can be likened to two political factions. The planets that belong to the sect in favor generally work on behalf of the individual, and their actions are generally favorable to guiding the life in the right direction. The planets that do not belong to the sect in favor either lead the individual off course or in directions that are not in the individual's best interests. The planets of the sect in favor are charged with the authority to run the life and their actions tend toward favorable outcomes. But these planets may or may not be well equipped to handle the task, depending on their overall condition in the chart.

There are certain "rejoicing" conditions pertaining to sect that enhance a planet's capacity to act in accordance with its nature in facilitating positive outcomes, but we won't consider these here. We will note the sect of the chart, which planets belong to the sect in favor and how this predisposes them to bring about more favorable outcomes to the individual, and which planets do not belong to the sect in favor and how they are less able to work for the best interests of the individual. Note that, when a benefic planet does not belong to the sect in favor, while its actions may be pleasant and enjoyable, those activities may lead the person off course (for example, partying through college and thus not graduating).

> Bill's chart is diurnal because the Sun is above the horizon. Thus the Sun is the sect leader, and its sect mates, Saturn and Jupiter, have the edge in terms of their authority to bring about success-ful outcomes. The nocturnal planets—the Moon, Venus, Mars, and Mercury (because it is an evening star)—do not belong to the sect in favor and thus their actions are at some disadvantage to the owner of the chart.

Zodiacal Sign Rulerships

Modern astrology approaches the delineation of planets in signs as the twelve various manners in which planets operate, and psycho-logical interpretation adds that the signs describe the twelve basic needs of the psyche. For example, a person with the Moon in Tau-rus may have an emotional need for stability and financial security, while appreciating the finer things in life. Someone with the Moon in Scorpio may have a powerful and penetrating emotional nature that tends toward secrecy and keeping feelings internalized. While all this may be true on the level of the personality and psyche, the modern approach does not take into account that someone with the Moon in Taurus may have a better chance of achieving financial security and high status with reference to the houses that the Moon both occupies and rules, or that someone with the Moon in Scorpio may have a more difficult time getting his or her emotional needs respected and understood and have difficulty manifesting the signifi-cations of the houses the Moon occupies and rules.

The notion that planets in each of the zodiacal signs are not equal in their capacity to indicate favorable life circumstances is politically incorrect in modern practice, but it is a fundamental operating principle in traditional astrology. It is the signs themselves that determine the resources that each planet has to accomplish its intentions, and some signs are more hospitable to certain planets than others.

This leads us to the doctrine of planetary rulership. Hellenistic and Medieval astrologers utilized four (and sometimes five) kinds of rulership: domicile, exaltation, trigon/triplicity, bound/term, and decan/face. Modern astrology retains knowledge of rulership by domicile and exaltation (for example, the Moon is the ruler of Cancer, or Saturn is exalted in Libra), but has lost the usage of rulership by trigon, bound, and decan. Hellenistic astrologers looked at each of these categories as equally important, but used them for different kinds of inquiries. Medieval astrologers did not differentiate between the various uses of each type of rulership, but instead ranked them in decreasing order of importance to determine the *almuten* or "victor." Here, we will investigate how to work with domicile and exaltation rulerships, but leave the others for more specialized studies.[5]

In general, when a planet occupies a sign in which it has rulership by domicile, it is especially powerful because it has the necessary resources and self-sufficiency to accomplish its significations. When a planet occupies a sign in which it is exalted, it will achieve honor, respect, and recognition with regard to its significations. When a planet occupies a sign in which it is in detriment (opposite its rulership sign) or fall (opposite its exaltation sign), it is less powerful because it is impoverished or not respected, and thus subdued in its capacity to be effective. Table 1 on page 42 gives the domicile, detriment, exaltation, and fall for each of the planets.

How were the planets assigned to the various signs in which they have rulership? The common assumption is that this was done according to the principle of affinity—that planets are similar to the signs they rule. However, the original reasoning was based on the geometrical order of the distances of the planets from the Sun and their speeds. The Hellenistic texts refer frequently to the *thema mundi*, the chart of the creation of the world. Firmicus Maternus tells us that this was a teaching device, not an actual chart, first taught by the mythic sage Hermes Trismegistus to illustrate the fundamental

Table 1. Rulerships and Exaltations

Planet	Domicile	Detriment	Exaltation	Fall
☉ Sun	♌ Leo	♒ Aquarius	♈ Aries	♎ Libra
☽ Moon	♋ Cancer	♑ Capricorn	♉ Taurus	♏ Scorpio
☿ Mercury	♊ Gemini & ♍ Virgo	♐ Sagittarius & ♓ Pisces	♍ Virgo	♓ Pisces
♀ Venus	♉ Taurus & ♎ Libra	♏ Scorpio & ♈ Aries	♓ Pisces	♍ Virgo
♂ Mars	♈ Aries & ♏ Scorpio	♉ Taurus & ♎ Libra	♑ Capricorn	♋ Cancer
♃ Jupiter	♐ Sagittarius & ♓ Pisces	♊ Gemini & ♍ Virgo	♋ Cancer	♑ Capricorn
♄ Saturn	♑ Capricorn & ♒ Aquarius	♋ Cancer & ♌ Leo	♎ Libra	♈ Aries

concepts of the astrological system.[6] This chart had Cancer rising, reflecting its Egyptian origins. In Egyptian tradition, the beginning of the new year (and hence also the birth day of the world) was timed to the heliacal rising of the star Sirius that took place in the summertime and heralded the rising of the Nile. In a summer chart, when the Sun is in Leo, the sign Cancer rises in the pre-dawn hours when the heliacal rising of stars or planets can be seen.

Thus the Sun was placed in Leo, and the Moon, the other luminary, was placed in Cancer. Both of the lights occupied the signs in which there were the most hours of daylight. Then, according to legend, Mercury, which followed the Sun in speed, had its dwelling in Virgo, the sign following Leo; then Venus in the next sign of Libra, Mars in Scorpio, Jupiter in Sagittarius, and Saturn in Capricorn. Further elaboration on this seminal chart had the same order of the planets fanning out from the Moon in Cancer in a clockwise direction, with Mercury in Gemini, Venus in Taurus, Mars in Aries, Jupiter in Pisces, and Saturn in Aquarius, forming a mirror image of the counterclockwise arrangement from the Sun. Each planet, except the Sun and Moon, resided in two signs, one masculine and one feminine. It was thought that the positions the planets occupied

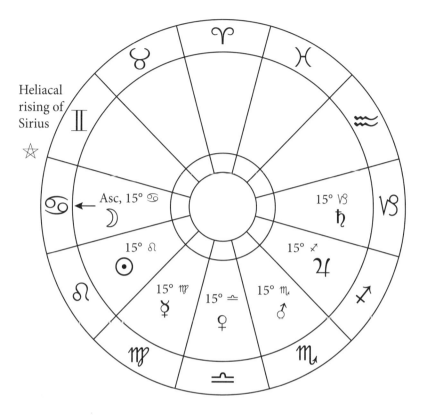

FIGURE 2. Thema mundi, *chart of the creation of the world.*

at the birth of the world were the signs in which they had the greatest power.

As you can see, the traditional assignments of planets as ruling certain signs were based on a geometric rationale of planetary distances and speeds. When the modern outer planets Uranus, Neptune, and Pluto were discovered, they were arbitrarily given certain signs to rule, displacing the traditional rulers of those signs. The reasoning behind these new rulerships is not altogether clear. Some astrologers attempt an explanation in terms of affinities in that the planets are *like* the signs. However, the modern rulerships do not conform to the inherent underlying order and symmetry that exists in the traditional system.

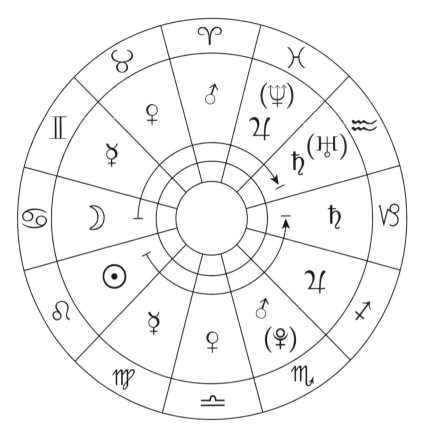

Figure 3. *Traditional and modern rulerships.*

Each sign was the domicile of a certain planet—the word used in ancient Greek was *oikos*, meaning "dwelling or home"—and the planet was said to be the master of the home, the manager of the household affairs. The relationship between a planet and its domicile can be likened to that of a lord or lady to an estate. This system of domicile lords mirrored the very important sanctity of the guest-host relationship in the ancient world—a relationship that fell under the auspices of Zeus himself.

If, at the birth, a planet is posited in its own domicile (for example, Mercury in Gemini or the Sun in Leo), it is as if it were at home, where it has great stability and is in command of all of its own resources to care for its needs and accomplish its intentions. We say that it has great power because it has the wherewithal—money, connections, education, credentials, opportunities—to bring about whatever it signifies. When a planet is in its detriment (the sign opposite its domicile), the logical assumption is that it is bereft of its own resources, needy, and thus unable to sustain and support the matters it represents. However, the ancient texts do not explicitly single out the difficulties of a planet in detriment, nor do the classical Vedic texts.

In most birth charts, however, a planet occupies another's domicile (for example, Mercury in Scorpio). In this case, Mercury is dependent upon the domicile lord of the sign Scorpio, which is Mars, to provide for its needs, in the same way that a guest in someone else's home is dependent upon the host to provide food and shelter. The host planet, (modern "dispositor"), depending upon its own condition, may or may not have the means or willingness to provide adequately for its guest. Thus we begin to see the important role that the domicile lord/dispositor of a planet plays in evaluating its condition and its interpretation.

The correlate to this is that each planetary lord or lady is responsible for providing for any planet that happens to occupy its own domicile. For example, no matter what sign the Moon is in in any given chart, as the domicile lady of Cancer, her duty as hostess is to welcome and provide for any planet that is posited in Cancer out of her own basket of significations in accordance with her sign and house position in that chart. This is the meaning behind the astrological term "reception," which describes how the host welcomes or receives a guest into the home—we say that the Moon "receives" Venus in Cancer. Mutual reception occurs when two planets occupy each other's domiciles (Jupiter in Taurus and Venus in Sagittarius). This is considered to benefit each planet, as they exchange places. Trading homes with someone, while not as good as being in your own home, certainly leaves you with more control over your circumstances than being a guest.

When a planet occupies a sign in which it is exalted, it is held in high esteem and treated as a favored guest. When a planet occupies the sign opposite its exaltation sign, it is said to be depressed or in its fall, being cast down and in disrepute. The rationale behind the

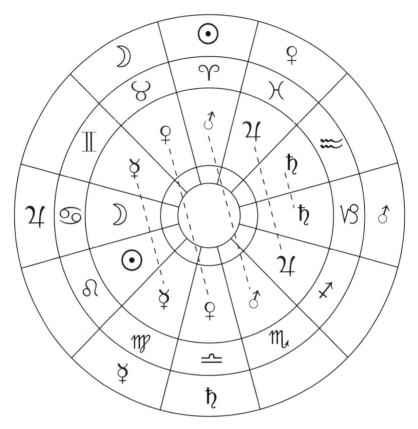

Figure 4. *Planetary domiciles and exaltations.*
The inner circle depicts the planets in their domicile signs.
The outer circle depicts the planets in their exaltation signs.

assignments of planets to exaltation signs is not yet completely clear, but the signs of a planet's exaltation are either trine (for diurnal planets) or sextile (for nocturnal planets) to one of the signs of their domiciles. Again, this hints at an underlying geometric order informing the assignment of planetary exaltation rulerships of signs.

Thus, when evaluating the condition of a planet according to its sign, determine whether or not it occupies its own domicile. If it does, this is a fortunate condition that denotes power and the potential for accomplishing its significations, both general and particular. If it doesn't, then determine the planet's domicile lord and the posi-

tion and condition of that planet to evaluate the kind and amount
of assistance it can expect to enable its events to manifest. When a
planet is in a sign of its exaltation, it bodes well for success through
recognition and honor; when a planet is in a sign of its fall, the
individual is less likely to receive honor and recognition in the areas
signified by that planet and the houses it rules.

> In Bill's chart, Jupiter occupying the fourth house (home and
> parents) and ruling the first and fourth has power and resources
> because it is in Pisces, one of its own signs of rulership. Mer-
> cury, occupying the first house and ruling the seventh (relation-
> ship) and tenth (profession), is problematic because it is placed
> in Sagittarius, one of the signs of its detriment. Saturn, occupy-
> ing the fifth house (children) and ruling the second (finances)
> and third (siblings) has some misfortune because it in Aries, the
> sign of its fall. But it is in mutual reception with Mars, which
> gives it power (Mars rules Aries and Saturn rules Aquarius).
> Mars in Aquarius is in mutual reception with Saturn. The other
> planets do not occupy any signs of their domicile or exaltation
> rulerships or their opposites. The Sun in Scorpio looks to Mars
> as its host and Venus in Sagittarius looks to Jupiter as its host.

How would you rank these planets in the order of most to least
powerful, based upon their sign rulerships as indications of their
access to resources to accomplish their effects? Think about why
someone might decide to rank the planets in the following order:

> Jupiter
> Mars and Saturn
> Sun, Moon, and Venus
> Mercury

Houses

The Whole Sign house system was the system of choice for the
first 700 years of astrological practice, during the Hellenistic cultural era. In the Whole Sign house system, the houses and signs are

co-incident—one entire sign occupies an entire house. This system was used to investigate the topics signified by each house—health, marriage, parents, children, or profession. The ancient texts discuss other house systems (for example, the Porphyry), but these were used for specific inquiries, particularly inquiries about how strong or energetic each planet is, especially for length-of-life considerations. Vedic astrology, like Hellenistic, uses Whole Sign houses for topical inquiries and a variation of the Porphyry system for determinations of planetary strength. Over the centuries, many other house systems have been developed and used by the various astrological traditions.

In Whole Sign houses, each house begins at 0 degrees of a sign and ends at 30 degrees of that same sign. The Ascendant sign determines the sign of the first house, and the degree of the Ascendant falls somewhere in that house. All the planets that are located in that sign are considered first-house planets in terms of the topics that the first house signifies. The Ascendant degree is not the dividing line between the first and twelfth houses (even if a chart has 29 degrees of that sign ascending), although it does determine the line of the horizon and placement of planets above and below the horizon for inquiries of sect. The sign following the Ascendant sign occupies the entirety of the second house, and so on.

Note that this is not the same as the Equal House system, in which the degree on the Ascendant becomes the beginning degree of the signs on the cusps of each successive house. (Firmicus Maternus discusses the Equal House system in his work). In Whole Sign houses, there are no intercepted houses, and ancient texts make no reference whatsoever to planets in intercepted signs. The use of Whole Sign houses brings the chart into more of an archetypal pattern. For example, as in our sample chart, everyone who has Sagittarius rising has Gemini occupying the seventh house and Virgo occupying the tenth. Thus all Sagittarius-rising individuals have the topics of marriage and career linked under the auspices of Mercury, which rules both Gemini and Virgo.

The houses are classified according to three categories that affect the condition of planets located in them: angularity, good and bad

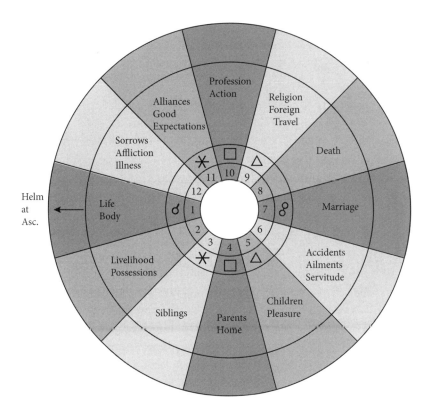

FIGURE 5. *Traditional meanings of the houses.*
Angular houses: 1, 4, 7, 10
Succedent houses: 2, 5,8,11
Cadent houses: 3, 6, 9, 12
Good houses: 1, 3, 4, 5, 7, 9, 10, 11
Bad houses: 2, 6, 8, 12

places, and joys.[7] In this book, I will emphasize relative angularity and make passing reference to good and bad places.

Modern astrology still retains the notion of angular, succedent, and cadent houses. The first, fourth, seventh, and tenth houses are angular. The second, fifth, eighth, and eleventh houses are succedent. The third, sixth, ninth, and twelfth houses are cadent. Before you go any further, however, divest yourself of any association of the angular houses with the cardinal signs (Aries, Cancer, Libra, and Capricorn), the succedent houses with the fixed signs (Taurus, Leo, Scorpio, and Aquarius), or the cadent houses with the mutable signs (Gemini, Virgo, Sagittarius, and Pisces).

In general, traditional astrology interprets the relative angularity of a house as giving a planet the strength to manifest its significations as external events. Planets located in angular houses are usually seen as having the greatest strength; planets in succedent houses are credited with a moderate amount of strength; planets in cadent houses are usually considered the weakest. Thus the significations of planets in angular houses tend to be much more dramatic and prominent in the life. But why is this?

Robert Schmidt, chief translator of the Hellenistic texts published by Project Hindsight, has proposed the following insight based on his interpretation of the meanings of the ancient Greek words used to describe this concept. The proper question, he claims, is: To what extent is the planet able to focus and direct its actions and activities upon the individual?[8] When a planet occupies an angular house, its action is totally centered or focused on the person's life agenda, and thus angular planets are more effective in getting the business of life accomplished. When a planet occupies a succedent house, its action is initially diverted away from the person's life agenda, but eventually comes back to it. Thus it is moderately effective in taking care of business. But the action of a planet in a cadent house is distracted and predominantly directed away from the business of the life agenda. Thus, at least on the level of the manifestation of outer events, not much happens. A modern understanding might speculate that activities of life occur in the inner world of the mind for planets located in cadent houses—a concept that was not articulated by ancient thinkers.

The second category—good and bad houses—speaks to whether the actions of planets located in these houses lead to favorable outcomes for the individual. Good houses are those that are linked by Whole Sign configuration to the Ascendant sign/first house by a sextile (third and eleventh), square (fourth and tenth), trine (fifth and ninth), or opposition (seventh) configuration. Bad houses are those that are not configured to the Ascendant by any of these aspects. Note that traditional astrology does not use the semi-sextile (30-degree) or quincunx (150-degree) aspects as valid configurations.

The bad houses are the second, sixth, eighth, and twelfth. These signify respectively livelihood; illness, injuries and slavery; death; and confinement, loss, and sorrow. All but the second-house meanings are obvious as topics that are not favorable to the life. Perhaps the notion of excessive materiality, wherein greed is the root of all evil, is implied in the negative association of the second house, but this is only a supposition on my part. According to traditional astrology, the good houses are ranked in descending order of goodness: first, tenth, eleventh, fifth, seventh, fourth, ninth, and third. The bad houses are ranked in ascending order of badness: second, eighth, sixth, and twelfth.[9] The third house was often said to be the "least good of the good" and the "least bad of the bad."

At this point in any discussion of good and bad houses, many students of modern astrology find the hairs standing up on the backs of their necks. Let us be clear. Planets in bad houses are not bad, nor are the actions of the individual in question bad. Nor is it certain that the life in question will turn out to be awful. It is simply that the outcomes of the activities associated with planets occupying good or bad houses are more or less favorable to the life force and the realization of ambitions. Some traditional astrologers have proposed that benefic planets in bad houses help to prevent some bad outcomes.

It may help to think of these good and bad houses as profitable or unprofitable, as these terms were often used as synonyms for good and bad by Hellenistic authors when referring to houses. Houses refer to location as places that are more or less conducive to doing business. Think of a store being placed in a good location—on a busy street with ample parking, or at the main crossroads of a mall where there is a lot of pedestrian traffic. Now think of that same store in an obscure alley or dangerous part of town where shoppers are less likely to venture or pass by. It is reasonable to assume that the store would be more profitable in the first location than in the second. So it is with good and bad houses. The actions of planets in these houses result in outcomes that are either profitable to the individual or not—not just in terms of money, but in terms of long-term implications for the life. When we begin to delineate the meanings of the planets, we will look at planets that are powerful by sign, but weak by house, and those that are weak by sign, but strong by house. And remember that bad houses can become good house when you use the system of derived houses for a particular investigation. (For example, if you are investigating the topic of profession, which is signified by the tenth house, the second house is the fifth from the tenth in a trine relationship; thus, in the context of profession, it is a good house.)

In our analysis of house placement, we will first examine the relative angularity of the planet to see how well it focuses on and conducts the business of the individual's life as an indication of how effective it is in getting its job done. Then we will determine whether its placement in a good or bad house points to the favorable or profitable outcome of its actions. We'll do this for both the visible planets, and the outer planets and major asteroids.

In Bill's chart, Venus and Mercury are in the first house, which is angular, good, and the best house. Moon, Mars, and Juno are in the third house, which is cadent and weak, but mildly good. Jupiter is in the fourth house, which is angular and good. Saturn and Vesta are in the fifth house, which is succedent and good. Uranus is in the sixth house, which is cadent and bad. Chiron is in the eighth house, which is succedent and bad. Pallas and Pluto are in the ninth house, which is cadent and good. Ceres and Neptune are in the tenth house, which is angular and good. The Sun is in the twelfth house, which is cadent and bad.

So the benefic Venus, Mercury (also probably a benefic due to its close association with Venus), the benefic Jupiter, the asteroid Ceres, and the outer planet Neptune are all in angular houses. Their activities are totally focused on the life agenda of the native and are likely to indicate dramatic and significant events. Because these houses are also good houses, their outcomes are likely to be favorable.

Vesta, malefic Saturn, and Chiron are in succedent houses, which indicates that only a moderate amount of their focus is directed toward the life and the achievement of the ambitions. However, the outcomes of Vesta and Saturn in the good fifth house are favorable, while those of Chiron in the bad eighth house are not. Moon, Juno, malefic Mars, Uranus, Pallas, Pluto, and the Sun are all in cadent houses, which suggests that the actions of these planets are distractive and divert Bill from his ultimate goal. Only the Sun in the bad twelfth house and Uranus in the bad sixth house indicate unfavorable or unprofitable consequences for their actions.

So far, based on the conditions of sect, sign rulership, and house angularity, which planet do you think will be the most effective and favorable? Consider that Jupiter, belonging to the sect in favor, occupying its own domicile Pisces, and located in an angular and good house, is shaping up to be a good contender for the best planet.

Aspects and Configurations

In addition to sect, zodiacal sign, and house location, there is another very important set of criteria that affect the manner in which a planet brings about its effects. This is the doctrine of aspects, which concerns a planet's relationship, or configuration, to other planets. Not only can a planet's significations be modified by its configurations with other planets, it can also be helped or hindered by them. The traditional astrological terms "bonification" and "corruption," which we will discuss later, refer to these conditions under which a planet's significations are made better or worse by its connection to other planets.

Hellenistic aspect doctrine, as taught by Robert Schmidt, is a highly sophisticated and complex system that describes how planets negotiate with one another through their configurations to see to it that the destiny of an individual's life is fulfilled. Based upon his reading of the ancient authors, Schmidt distinguishes between two kinds of configurations. One is sign-based and refers to a process of testimony whereby planets witness certain topics (such as marriage or children) that are signified by a house, and then provide testimony concerning what they have seen to the planet that has jurisdiction over the matters of that house. The other is degree-based and describes how planets that are within 3 degrees of one another can actually look upon each other and, by their gaze, influence each other's significations. He also explains all the conditions of maltreatment whereby planetary combinations lead to the more problematic qualities of a planet being emphasized. I am going to simplify Schmidt's model substantially, with apologies in advance for any omissions and over-generalizations. Hopefully, the foundation you receive here will allow you to grasp the more advanced teachings concerning aspect doctrine if you decide to pursue them. I take responsibility for any errors in the following discussion.

The focus of this section is not to explain how to interpret aspects between planets, but rather to lay out the criteria by which a planet's configurations to other planets contribute to the determination of its capacity to bring about favorable outcomes. There are two ways in which planets can have a connection with one another. One is through sign-based configurations and the other is through degree-based aspects. First, we'll investigate how planets are related to one another by whole sign, as well as by an orb of degrees. Then we'll discuss under what circumstances a planet's ability to produce favorable outcomes is enhanced or impeded by these relationships.

Sign-based configurations arise from the natural connections that certain signs have with one another, based on the inscription of regular polygons within the zodiacal circle that link various sets of signs. The hexagon links signs of the same gender (the masculine fire and air signs, and the feminine earth and water signs). The square links signs of the same modality (the quadruplicities of cardinal, fixed, mutable). The triangle links signs of the same element (the triplicities of fire, earth, air, and water). Because the signs themselves are connected by a geometrical formation, planets that occupy configured signs likewise have a natural connection to one another due to their presence in these signs, regardless of the number of degrees that separate them.

These geometrical configurations yield the sign-based sextile connection from the hexagon, the square and opposition connection from the square, and the trine connection from the triangle. In traditional astrology, the modern conjunction was understood, not as a configuration, but rather as a co-mingling of the natures of planets in the same sign. Likewise the modern semi-sextile and quincunx were not considered to be configurations, as no regular polygon could link these signs. Planets in these disjunct signs were said to be in aversion, turned away from one another and having no connection whatsoever. This was thought to be a most unfortunate situation. In sign-based configurations, it is the planets' presence in geometrically related signs that gives them their connection or lack of connection to one another, not their orb or arc of separation.

This type of configuration between two planets describes the nature of their interaction, as does modern aspect doctrine. According to Hellenistic authors, the conjunction designates a generally harmonious mingling of the individual natures of the planets.[10] The trine, and to a lesser extent the sextile, describes a helpful and sympathetic relationship, even with a malefic planet. The square denotes a harsh and discordant contact, capable of giving pain if a malefic is involved. The opposition indicates adverse dealings—and worse if a malefic is involved. When planets are configured by sign rather than by degree, this is called whole-sign based configurations.

A second Hellenistic aspect doctrine is degree- rather than sign-based. In this construct, each planet is said to emit seven visual rays at the partile- (exact) arc distances designated by the right and left sextiles (60 degrees), right and left squares (90 degrees), right and left trines (120 degrees), and the opposition (180 degrees). This is the means by which one planet can "look upon" and "see" another planet. The Greek words in the Hellenistic texts that referred to aspects all had meanings related to sight—"to see," "to look upon," "to gaze at," "to scrutinize," "to behold." In Latin, the word *adspicere*, from which the word aspect is derived, means "to look at." According to this doctrine, planets can only "see" one another when they are within a 3-degree orb of a conjunction, sextile, square, trine, or opposition and a 13-degree orb for the Moon. And this orb can cross sign boundaries. This is the strict and formal definition of aspects. When such a degree-based aspect exists between two planets, these planets have entered into a direct relationship with one another and, by their "gaze," they can actually impact each others' significations. Robert Schmidt suggests that many of the aspect delineations given in the ancient texts refer to these kinds of degree-based relationships. We will refer to this type of relationship as degree-based aspects.

While configurations and aspects describe the various ways in which planets relate to and affect one another, there are certain other conditions under which planets can be either greatly enhanced or severely damaged in their capacity to act effectively for the best interests of the person. This is traditionally called "bonification" and "corruption." When a planet is "bonified" by its relationship with another planet, it gets assistance in bringing out its more positive qualities. It can act better than it normally would, resulting in favorable outcomes for the life. When a planet is "corrupted" or mal-treated by its relationship with another planet, it is harmed in its capacity to bring about favorable outcomes. It can act in ways that are worse than its usual behavior at the more problematic range of its expression, or at least it is prevented from doing good. Not only are the planet's individual significations improved or worsened, but also the topics they govern as a result of the houses they rule.

Ancient authors write of seven conditions of maltreatment by the malefic planets (Mars and Saturn),[11] and imply that there are seven corresponding conditions of bonification by the benefic plan-ets (Venus and Jupiter). These include being struck by the aspect ray of one these planets, or being enclosed by them,[12] or occupying the domicile of one of these planets whose lord is, itself, in a house not conducive to business.

Here, we will use a simplified form of this doctrine. Remember that, at this point in our process, we are only looking at a planet's relationship to other planets by configuration and aspect. We are not interpreting what the combination means in terms of delineation, but rather determining how planets help or harm one another in their capacity to bring about favorable outcomes for the individual. A planet can be strong and powerful in terms of its capacity to mani-fest its events, but may use that strength against the best interests of the person. For example, a strong Mars in the sixth house may be able to produce a great illness that is detrimental to the person's health and well-being.

If a planet is configured in a sign-based conjunction, sextile, or trine configuration with the benefic planets Venus and Jupiter, it is receiving sympathy, help, support, and affirmation for its significations. If there is a 3-degree orb (or 13 degrees for the Moon) with a benefic or it is enclosed by the benefics, the planet is being bonified. Bonification enhances a planet's positive significations, making it more benevolent, and suppresses its negative significations. If a planet is being witnessed in a sign-based conjunction, square, or opposition configuration with the malefic planets Mars and Saturn, it is receiving discord, conflict, and negation for its significations. If there is a 3-degree orb (or 13 degrees for the Moon) with a malefic, or it is enclosed by the malefics, the planet is being corrupted or maltreated. Maltreatment suppresses a planet's positive significations, preventing it from doing good; it damages it in some way, and may contribute to its malevolent tendencies.

We will use traditional configuration and aspect doctrine in the following modified and greatly simplified manner:

- We will examine only the five "Ptolemaic aspects"—conjunction, sextile, square, trine, and opposition.
- We will consider configurations by whole sign, but assume that the closer the two planets are to an exact orb, the more active the relationship. We will designate interactions as harmonious or inharmonious.
- We will assume that planets within a 3-degree orb of another planet, or the Moon within a 13-degree orb of another planet, impact and affect each others' significations. This 3-degree range can extend across sign boundaries (such as the Sun at 1 degree Leo in opposition to Mars at 29 degrees Capricorn).
- We'll pay special attention to sign-based conjunctions, sextiles, and trines with the benefic planets as sympathetic and affirming, and sign-based conjunctions, squares, and oppositions with the malefic planets as harsh and negating.
- We'll also pay special attention to planets having a 3-degree aspect orb with the benefic planets or being enclosed by them as an instance of bonification. We'll interpret planets having a 3-degree aspect orb with the malefic planets or being enclosed by them as an instance of corruption/maltreatment.

Remember:

- Configurations can be harmonious (co-presence/conjunction); helpful and sympathetic (trine and weakly the sextile); harsh and discordant (square) and capable of giving pain (if a malefic is involved); or adverse (opposition) and worse if a malefic is involved. These conditions in themselves, however, are *not* the conditions of bonification or corruption/maltreatment.
- A malefic planet trine or sextile does not cause as much harm, and a benefic planet squaring or opposing does not do its full measure of good, but it also doesn't do damage.
- Bonification entails a conjunction, trine, or sextile from a benefic—Venus or Jupiter—and makes the significations of the planet more favorable for the individual by enhancing its ability to act in ways that are beneficial to the person.
- Corruption/maltreatment entails a conjunction, square, or opposition from a malefic—Mars or Saturn—and makes the significations of the planet unfavorable for the best interests of the individual by damaging its ability to act in ways that are beneficial for the person.
- Configurations speak to how both planets interact with one another; aspects speak to how planets impact one another. Bonification makes one of the planets act better; corruption/maltreatment makes one of the planets act worse.

In Bill's chart, Venus in Sagittarius receives neither affirmation (no conjunction, trine, or sextile from Jupiter) or negation (no conjunction, square, or opposition from Saturn). Mercury in Sagittarius receives help and bonification by a conjunction with Venus, but no harm from either malefic, while the Moon and Juno receive weak help by a sextile from Venus and harm by a conjunction with Mars. Note that Juno is making application to Mars within 3 degrees, thus it is being maltreated by Mars, while Mars is weakly helped by a sextile from Venus.

Jupiter receives neither a sextile nor trine from Venus and hence no assistance, and does not receive a square or opposition from Mars or Saturn. However, it is enclosed by the two malefics, hence some maltreatment may be present (a finer analysis would note the intervention by ray from Venus). Vesta and Saturn are helped by a trine from Venus and are not harmed by the malefics. Uranus is weakly helped by a sextile from Jupiter, and harmed by a square from Mars.

Chiron is helped by a trine from Jupiter and harmed by a square from Mars, while Pallas and Pluto are helped by a trine from Venus and harmed by an opposition from Mars. Ceres and Neptune are neither helped nor harmed, but the Sun is helped by a trine from Jupiter, and this is within 4 degrees, but harmed by a square from Mars.

From the above considerations, which planet would you say is getting the most help and least harm in expressing its favorable outcomes?

SOLAR AND LUNAR PHENOMENA

A planet's cycle relative to the Sun is called its *synodic cycle*, also referred to as the solar-phase cycle.[13] As planets orbit the Sun, certain relationships occur when they are at various distances from it as measured along the ecliptic. These critical points in the cycle also affect their capacity to be effective and favorable. Planets display regular observable phenomena at various distances that have to do with their visibility, speed, apparent direct or retrograde motion, and their relative position as rising before or setting after the Sun. The speed and visibility of all the planets except the Moon are dependent upon their elongation from the Sun.

In general, we can say that, when a planet is visible when crossing either the eastern or western horizon, its events are more likely to manifest, for better or worse, depending upon its nature and condition. All of the planets are invisible when they are either 15 degrees preceding or following the Sun. The term for this situation is "under the Sun's beams (USB)." In Medieval terminology, the planet is sometimes called "combust" at the 8-degree interval.

When a planet is under the Sun's beams, its power is weakened by the intensity of the Sun's glare, and its significations are absorbed or taken up by the Sun. For example, if Venus is under the beams,

while the Sun will benefit from contact with a benefic and act in a
more Venusian manner, the significations of Venus, both in terms of
what the planet represents in itself and the houses it occupies and
rules, will have greater difficulty in eventuating, or they may occur
in ways that are ineffectual for the individual. The effects of a planet
that is under the beams do not come to anything, or may not be
apparent to the external observer. One author notes that if a planet
is "in the heart," that is conjunct the Sun in the same degree or on
either side, it is an exception to this rule.[14] If a planet occupies the
sign of its rulership or exaltation, it is much less likely to suffer the
effects of being burnt and diminished by being under the beams of
the Sun.

The speed at which a planet moves—fast, average, or slow—
is a determining factor in how active it is. In general, the faster a
planet moves (unless it is under the beams), the more active it is.
From this, we can infer that there are more events associated with
its significations—more marriages, more children, more gifts, etc. By
contrast, the energy of a slower-moving planet is weaker, and thus
fewer occurrences emerge from its significations.[15] All of the planets
move the fastest when closest to their conjunction with the Sun,
and they begin to slow down as they approach their retrograde station (around the waxing trine from the Sun for the outer planets).
Planets remain slow during their retrograde period, and begin to pick
up speed again after they turn direct (around the waning trine for
the outer planets). If you have an astrology computer program that
gives the speed of each planet, you can compare that speed to the
average speeds given in Table 2 to determine if the planet is moving at a rapid, average, or slow speed. Alternatively, you can use an
ephemeris to subtract the zodiacal longitude of a planet's position
from its longitude on the preceding day to see how far it has traveled
during that day. Then compare this number to its average motion as
given in the table.

The direct and retrograde motion of planets is connected to their
speed. When a planet appears to be moving in a forward direction
according to the diurnal motion (rising in the east and setting in
west, moving in a clockwise direction), we call it direct. When it is
direct, it is moving with faster-than-average or slower-than-average

Table 2. Average Planetary Speeds

♄ Saturn	0 degrees	2 minutes per day
♃ Jupiter	0 degrees	5 minutes per day
♂ Mars	0 degrees	31 minutes per day
♀ Venus	0 degrees	59 minutes per day (same as Sun)
☿ Mercury	0 degrees	59 minutes per day (same as Sun)
☉ Sun	0 degrees	59.16 minutes per day
☽ Moon	13 degrees	11 minutes per day

speed. However, as the Earth orbits the Sun, at certain times in the cycle of that orbit, it appears as if the planets are moving backward against the background of the constellation stars. This backward motion is called retrogression; when a planet is retrograde, it moves extremely slowly.

According to ancient astrologers, a retrograde planet is "ineffectual, unavailing, and insignificant" and "inactive, weak and irregular."[16] These definitions are in accordance with the guidelines given for planetary speed in general. The Greek word for retrograde means "to walk backward," "to retrace steps," or "to recall." Thus a retrograde planet may also be interpreted as recalling, or taking back, what it has given at a prior time. The modern definition for retrograde points to an internalization of that planetary function in the psyche, with the accompanying need to rethink and reformulate its expression in a more individualistic manner than that which is the norm for the general population.

When a planet makes a heliacal rising or heliacal setting (rising soon before sunrise at a 15-degree interval from the Sun or setting soon after sunset at a 15-degree interval from the Sun), or makes a station direct or retrograde within seven days before or after the birth, a special condition called *phasis* occurs. A planet making a phasis indicates an intensification of its energies; the significations of that planet saturate the life, for better or worse, depending upon its other factors. If the planet is in poor condition, badly situated, or of a malefic nature, its problematic significations can dominate the life experience. If the planet is in good condition, well situated, and of a benefic nature, its more fortunate manifestations can permeate the life circumstances.

In this introduction to planetary condition, let us defer consideration of heliacal rising and setting. But we shall look to see if any planet makes a station within seven days of the birth by consulting an ephemeris for the birth date.

> There are no planets within 15 degrees of the Sun in Bill's chart, and thus no planets are under the beams. Jupiter, Saturn, Uranus, Chiron, and Neptune are all retrograde and thus either are less effectual or less active, recall their significations, or internalize and individuate their expressions. Consulting an ephemeris for November 17, 1939, we see that Mercury made a station and turned retrograde on November 19, two days after the birth, and thus can be considered in *phasis* and intensified. With Mercury as ruler of the seventh house (relationships) and tenth house (career), we may suspect that two areas permeate Bill's life experiences. On November 25, eight days after the birth, Jupiter made a station and turned direct. While this is one day more than our rule, we must nevertheless take this information into account in our analysis of Jupiter as the ruler of the first house (life force) and fourth house (home and parents) as being especially emphasized.

When considering lunar phenomena, we note whether the Moon is waxing and increasing in light (from the New Moon to the Full Moon), or waning and decreasing in light (from the Full Moon to the New Moon). In general, a waxing Moon is more favorable than a waning Moon, as the light force is increasing. We also note the speed of the Moon, which travels at a variable rate of between 11 and 15 degrees per day, with around 13 degrees being the average rate of motion. The faster the speed, the more active the influence, and the more events, and hence opportunities, occur. Then we determine if the Moon is making applying aspects to the other planets in the chart.[17] Because in ancient philosophy the Moon was thought to transmit the effluences of the other planets to the Earth, the Moon by means of her applications assists in the realization of the planets' significations.

Finally, we investigate if the person was born with a "void-of-course" Moon. The Hellenistic astrologers defined this as the Moon making no applying aspects to another planet (remember to use only the seven visible planets) for a day and a night, or the span of 13 degrees, and this span can cross sign boundaries. Other authors specified a 30-degree range. Unlike the modern void-of-course Moon, this is a relatively rare phenomenon. In the Hellenistic texts, a void-of-course Moon indicates vagabonding, troubadours, or aimless wandering in general. It may signify a person who does not function well or is not grounded in this earthly world, not tending to ordinary householder concerns or bringing matters to completion.

> In Bill's chart, the Moon is waxing, traveling slower than average at 12 degrees 3 minutes, and will make applying aspects to Venus, Mercury, Uranus, Sun, Juno, Vesta, Saturn, and Mars during its passage in its home sign of Aquarius. Hence it is not void-of-course, but a generally active and beneficent Moon.

Before you make any judgment as to what a planet means in a chart, you must first assess its capacity to produce its effects and whether or not these outcomes are in the best interests of the individual. Table 3 on page 65 summarizes all the information we have gathered about each planet and specifies what each factor indicates.

- Belonging to the sect in favor gives a planet the authority to promote its agenda and work on behalf of the individual to bring about better outcomes for the life.
- Power comes from a planet being in its own places of rulership with command of its resources (domicile) and high status and honor (exaltation).
- Strength and focus come from placement in angular or succedent houses, and placement in good houses is similar to having a good location that is profitable to conducting the business of life.

- Configurations and aspects show the planets' interaction and the impact they have on one another as they negotiate about the destiny of the individual.
- The conditions of bonification and corruption enhance or harm the significations of the planets that help or hinder the happiness and well-being of the person.
- Visibility brings a planet into the spotlight, where its agenda can be seen and realized; speed equates to activity, creating more energy and opportunities for the significations to come about; direct motion ensures forward momentum.

Thus the best condition for a planet is to belong to the sect in favor, occupy one or more of its signs of rulership, be located in an angular and good house, be bonified by the benefics, be visible, fast, and direct in motion, and rise or set heliacally. The worst condition for a planet is not to belong to the sect in favor, occupy the signs of its detriment or fall, be located in a cadent or bad house, be corrupted by the malefics, and be under the Sun's beams and retrograde. Most planets fall somewhere along this continuum. It is your job as an astrologer to weigh all the positive and negative factors and arrive at a judgment as to a planet's overall capacity to function effectively and favorably.

As you look at a chart, fully analyze only the seven visible planets, because these and only these are the rulers of the houses, and thus of all the topics of life. Train yourself to identify not only the house a planet occupies, but also the house(s) it rules, so you determine over what exactly it has jurisdiction. Look at the house positions of the outer planets and the asteroids to get a sense of how focused they are on the ambitions of the person, to what extent they are helped or harmed by configurations with the malefics or benefics, and if they are direct or retrograde or under the beams. But remember that the categories of sect and sign rulership do not apply to outer planets and asteroids.

The Sun in Scorpio occupying Bill's twelfth house (affliction/ transcendence) and ruling his ninth (religion, travel, education) has great authority as the sect leader to bring about favorable

Table 3. Planetary Conditions

Planet	Sect	Sign	House	Configuration	Solar/Lunar
☉ Sun	favor		cadent/bad	helped 1x; harmed 1x	
☽ Moon				harmed 1x	visible, waxing, slow
☿ Mercury	not in favor	detriment	angular/good	helped 1x	visible, direct, phasis, station retrograde
♀ Venus	not in favor		angular/good		visible direct
♂ Mars	not in favor	mutual reception with Saturn	cadent/good	helped 1x	visible, direct
♃ Jupiter	favor	domicile	angular/good	maltreated by enclosure maybe	visible retrograde, phasis, station direct (8 days)
♄ Saturn	favor	fall, but mutual reception with Mars	succedent/good	helped 1x	visible, retrograde
♅ Uranus			cadent/bad	helped 1x, harmed 1x	retrograde
♆ Neptune			angular/good		visible, direct
♇ Pluto			cadent/good	helped 1x, harmed 1x	visible, retrograde
⚳ Ceres			angular/good		visible, direct
⚴ Pallas			cadent/good	helped 1x, harmed 1x	visible, direct
⚵ Juno			cadent/good	helped1x, maltreated 1x	visible, direct
⚶ Vesta			succedent/good	maltreated 1x	visible, retrograde
⚷ Chiron			succedent/bad	helped1x, harmed 1x	visible, retrograde

outcomes, but it does not occupy any signs in which it has rulership. Thus it does not have command of its own resources or the expectation of status, but looks to its dispositor, Mars, for its resources. The Sun is placed in a cadent house, which makes its actions distractive, and in a location not conducive to business. However, it is helped and affirmed by a trine from an almost *phasis,* very strong Jupiter.

The Moon in Aquarius occupying Bill's third house (siblings, communications) and ruling his eighth (death, inheritances) does not belong to the sect in favor, does not occupy any signs of its own rulership, and thus must look to its dispositor, Saturn, for its resources. It is located in a cadent, weak, but good house. It receives slight help by a sextile from Venus and is harmed by its co-presence in the same sign as Mars. It is waxing, slow in motion, but makes many applications to other planets. Overall, the Moon does not have a whole lot going for it, but it is not in deplorable condition by any means.

Mercury in Sagittarius occupying the first house (character, self) and ruling the seventh (relationships) and tenth (profession) is interesting. It does not belong to the sect in favor and is impoverished in the sign of its detriment, having neither the authority nor the resources to be effective in the areas it rules. It must look to its dispositor, Jupiter, which can give great support. However, it is in a strong, good house, and thus its concerns will be of major focus in the life. Its *phasis* condition, the result of making a retrograde station two days after the birth, intensifies all its issues and, more than otherwise, favorable results may come about by bonification through the conjunction with Venus and not receiving harm from Mars or Saturn. The Moon is making an application to Mercury.

Venus in Sagittarius also occupies the first house, but rules the sixth (health) and eleventh (friends). It does not belong to the sect in favor, is not in any signs of rulership or their opposites, and is neither helped nor harmed. It must look to its dispositor, Jupiter, and it is strong and focused upon Bill in the good first house. The Moon is making an application to Venus.

Venus has strength by location and by virtue of being a natural benefic, but otherwise is moderate and neutral in its overall condition.

Mars in Aquarius occupies the third house and rules the fifth (children) and the twelfth (afflictions, loss). It does not belong to the sect in favor and thus does not have the authority to pursue its agenda. It is in a weak, but good, cadent house, and is neither bonified nor maltreated. This may seem like an overall feeble condition, but Mars gains much power through being in mutual reception with Saturn, which is also its dispositor, and thus has the resources to be effective as if it were in its own domicile. Yet, even with its resources, its position puts it at a disadvantage as to the topics it rules.

Jupiter in Pisces occupies Bill's fourth house (home, parents) and rules his first (self) and fourth. Belonging to the sect in favor, it is in the sign of its own domicile, giving it much power through full access to its own resources. It is located in a strong, angular, good house. While seemingly enclosed by the two malefics, Venus interposes a benefic ray at 13 degrees of Pisces, shielding the malefic containment. Jupiter is retrograde, which is its only difficulty, but it will turn direct in eight days, putting it on the edge of *phasis,* a condition of intensification. Overall, Jupiter is in excellent condition, and the strongest planet in the chart.

Saturn in Aries occupies Bill's fifth house (children) and rules his second (finances/livelihood) and third (siblings, communications). It belongs to the sect in favor and is located in a moderate succedent good house. Even though it is seemingly held in low repute due to its fall in the sign of Aries, it is saved from dishonor through its mutual reception with Mars, which is its dispositor, giving it the power of being in its own domicile. Saturn is also helped by a trine from Venus, but retrograde in motion. Thus Saturn, through its sect status, sign rulership, and house location, is in fairly decent condition, with its slow retrograde motion its only real drawback.

Study Guidelines

- Create a table of planetary condition for each planet in your practice chart following the example given in this chapter.
- Write out an analysis for each planet, detailing its condition, and make a judgment about its overall capacity to bring about the matters it signifies in a favorable manner. Be sure to include the house it occupies and the house or houses it rules, its sect status, its zodiacal sign rulerships, the relative angularity and profitability of its house location, the help or harm it receives from other planets, any special solar phenomena (like being under the beams, retrograde motion, or phasis condition), and if the Moon is making an application to it.
- Remember, you are not yet interpreting the meaning of the planets in the chart, just evaluating their condition.
- List the planets in order, from the most effective and favorable to the least effective and favorable.

Part II
Establishing the Framework

CHAPTER THREE

AN OVERVIEW OF THE CHART

Now that you have carefully examined the condition of the planets, you can begin to delineate their meanings in the chart. In this chapter, we'll discuss how to assemble the information you need to begin interpreting a chart to a client. First and foremost, you must feel confident about the birth data you are given. Then decide on the defaults you will use for your charts, prepare the charts themselves, and get an overview of the chart by familiarizing yourself with the placements of important natal points and current timing factors. Before you begin the client session, conduct an initial interview with the client.

Verifying Birth Data

The first step in reading a chart is to obtain the client's birth data. If this is communicated to you orally instead of being written down, verify it by repeating the information back to your client. Ask for the source of the data and determine its relative credibility. The most reliable source is a birth certificate. If you have access to the birth certificate, use its data. If the time of birth recorded appears as the hour, half hour, or quarter hour (e.g., 3:00 P.M., 3:15 P.M., 3:30 P.M., or 3:45 P.M.), assume that it may have been rounded off and proceed with caution in giving exact timing over the angles. Four minutes of birth time equates to approximately one degree of change in the angles. Two to three degrees difference in an angle means that a slow-moving outer-planet transit occurred several years earlier or will occur several years later.

71

Not all birth certificates contain this information. If your client cannot find the birth time on the certificate, ask if the certificate is a birth record (an official stamped document that certifies some of the information needed for obtaining licenses and passports, but omits the time) or a photocopy of the original certificate. If it is a birth record, have your client contact the Bureau of Vital Statistics in the capital of the state in which he or she was born, and specifically request a copy of the original certificate rather than the birth record. If the time is not on that, then you must rely on the memory of parents or relatives.

A mother's memory can be tricky. After the 1940s, most births occurred in hospitals; women were enclosed in rooms with no windows and given anesthetics that could cloud the memory. On the other hand, many participants of home births do not think to record the birth time at all. Sometimes, you can get corroboration from the father or another relative who may remember getting a call about the birth at work in the morning, or after dinner, or some general timeframe like that. Baby books and birth announcements may also contain the time.

Always ask your clients if the birth times they give you are based on a rectification by some other astrologer, or by someone dowsing with a pendulum, or a psychic. I am always extremely hesitant about using these times. Personally, I question the validity of the doctrine of astrological rectification, which proceeds on the assumption that transiting, progressed, or solar-arc planets crossing the angles manifest as dramatic outer events. I have repeatedly seen in charts with very reliable data that there are many times when planets cross angles and no outer event occurs.

If you have no birth time to work with, or if the time is highly uncertain, you can still do the chart, but some parts of the session will be more general than specific due to lack of information. In these cases, I set the chart for 12:00 noon so the Moon is at the midpoint of its possible range of degrees, and I look at planets in signs, aspects between planets, and transits over planets. I exclude any considerations that involve houses or angles. If you have access to a time that is accurate to within an hour or less, and the Ascendant does not change, then you only have to exclude transits over angles from the delineation. Later, I will give you clues about how to determine which Ascendant to use if the Ascendant changes within that hour.

Some astrologers prefer to use a sunrise chart, in which the Sun is on the Ascendant; in this case, the succeeding houses are called solar houses. They interpret the meanings of these solar houses relative to the Sun in the usual way. There is indeed some value in this approach, but be careful not to use planetary rulers of the houses when you interpret a solar chart.

CHART DEFAULTS

Before you set up your charts, decide which house system (Whole Sign, Equal House, Placidus, Porphyry, Koch, Regiomantanus, Alcabitius, etc.) and zodiac (tropical, sidereal, heliocentric) you will use, whether or not you will include the minor planets, and, if you are a traditionalist, whether you will include the outer planets, Uranus, Neptune, and Pluto. Then decide which formula (day/night) you will use for the calculation of the Lot (Arabic, Part) of Fortune, whether you will use the mean or true node positions, and which aspects you are going to consider and their orbs. In addition, if you are preparing a Solar Return chart, decide if you are going to use the birth location or the current location, as well as whether or not the Sun is precessed.

My current defaults, and the ones I use in this book, are:

- Whole Sign house system
- Tropical zodiac
- The four major asteroids (Ceres, Pallas, Juno, and Vesta)
- Several dozen minor asteroids, including Chiron
- The five Ptolemaic aspects (conjunction, sextile, square, trine, and opposition)
- Aspects considered primarily by sign rather than by degree of orb, although the closer the degree, the more active the aspect

- Out-of-sign aspects not considered unless the faster planet is within a 3-degree range of application to the slower planet
- Birth location and non-precessed Sun used for the Solar Return

SETTING UP A CHART

Giving your client a printed copy of the natal chart is a good idea. If your software has the option of displaying a legend for the symbols of the signs and planets, that is even better. A wheel that contains lines drawn in for the aspects or an aspect grid can be confusing, however, because of the various opinions on aspects and orbs. So if you include aspects, be clear about your preferences and make sure your printout accurately reflects those preferences. Some programs display a tabulation of planets by elements and modalities, but these numbers can be deceiving, as we will discuss later. Use your judgment about whether or not to include that.

The bi-wheel natal/secondary-progression chart in which the natal chart occupies the inner wheel and the progressed chart occupies the outer wheel is my main chart (see figure 6). To this, I add the following notations by hand:

- Using the list of minor asteroids that are arranged in a zodiacal sort, I list the ones I use in every chart.
- I note which asteroids are conjunct the four angles, especially the Ascendant and the Midheaven as well as conjunct the Sun, Moon, and Ascendant ruler.
- If the client's personal-name asteroid is on the list, or that of their partner, I add them.
- If I see a theme developing, I add other asteroids associated with that theme.

I will explain these notations in more detail later. Unless you already have experience working with the asteroids, for the time being don't do anything except locate and familiarize yourself with the glyphs for Ceres, Pallas, Juno, Vesta, and Chiron.

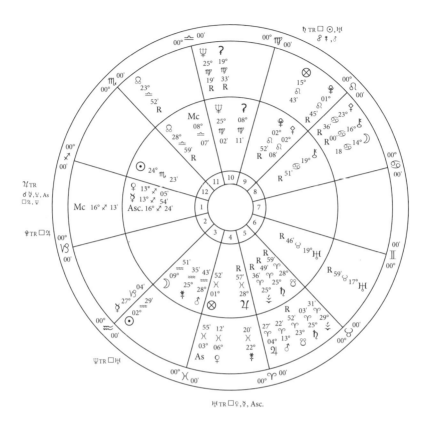

FIGURE 6A. *Bi-wheel natal chart with secondary progressions and annotations.*

Now you are ready to scan the chart:

1. Determine the natal lunation phase, the progressed current lunation phase and its beginning and ending dates, and the dates of the previous progressed New Moon phase. We will cover this in more detail later.

2. Scan the progressed chart, comparing the positions of progressed planets to natal planets.

3. If there is a conjunction or opposition of a progressed angle (Ascendant, Midheaven, Descendant, IC) or inner planet (Sun,

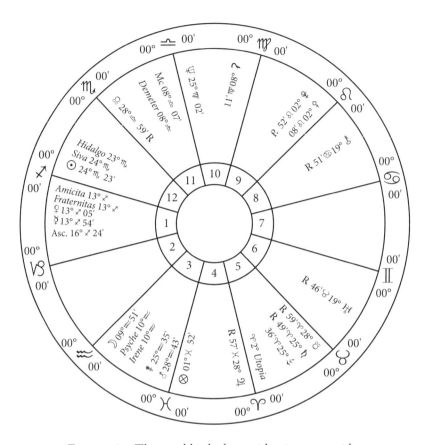

Figure 6b. *The natal birth chart with minor asteroids.*

Mercury, Venus, Mars, Ceres, Pallas, Juno, or Vesta) to a progressed or natal angle or planet within a 1-degree orb, circle it.

4. If there is conjunction of a progressed outer planet (Jupiter, Saturn, Uranus, Neptune, or Pluto) to a progressed or natal planet,
or an angle within an orb of 15 minutes, circle it.

5. Note the sign and house of the progressed Moon.

6. Note if a progressed planet has just entered a new sign, or turned
direct or retrograde this year (for this, look in an ephemeris at
the progressed date).

While many other factors of the progressed chart may be important,
these are the only ones you need to consider now. It is not unusual

for there to be limited activity in this kind of scan of the progressed chart.

While you may be tempted simply to print out a chart of the current transits, or create a third wheel with the transits, I advise against this. One of the drawbacks of astrology students using computer software instead an ephemeris to determine the current transits is that they often do not have a sense of the various speeds of the planets, their cycles or their retrograde motions, and the range that the planets travel within a given period. Look in an ephemeris and note how far each of the outer planets, Jupiter through Pluto, travel in the course of the year around the time of the consultation, and note if they make stations, turning direct or retrograde. Fix those degrees for each planet in your mind. Then, on the outside of the progressed chart, write in the symbol for each transiting planet in the appropriate sign, noting if it is making an exact aspect to any natal planet during the course of that year's travel. The hard aspects (conjunctions, squares, oppositions) are often more dramatic in their effects, but the soft aspects (sextile and trine) are not always insignificant. If the inner planets—Mercury, Venus, and Mars—are making stations on natal planets or going retrograde in a particular house, this is also important information to note. Do not factor in transits to progressed planets.

Finally, familiarize yourself with what solar and lunar eclipses will occur in the next year or have recently occurred, what natal house they activate, and if they conjunct any particular planet within 3 degrees. If you are a Hellenistic or Medieval astrologer, note the profected house of the year, and the annual profected time lord and its position in the Solar Return chart.

If you are not familiar with some of these astrological terms, they will be defined and discussed more fully in later chapters, or you can check them in the Glossary. After completing the book, you can return to this section and complete your checklist.

GETTING AN OVERVIEW

Now you are ready to let your eye flow around the chart and obtain an overview of it as a whole. Here, you must familiarize yourself with the layout of the chart, and strike a fine balance between making some very general observations and formulating specific judgments. With practice, you will come to recognize what stands out and thus is most likely important. First, note the sign of the Ascendant, any planets conjunct the Ascendant, and the sign, house, and configurations of its ruler. Then note the sign and house placements of the Sun and the Moon, and determine if there are any planets or asteroids in close conjunction with these luminaries. To the extent that the Ascendant, Sun, and Moon are three principle significators of the life, an analysis of these factors by element can give you clues to the basic predisposition of the client.

The fire element is associated with freedom, the air element with change. The earth element is associated with stability, the water element with emotional safety. The fire and air elements are sympathetic with one another, as are earth and water elements. Based on the elements of the Sun, Moon, and Ascendant, is there a dominant theme and sub-theme that emerges? This will affect the kind of advice you give your client.

For example, a woman who has Sun and Moon in earth elements and a water sign ascending will have a strong disposition toward maintaining safety and security in her life. If she finds herself in a problematic marriage, but one that provides financial security, don't be too quick to urge her to divorce under a difficult transit. Rather, advise her to seek alternative solutions, especially if she has no skills or resources to provide for herself and her children. However, if the dominant theme is one of freedom and change, marked by fire and air elements for these three factors, she may be more suited to strike out on her own. The point is to establish a general baseline, a frame of reference that can and should influence how you slant all subsequent specific delineations.

Another consideration that lets you get an overview of the chart is whether any signs or houses are emphasized by the presence of *stelliums* (three or more planets in the same sign or house). These will designate areas of significant activity. In addition, any angular planets or asteroids conjunct the four angles or located in the angular houses will play a dominant role in the life. Note the natal lunation phase to assess how the Sun/Moon energies operate together. As you become skillful in scanning aspect patterns, note if there are any T-squares or grand trines. Remember that configurations involving the outer planets are generational, rather than specifically personal. Also check to see if any planets are retrograde, and fix in your mind the placements of the lunar nodes and the Lot of Fortune.

I advise against resorting to any mechanical tabulation of planets in elements and modalities using a gradated pointing system for the various planets, angles, nodes, and lots to determine overall elemental emphasis. As you start adding more minor planets and lots and choosing different house systems, these tallies will vary radically and the results can be deceiving. I don't find the doctrines on hemispheric emphasis (above-extrovert/below-introvert) useful. The doctrine of chart patterns (such as the bowl, where all the planets are within an arc of 180 degrees, and the bucket, which is similar to the bowl but with one planet opposite all the others and acting as the handle) was developed by 20th-century astrologers. It can give some insights when the 10-planet system is used; however, when you add asteroids to the chart symbols, these patterns become meaningless because of the number of bodies. So keep in mind that, if you use chart patterns, you must remain within the 10-planet system.[1]

Finally, look to see what areas of the chart are receiving challenging outer-planet transits. These areas are likely to be of concern to your client. Again, transits (conjunct, square, opposition) to the four angles (the Sun, the Moon, the Ascendant ruler, and Mercury, Venus, and Mars) are the ones to take special notice of here. Note the houses through which the transiting planets travel and if they have recently made an ingress into a new sign or are about to do so.

At this point in your analysis, simply identify how the chart is assembled and where the concentrations of energies exist, without trying to determine specifically what they mean. Here is a checklist for getting an overview of a chart that helps you determine the areas you potentially want to address:

• List the element of the Ascendant, Sun, and Moon signs. Is there a dominant theme involving fire/air or earth/water? Is there an equal distribution? Which elements are missing? What does this indicate about the basic orientation of the individual in terms of freedom, change, security, and safety?

- Note the Ascendant sign and any planets/asteroids in the first house or fixed stars conjunct the Ascendant. Note the planet that rules the Ascendant sign using traditional rulerships (Mars for Scorpio, Jupiter for Pisces, Saturn for Aquarius) and the house and sign placement of its ruler. Does it also rule another house? What planets/asteroids/fixed stars are conjunct or opposite the ruler? Do not use oppositions for fixed stars.

- List the sign and house position of the Sun and the Moon, as well as the houses that they rule. What planets and asteroids are conjunct or opposite the luminaries? What fixed stars are conjunct the luminaries?

- Note if any planets occupy the signs of their domiciles or detriments, or exaltations or falls.

- List the natal and progressed lunation phases.

- List the placement of the lunar nodes and the Lot of Fortune. Note if the person was born during an eclipse. Make sure your computer software is set to calculate Fortune differently for day and night births.

- List any angular planets

- List any stelliums or other aspect patterns.

- List any retrograde planets or planets that are under the beams (within 15 degrees of the Sun).

- List the significant progressed and transiting aspects, as well as the degrees of the solar and lunar eclipses for the year.

Now refer to our sample chart and see how the above points are tabulated.

Male, November 17,1939, 8:30 a.m., Seneca, Nebraska
Whole Sign houses

1. Elemental analysis of the three principle places of life: Ascendant in fire, Sun in water, Moon in air. Distribution and balance of elements, with earth missing. From an elemental analysis of

the Sun, Moon, and Ascendant, the Ascendant and Moon in fire and air have a compatible interaction around the themes of freedom and change, while the Sun is focused upon emotional safety and connection. Earth, as the propensity for obtaining physical and financial security, is lacking.

2. Sign of Ascendant—Sagittarius with Venus and Mercury conjunct the Ascendant, its ruler Jupiter retrograde in Pisces in the fourth house (home, family) and ruling the fourth house of home opposite Neptune in the tenth house of career.

3. The Sun in Scorpio in the twelfth house (suffering, transcendence) ruling the ninth (higher wisdom) opposite retrograde Uranus in Taurus in the sixth (injuries, ill heath, job). The Moon in Aquarius in the third house (communication, siblings) ruling the eighth (death, inheritance), widely conjunct Juno and Mars and opposite Pluto and Pallas.

4. Jupiter is strong in its own domicile, Pisces; Mercury is weak in its detriment, Sagittarius; Mars and Saturn are in mutual reception.

5. Crescent Moon lunation phase.

6. Nodes in Aries-Libra across the fifth-eleventh house (children/ friends) axis; Fortune in Pisces in the fourth house (home, family).

7. Stellium in the third house (communication, siblings) with Moon, Juno, and Mars in Aquarius.

8. Angular planets—Neptune in the tenth house, Jupiter in the fourth house, Venus and Mercury in the first house (profession, home life, self). MC/IC axis in the eleventh/fifth houses.

9. Major aspect patterns by whole sign aspects—mutable T-square between Neptune, Jupiter Rx, and Venus/Mercury in angular houses; fixed T-square between Sun, Uranus Rx, and Mars/Juno in cadent houses; grand trine between Sun, Jupiter Rx, and Chiron Rx in water signs. (Rx is often used as an abbreviation for retrograde.)

10. Jupiter, Saturn, Vesta, Uranus, Pluto, and Chiron retrograde.

11. As of Fall 2006, transiting Pluto square Jupiter (Asc. ruler and about to enter the first house by sign); transiting Saturn opposing Juno and Mars; transiting Jupiter conjunct the Sun; pro-

gressed MC/IC axis conjunct natal Acs./Desc. axis; progressed lunation phase Gibbous October 2004 to March 2008 and progressed New Moon phase October 1992 at 19 Capricorn.

THE INITIAL INTERVIEW

While you may use this same basic procedural structure with every session, your manner and tone, and the level of complexity of your delineation will differ for each individual client. Once you have set up and familiarized yourself with your charts, but before you actually begin to interpret the data, you should conduct an initial interview with your client. You must determine your approach within the first three minutes of this session. There are two important sets of questions to ask that will help you determine how to proceed. Ask your client:

- What is your previous astrological background? Is this the first time you have had a reading or have you had other sessions? Are you a student or practitioner of astrology? Are you familiar with the basic meanings of the planets, signs, houses, and aspects? Do you know what transits are?
- Do you have any particular questions or concerns that you want me to address in this session?

If this is a first-time reading and your client has no knowledge of astrological terms, keep everything simple and straightforward, with a minimum of technical jargon in your explanations. For clients with a lot of astrological experience, a basic reading may be tedious and not worth their time and money, so cover more material and use a variety of technical terms. Practice both approaches with the same chart, and work on your oral delivery of the information for each. It is not enough to know what a chart means. You must be able to present the information at a level at which each client can comprehend it.

The second determination you must make before beginning a session is why the client has come to you. Ask clients to give you a brief (less than three-minute) summary of who they are, the circumstances of their lives, and their pertinent questions. Their responses will also inform you about their expectations and the level on which they want you to approach the consultation. If a client's stated concern is when to sell a home, then discuss that and not an abusive relationship with a partner. If, on the other hand, a client wants to know what the chart indicates about an intended path in life, don't bother talking about whether it's a good time to buy a new car. While you want to give an integrated summary of the client's chart, always leave enough time in the session to focus on his or her stated concern.

We will discuss these and many more issues later, but for now, you want to know how simple or complex to make your explanations and what the specific focus of the session should be in the context of your general synthesis of the chart. While your client is speaking, scan the charts you have prepared and note the areas where your client's stated concerns reside. What is going on in these areas of the chart? While the ultimate goal of the model presented in this book is to discern your client's life purpose, you must also know how to address specific concerns.

Study Guidelines

Using your practice chart:

- Obtain and verify the birth data, and state its source and reliability.
- Prepare the necessary charts.
- List the factors described in the chapter above.
- Designate a topical concern (relationship, health, vocation, education, etc.) to keep in mind and to investigate.
- Determine where the energies are concentrated in the natal chart and what areas are receiving the most current activation.

CHAPTER FOUR

THE ASCENDANT, ITS RULER, AND THE LIFE DIRECTION

THE BIRTH CHART can be read, not merely as a description of the personality or a prognostication of events that will take place, but also as a guide to activities that can facilitate the living of a purposeful life. While the art of interpreting a chart can be infinitely complex in the details, it can be quite simple in the essentials. Ancient astrologers looked upon the Sun, the Moon, and the Ascendant as the "places of life." You can construct the basic framework of the life purpose considering just these three factors. Everything else adds detail to the essential theme that is established by these places of life.

The Sun and Moon represent the soul and the body. The Sun represents the intention of the soul as the divine part of the human mind and the contents of the life purpose. The Moon symbolizes the body that gives the soul life, the senses by which to perceive the world, and the vehicle through which to actualize the purpose in the affairs of daily life and worldly existence. The Ascendant indicates the basic motivation that drives the soul, and the planet ruling the Ascendant guides the life to its destination.

In this chapter, we will examine the roles that the Ascendant sign, any planets occupying the first house, and the ruler of the Ascendant play in the delineation of the life purpose. In the next chapter, we will look at what the Sun and the Moon contribute to the articulation of the essential meaning of the life.

A few words before we begin. There are two approaches to chart delineation. One is descriptive, the other proscriptive. The descriptive approach simply describes a person's personality and behaviors. The proscriptive approach provides information that can help clients use their resources to live a meaningful, purposeful life. From this point on, our inquiry will be proscriptive. We will focus on how to extract meaning from the chart to describe a possible life purpose for the client. The point is not just to tell clients they are communicative, rigid, analytical etc., but rather advise them on how they can use these qualities to provide meaning in their lives.

THE ASCENDANT

The Ascendant is perhaps the most sensitive and personal factor in the chart, as it designates the zodiacal sign and degree that rose above the eastern horizon at the precise moment and place of a child's birth. The Ascendant marks the spot where heaven meets the Earth at the location of sunrise on the day of birth. It is what makes a child unique from any other child born on that day. The ancients knew the Ascendant as the *horoskopos,* the "hour-marker." As a place of life, it designates when the newborn takes its first breath as an independent entity at the moment the life comes into physical incarnation.

Sometimes, the term Ascendant refers to the exact degree of the rising sign—the 23rd degree of Taurus—and at other times, it refers to the entire sign occupying the first house. The Ascendant degree establishes the line of the horizon, marking both the sunrise and sunset points on the birth day, and hence distinguishing the boundary between the location of the other planetary bodies that are in the visible upper hemisphere of Earth and those in its invisible lower hemisphere. The sign in which the Ascendant is located occupies the first house. Hellenistic astrologers named this house Breath, Spirit, Life, and Helm. The helm contains the steering mechanism of a ship and, in this context, refers to a nautical metaphor used in ancient texts that envisioned the life as a seafaring journey. With the Ascendant, a soul with an intention and occupying a physical body with which to accomplish it is born into time and space and begins its journey. This is where life emerges into the world of becoming.

In Hellenistic astrology, the investigation of the planet ruling the Ascendant was one of the universal techniques that spoke to the overall success of the life. The domicile lord of the Ascendant was likened to the helmsman or steersman, whose commands guided the ship of life to its destination. In Indian/Vedic astrology, the Ascendant, called the *Lagna*, is also a major component of interpretation. The importance of this planet has continued into the modern tradition, where it is sometimes called the chart ruler.

Let's begin with a thorough examination of the Ascendant, and then illustrate the teaching using our sample chart. Then we will discuss how to interpret the Ascendant ruler in our sample delineation, so you can see how to build the interpretation step by step.

The Ascendant Sign as Character Description

On the outermost level, the Ascendant by sign describes the outer character, appearance, and personality of an individual motivated by a certain psychological need. It signifies the kind of image that the person projects to the world at large. This outer image is often not the same as the essential identity, but it is the personality that is displayed in initial and everyday encounters with others. You could call it the individual's "packaging." To the extent that, in many of our casual and ordinary interactions with others we do not reveal our inner selves, the persona designated by the Ascendant sign governs a considerable portion of the qualities that are displayed to others.

Each of the twelve zodiacal signs can be conceptualized as representing one of the basic psychological needs that are common to all human beings. The way in which we express our personalities also incorporates the psychological features of the ascending sign. For example, if you have Gemini rising, your personality is communicative, versatile, curious, changeable, and seeks breadth rather than depth in your experiences. The outer display of this persona is informed by a psychological need to make mental contacts and communicate with others.

Modifying the Expression of the Persona

Planets or asteroids conjunct the Ascendant, and planets occupying the first house, will add their natures to the expression of the personality. They represent the archetypal personalities that stand front and center, having a strong influence in directing the course of the life. Thus, if you have Saturn the Elder conjunct a Gemini Ascendant, you will tend to be more serious, taciturn, and conservative with your thoughts and words. If Mars the Warrior is conjunct the Ascendant, your personality may be more aggressive and you may use words as weapons. Note that you do not have to delineate the planets conjunct the Ascendant by sign, or even discuss their condition, at this point in the delineation. When you investigate the topics that planets rule, then you can consider their condition.

In your delineation, begin by describing the personality in terms of the qualities associated with the zodiacal sign rising, both as descriptive characteristics and as a psychological need. Modify its expression due to the presence of any planets or asteroids conjunct the Ascendant. These planets will be in the same sign as the Ascendant (when using the Whole Sign house system), so you have the option of whether or not to discuss how they are modified by the sign. If they are in a sign of their rulership, exaltation, detriment, or fall, this may be important to mention.

> Bill has Sagittarius rising, with Mercury and Venus conjunct the Ascendant. The asteroids Amicita and Fraternitas are conjunct Venus and Mercury to the exact degree, and they are within a 3-degree orb of the Ascendant.
>
> Bill's outer personality is characterized by an expansive, intellectually questing nature that has strong idealism and broad-ranging visions (skillful Sagittarius attributes). However, he can sometimes be dogmatic in his views and overly blunt, bordering on tactless (unskillful Sagittarius attributes). With Mercury conjoined to the Ascendant, he projects the image of a good communicator who is knowledgeable in a variety of topics, although he may wander about verbally, more con-

cerned with conveying the big picture than the details (Mercury in its detriment). The placement of Venus in the ascending sign lends charm, magnetism, and physical attractiveness to his image. The asteroids Amicita and Fraternitas speak for themselves—Bill's outer personality is characterized by his concern for friendship and brotherhood, as an expression of the kind of person he is.

The Drive that Motivates the Soul

On a deeper level, the element of the Ascendant sign also points to the primary motivation of the soul. What core drive motivates the person to action and sustains the continuity of that action?

- People with a fire sign rising are motivated by the drive for freedom of action, power over their own lives, and the influence or wherewithal to bring their visions into manifestation.
- People with an air sign rising are motivated by the drive to explore and express their ideas without restriction, and to receive positive acknowledgment for what they think and say.
- People with an earth sign rising are motivated by the drive for physical and material security in their lives—a roof over their heads, money in the bank, and the knowledge that they will not become homeless and destitute.
- People with a water sign rising are motivated by the drive for emotional support, security, bonding, and intimacy, with the continual reassurance that things are as they seem and will turn out all right.

To the extent that life circumstances—relationships, jobs, belief systems, or group affiliations—foster and permit the expression of these core drives, the individual is functional. However, when circumstances deny or negate these basic needs, sooner or later the situation becomes intolerable. The person has to disengage him or herself, because the bottom line is not being met. This information concerning what motivates the soul in accordance with the element of the sign can help you determine the Ascendant sign when the birth time is uncertain. Determine what motivates Bill's soul according to the characteristics of the element of his Ascendant sign.

> Because Sagittarius is a fire sign, the core drives that motivate Bill's soul to action are freedom and autonomy, the desire for power over others (or, minimally, not wanting anyone else to have power over him), and the capacity to have influence in his world. When he feels restricted, dominated, or thwarted in his efforts, his fire-sign-rising nature may induce him to push back and become overly aggressive. Remaining in situations where he is disempowered is not an acceptable option.

Transits or Progressions to the Ascendant

At this point, you have to make a decision about what to discuss next. The immediately obvious choice is to see the planet that rules the Ascendant as providing the key to how that core need is met. However, this move will take you away from the Ascendant, and there may be a few more things that could happen first. In particular, if there are any transits or progressions to the Ascendant degree, this is the time to integrate them. Another possible time to bring this up is after you discuss the ruler of the Ascendant. Then look at timing activations to both these points before moving on to other factors.

In your delineation, discuss any timing activations to the Ascendant by transit or progression, or eclipses that have recently occurred or will occur within the coming year.

> In looking at Bill's chart on the date of this writing, November 2006, we see that the progressed MC at 16 Sagittarius 09 is within a partile (same-degree) orb of the natal Ascendant at 16 Sagittarius 24. Also, the transit of Jupiter will shortly enter the sign of Sagittarius, activating his first house, and conjoin Venus, Mercury, and Ascendant degrees by February 2007, retrograding back and forth until November 2007. A quick glance tells you that the transit of Pluto will also be squaring Jupiter, the Ascendant ruler, during this same period, and the transit of Uranus will square the Ascendant in 2007.

You may decide to wait and discuss all of these timing activations at the same time later in the reading. In any case, you know that the most sensitive point in Bill's chart is being triggered during the coming year, and this is likely to precipitate significant change. We will discuss the interpretation of transits and progressions more fully in chapter 6.

The Ascendant as Helm

Now we arrive at one of the most important planets in the chart—the ruler of the Ascendant. Once you establish the fundamental motivation as indicated by the element of the Ascendant sign, you can determine how the person instinctively goes about expressing that drive. The planet that rules the Ascendant gives information about how and where the person is motivated to act, and to what extent the actions will lead to realization of the life purpose. In a broader sense, the condition of the planetary ruler of the Ascendant and its relationship to the Ascendant itself speaks to the issue of whether or not the individual has the resources and capacity to direct the course of the life to a clearly defined goal. If not, the life may emerge in a manner that drifts about aimlessly; the person may have difficulty defining or accomplishing a clear purpose, or may seem to be carried along by forces outside his or her control.

In Hellenistic astrology, Helm was one of the significations of the first house where the rudder, the steering mechanism of a ship, is located. A successful life can be likened to a successful seafaring voyage where a ship reaches its destination with its cargo intact. Planets occupying the first house stand close to the rudder, perhaps having their hands on it, and their agendas are considered very influential in moving the ship of life forward. But it is the steersman who issues the commands that guide the ship toward its destination. Here, this role is attributed to the planet that is the domicile lord, or ruler, of the Ascendant.

The Ruler of the Ascendant as Steersman

The domicile lord, or ruler, of the Ascendant is an extremely important planet because it guides the life to its destination. This planet indicates the archetypal personality of the steersman. For example, if the ruler of the Ascendant is Venus, the Lover guides the life journey; if Mars, the Warrior; if the Moon, the Mother. Its house placement determines which topic steers and directs the life. For example, if the ruler of the Ascendant is located in the seventh house, relationship steers the life; if it is located in the tenth house, profession moves the life toward its destination. The sign of the Ascendant ruler tells the manner in which this is done. For example, an Ascendant ruler in the sign of Aries signifies strong, autonomous, decisive action; an Ascendant ruler in Capricorn signifies methodical, strategic planning; a ruler in Pisces signifies emotional and artistic sensitivity. The sign and house placements of the Ascendant ruler together point to how and where individuals take action to move their lives forward based on the core drive that motivates their souls.

The condition of the Ascendant ruler, as gauged by its sect, zodiacal sign rulership, house angularity, help and harm from benefic and malefic planets, and relationship to the solar-phase cycle of the Sun, determines its capacity to be effective in its job and regulates its ability to produce favorable outcomes for the life and its competency to bring the life journey to a successful conclusion. Planets and asteroids configured to the Ascendant ruler give more detail about how this planet operates. Once you have considered these chart elements, you can discuss the timing activations to both the Ascendant and the ruler of the Ascendant. I listed them for Bill's chart earlier in this lesson, but we will defer their interpretation until chapter 6.

INTERPRETING THE ASCENDANT IN THE CHART

There are two levels of interpretation for the ruler of the Ascendant. On the first level, you describe the planet itself, and how its expression must incorporate the significations of other planetary bodies to which it is configured, especially the conjunctions. Then you must synthesize how that planet's expression is filtered through the sign in which it is located and how it impacts the houses it occupies and rules. This constitutes a thorough analysis from a modern perspective. However, the traditional approach adds a second level of interpretation—assessing the planet's condition to gauge how effectively it can do the job of directing the life to its intended destination. If you are a beginning student, you may want to start with the first level. However, if you are an intermediate student or feel ready to take on an additional challenge, try the second, which is based upon a full analysis of a planets' condition as understood by traditional astrologers.

LEVEL 1: WHO, HOW, WHERE?

1. Identify and describe the nature of the planet that rules the Ascendant.
2. If the planetary ruler is conjunct another planet or asteroid, a fixed star, a lunar node, or the Lot of Fortune, factor in those influences.
3. Delineate the sign and house placement as they point to how and where the personality seeks to secure the core need that motivates the soul.
4. What other house does that planet rule? The topical meanings of that house will also play a part in identifying the dynamics involved.

LEVEL 2: EFFECTIVE OR INEFFECTIVE; FAVORABLE OR UNFAVORABLE?

1. Is the sign of the planet that rules the Ascendant configured to the sign of the Ascendant itself? Use only the five Ptolemaic aspects (conjunction, sextile, square, trine, opposition) for this consideration—in other words, determine if the planet is located in the good houses that are conducive to the business of life. If the sign is so configured, there is a connection and line of communication between the agent responsible for accomplishing the goal or fulfilling the core motivational drive and the

steering mechanism itself. If there is a clear line of communication between the articulation of the order and the execution of the action, conscious directive movement can occur. If there is no configuration between the sign of the Ascendant ruler and the sign of the Ascendant, there is not a clear line of communication; the life can drift about with no clear sense of direction and can easily be taken off course.

2. Is the planet in a sign in which it has rulership (domicile, exaltation)? If so, it has ample resources to accomplish its aims or achieve high status as to its significations. Is it in a sign of its detriment or fall? If so, it may be bereft or needy of resources or not respected, and thus be challenged in its capacity to produce the desired result.

3. If the planet does not have access to it own resources due to its sign, can it expect assistance from its own domicile lord (also called the dispositor) based upon its condition and configuration to the planet in question?

4. Is the planet in an angular, succedent, or cadent house? How much of its focus is directed toward the destination of the individual?

5. Is the planet assisted in its quest by means of a conjunction, trine, or sextile from Venus or Jupiter? Is the planet hindered in its quest by means of a conjunction, square, or opposition from Mars or Saturn?

6. Is the planet retrograde? From the traditional point of view, a retrograde planet is weakened, making it more difficult for the person to actualize its significations in the life. The significations that it produces may later be taken back, or the outcomes may occur later in life. From a modern point of view, the individual is challenged to discover alternative ways of expressing the planet's function that speak to inner rather than outer processes, and thus becomes a more individualized expression of that planet's nature.

7. Is the planet under the Sun's beams? If so, its nature is absorbed by the Sun, which then becomes more like that planet. But its own significations and those of the houses that the USB planet occupies and rules are diminished.

8. Does the planet receive an application from the Moon that assists in the manifestation of its significations?

The ruler of Bill's Sagittarius Ascendant is Jupiter. Bill seeks to secure these (fire-sign-rising) needs through the significations of the planet Jupiter, seeking philosophical meaning and dissemination of knowledge as it is applied to the area of home, family, parents, land, and real estate (fourth house) in a Piscean manner marked by a spiritual vision and artistic creativity. By holding to a moral highroad (Jupiter) from a spiritual motivation (Pisces) in family- and home-related matters (fourth house), he gains in power and influence (fire sign rising). Since Jupiter is in Pisces, one of the signs of its own rulership, it is located in the house Pisces rules, so there is no other house to consider. The asteroid Utopia at 2 Aries is within a 3-degree across-sign boundary conjunction with Jupiter, and Bill's philosophical inclinations superimpose visions of the ideal state onto his personal domestic environment. Neptune, the planet of illusion and imagination, in the tenth house of profession placed in the technically proficient sign of Virgo, opposes Jupiter and draws the life force into the arena of social recognition from Bill's artistic or spiritual actions in the world. The Sun as sect leader forms a favorable applying trine to its sect-mate, Jupiter, illuminating the insights that arise from deep contemplation of universal truths.

While Mercury and Venus in the first house may have their hands on the rudder and thus exert a strong force in guiding the life forward, putting their concerns for relationship and profession (Mercury ruling the seventh and tenth) and health and group affiliations (Venus ruling the sixth and eleventh) as the leading issues, it is the natural benefic Jupiter, as the ruler of Ascendant and steersman of the ship, that has the authority to bring the life to its destination.

In our previous analysis of each planet, we determined that Jupiter was in the best condition of all. Because Jupiter in Pisces configures by sign to Sagittarius on the Ascendant, there is a line of communication, albeit stressful, between the ruler of the Ascendant and the Ascendant itself. This indicates the issuance of commands that can bring the life to a favorable completion of its purpose, although there may be obstacles to overcome on the way. Jupiter occupies Pisces, a sign of its own domicile rulership, and thus has access to significant resources for the accomplishment of its endeavors that may arise from the parents and real estate assets (fourth house). Jupiter gains strength placed in a good angular house that is conducive to business and all of its actions are focused upon his purpose.

Jupiter is neither helped and assisted by the benefic Venus, nor harmed and negated by either of the two malefics. (An advanced analysis might consider Jupiter's possible containment by Mars and Saturn, but that is nullified by the interposition of a ray from the Sun). Jupiter is visible, so its significations can appear and eventuate, but its retrograde motion suggests, from a traditional perspective, that some of its benefic events will be recalled or occur later in life. From a modern psychological perspective, the retrograde motion suggests Bill will be in a continual process of re-thinking his belief system and coming to an internal verification of truth rather than relying automatically on external authority. Jupiter is one day past a phasis condition, as it turns direct eight days after the birth, and has residual intensity in its effects permeating the life. Jupiter receives an application from the Moon by sextile aspect, which assists in the manifestation of its significations.

Now you can make a statement about this chart that takes into account your analysis of planetary condition, but reframes your understanding in terms of life purpose. Bill projects an expansive, idealistic, philosophically questing nature (Sagittarius Ascendant) that seeks to have power and influence (fire sign) in manifesting his Utopian ideals (Jupiter as ruler of Ascendant) concerning land and home matters (Jupiter in fourth house) in a manner that is compassionate and arises from spiritual insight (Jupiter in Pisces). He has the necessary resources (Jupiter in its own domicile) and focus (Jupiter angular) to accomplish this intention, and the capacity to overcome obstacles along the way (Jupiter configured to Ascendant sign by square). The final outcome may eventuate in the latter part of his life (Jupiter retrograde).

Study Guidelines

Examine all the factors involved for a delineation of the Ascendant sign and its ruler for your practice chart. Prepare a written analysis, following the example in Bill's chart.

- Describe the persona by the qualities associated with the zodiacal sign rising, and modify its expression due to the presence of any planets or asteroids conjunct the Ascendant.
- Describe the primary need that motivates the soul by the elemental characteristics of the rising sign.
- Delineate the ruler of the Ascendant in terms of how and where the individual seeks to meet the core need that motivates the soul, its condition, and how this factor influences the capacity to accomplish the life goal.
- Mention any important transits and/or progressions to the Ascendant or to its ruler, but delay interpreting them until later.
- In your summation, reframe the material into a concise statement that addresses the life purpose.

CHAPTER FIVE

THE SUN, THE MOON, AND THE LIFE PURPOSE

Now that you have delineated the Ascendant and its ruler, you have a sense of what core drive motivates the soul to action, what planet and house guide the person to his or her destination as the purpose of the life incarnation, and to what extent this will be a successful journey. Next, we will investigate just what this purpose is and how it can be expressed in the daily life. For these answers, we turn to the Sun and the Moon.

Hellenistic astrologers called the Sun and the Moon "the rulers of one's all," and described them as having authority over the whole life.[1] Of the seven visible planets known to the ancients, the Sun is the largest body and the Moon is the smallest. Yet, by some exquisite piece of geometry and proportion, at the moment when the Full Moon rises in the east, just as the Sun sets in the west, they appear to be the same size from the perspective of Earth. Together, the Sun and Moon regulate the cycle of day and night, wake and sleep, activity and rest—a tempo that moves us through the days and months and years of our lives.

What distinguishes the Sun from the other planetary bodies in the horoscope is that it is a star. The nature and composition of a star, an enormous generator of fiery energy, is different from that of a planet. In fact, since the ultimate energy source for most of the biological processes on Earth is sunlight, the ancients were not mistaken in their worship of the Sun as the fount of life. Plato thought the stars were a more divine order of celestial entities than the planets, because they moved with a regularity quite different from the erratic movements of the planets. Today we know that the Sun is the center of our solar system; all the other planets revolve around it. As such, it can be said to be the center or heart of our being, around which all other astrological factors constellate.

The Sun is the domicile lord of the zodiacal sign Leo, which is associated with both the heart of the cosmic animal and the heart of the human being. Many medical schools of antiquity held that the mind was located in the heart. In the second century c.e., the Hellenistic astrologer Vettius Valens wrote that the Sun signifies the king, the soul, and the mind.[2] In Mesopotamia, where astrology originated and was practiced for 2000 years before it was taken up by the Greeks, astrologers were the priests who interpreted the movements of the planets as communications from the gods. They conveyed this information to the kings so that they might rule in accordance with divine intent. The ancient Greek philosophers understood the soul as the divine part of the human mind. In astrology, it is through the Sun that the human mind has a direct link to the divine, and thus it is through the Sun that the divine intention for the individual is most clearly indicated.

The Moon is neither a star nor a planet, but rather a satellite that orbits the Earth. Its light is reflected light, and yet it is the most brilliant object illuminating the night sky. Aristotle proposed a model of the cosmos whereby everything in the celestial realm was composed of *aither*, a divine substance, and everything beneath the sphere of the Moon consisted of a mixture of the four qualities of fire, earth, air, and water. These elements changed into one another through the qualities hot, cold, wet, and dry. It was the Moon that transmitted the influences of the divine celestial bodies via effluences to the elemental terrestrial realm, and thus aided in the process of making their significations manifest and embodied in the physical realm. The heating and cooling actions of the Sun and Moon governed the process of what Aristotle called the "generation and corruption" of the elements, or the periodic cycles of coming to be and passing away. Because the Moon is nearest to Earth, it was considered to have the closest connection to the human body and consequently to matters of health.

Vettius Valens wrote that the Moon signifies the queen, concep-
tion, and the body.[3] As the Sun is the lord of the day, the Moon is
the queen of the night; together king and queen are the archetypal
earthly representatives of the god and goddess in the heavens. Buddhist philosophy speaks of the "precious human birth," because they
hold that we can only achieve enlightenment while in a human body.
The life and death of the body demarcates the boundary between the
life and death of a human being. When a soul/mind can occupy a
body that is alive, it has the potential to actualize itself. What can
be actualized, however, is often determined by the nature, strength,
and capacities of the body.

The Moon is the final link in the chain between celestial and
terrestrial. It receives the vital fiery energy of the Sun and, via reflection, focuses it on the Earth in incremental phases. From an astrological perspective, the Moon signifies how the divine intention represented by the Sun can find physical actualization in a human body
and then be applied to the affairs of daily life and worldly existence
so that our actions can benefit others.

We can say that the two lights, the Sun and the Moon, are the
places that contain the vital essences of the life force. The recep-
tacles of the most concentrated, vital, life-sustaining energy are
the very places whose outflow is directed toward the essential life
purpose.

The Sun and Moon are the two primary symbols of human personality, and each has a wide range of individual meanings. In fact,
all the planets have at least three distinct categories of significations. First, each planet has a general signification that is common
to all charts and corresponds to some quality of a person's essential
nature. The term that the Greeks gave to this faculty was *ousia,* or
"soul essence." Each planet represents this same faculty of the soul
in every chart.

Each planet also signifies concrete objects, personality traits,
and types of people, and is associated with particular colors, metals,
stones, plants, smells, and tastes. These comprise its Hermetic correspondences. Robert Schmidt points out that, in terms of the cosmological model underlying the discipline of astrology, here we see
the role of the planets as mediators between some faculty of the soul

on the divine level and the concrete manifestations of that principle on the earthly level.

In addition to these general significations, each planet influences the significations of the house it occupies and also governs one or two particular topics, based upon the house(s) that it rules in a particular chart. This category will vary from one chart to another, as the signs occupying the houses are generated from the hour of the day a person is born.

As an astrologer, you must be familiar with all the significations that each planet represents; in the course of your delineations, you will draw upon this knowledge. However, for the purposes of this inquiry, we will consider that the Sun points to the content of the life purpose and the Moon represents how this purpose is applied in our daily activities. The Sun symbolizes the conceptual image, which then takes shape in an embodied form as defined by the Moon. Our hypothesis is that the birth chart contains this innate pattern that asks to be lived. If the individual can express and live out this pattern, it will give a sense of purposeful meaning to the life. In a detailed and comprehensive study of Hellenistic astrology, other planets besides the Sun and Moon are involved in the determination of the nature of a person's destiny. Here, we'll use the primacy of the solar and lunar symbols as guideposts by which to uncover the essential meaning of the life.

The Sun

The Sun signifies the radiant core of a person's essence—the soul, the mind and consciousness, the life force and vitality, the basic sense of selfhood, the purpose of the life, and the source of the will for accomplishing that purpose. Keep in mind that the Sun describes both the basic nature of the individual and the life purpose as an expression of that nature. Thus, what we do in terms of living a meaningful life is simply *who we are* on an essential level. The Ascendant ruler points to the capacity of the personality to accomplish a life goal that is motivated by the core drive. The Sun, by its sign and house positions, describes the nature of the underlying purpose striving toward expression.

House Considerations

As you become proficient in the art of delineation, you will develop the ability to take in all the factors in a chart in one initial glance before saying anything. If we had to rank those factors, however, perhaps the most important is the house a planet occupies and the houses that it rules. The Sun's house placement signifies the area of life activities in which the purpose will be expressed and the house that the Sun rules points to the topics of life that have a role in the expression of the purpose. A more formal statement based upon the tenets of traditional astrology as to the exact relationship between the house a planet rules and the house it occupies can be stated thus:

> A planet has the responsibility to render judgment upon and bring about the affairs of the house it rules, and it does so by means of the activities of the house it occupies.

For example, if the Sun occupies the seventh house of relationship and rules the tenth of profession (which contains the sign Leo), you know that the ruler of the tenth house is located in the seventh house. Thus the content of the life purpose as signified by the Sun has to do with bringing about the affairs of the profession by participating in relationships and partnerships. This may mean that building or participating in a career with a marriage or business partner is the kind of activity that can support the development of the professional life. Furthermore, participation in relationships that are linked with professional goals is what this person is here to do in this life.

Meanwhile, on a secondary level, you consider the kind of house the Sun occupies. Its relative angularity will tell you how much strength stands behind the Sun to focus on its task and the good/bad nature of the house tells you something about how favorable the outcomes will be. As a counselor, you may not necessarily share this information, but, as an astrologer, it informs you how to proceed with the discussion. Not everyone has the same amount of energy or priority to put into the effort of expressing life purpose, or it may be that the purpose is quite straightforward. Some may see financial security or fulfilling familial expectations or enjoyment of the moment as purposeful self-expression. As a counseling astrologer, you must discern where your clients are and what is most important to them, and extend respect for the choices they make.

Sign Considerations

From the perspective of descriptive delineation, the zodiacal sign in which the Sun is placed describes the manner in which the soul purpose will be expressed, the qualities that fuel the Sun's ability to shine and be important in some way, and the source of the will that makes the purpose manifest. If the Sun in the above example is in the seventh house and rules the tenth, which is occupied by the sign Leo, in the Whole Sign house system, by necessity, that Sun occupies the sign of Taurus (and Scorpio is ascending). The soul purpose will express itself in a stable and productive manner. Its perception and sensory appreciation of the physical world fuels its ability to shine, and its consistent and practical nature are the source of the will that makes the purpose manifest. Furthermore, professional partnerships that involve working with land, art, or financial resources (all Taurus-ruled activities) may contribute to the content of the business.

To assess the condition of the Sun based on sign rulerships, you take note of what kind of sign the Sun occupies. Mentally place a plus mark if it is Leo (the sign of its domicile rulership) or Aries (its exaltation sign) to indicate resources or honors. If the Sun is in its detriment in Aquarius or fall in Libra, however, place a mental minus sign and be aware that there may be a problem with a lack of resources or with disrespect. From a psychological perspective, because Libra and Aquarius are both "other-directed" signs, the unique individuality of the Sun is eclipsed or overshadowed by its consideration of and connection to others, either one-to-one with Libra or in groups with Aquarius. By reframing the interpretation, you can also propose that the individual purpose *is* to merge one's self with others. If the Sun is in some other sign, then look to that sign's domicile lord (its dispositor) for information about the nature, amount, and availability of resources it is likely to receive from its host. In the above example, the Taurus Sun is not in any signs of its own rulership, so look to the placement and condition of its dispositor, Venus, in the chart.

Aspect Considerations

Look to see if the Sun is in the same sign as another planet, asteroid, fixed star, Lot of Fortune, or lunar node. The significations of these celestial bodies or points will contribute their own natures to the expression of the life purpose, and this is the time to bring their meanings into the delineation. The closer they are to the degree of the Sun, the more active their influence. For the minor asteroids, I generally do not go beyond a 3-degree orb.

Here we encounter a major difference between modern and traditional astrology—but not an irresolvable one. In modern astrology, a planet gains in importance and influence if conjoined with the Sun; the two archetypes merge and function as a team. The basic life purpose incorporates the qualities of the planets and asteroids that conjoin the Sun.

In traditional astrology, if a planet or Fortune is under the Sun's beams within a 15-degree orb, it becomes burnt up by the Sun's glare and its own significations and the topics of the houses it rules are weakened. What actually happens is that the Sun takes up and absorbs the qualities of these other planetary bodies and radiates them outward as part of its own expression. Thus Mercury conjoined to the Sun results in a more mercurial kind of Sun. While the power of the planet is weakened when absorbed by the Sun, the Sun itself is strengthened. But if a planet is in its own sign of rulership, it has more strength and resilience to withstand the ill effects of the Sun's beams.

Any planets or asteroids that square or oppose the Sun produce a state of dynamic tension, because their own agendas are often at cross-purposes with, or going in an opposite direction from, the expression of the solar purpose. When evaluating the condition of the Sun, be sure to determine if it is being corrupted and harmed in its capacity to produce favorable significations due to a conjunction, square, or opposition by Mars or Saturn. Also check to see if it is

bonified and enhanced due to a conjunction, sextile, or trine from
Venus and Jupiter.

The Sun is never retrograde.

General Considerations

The rubric I have given you for delineating the Sun can be used,
with modifications, to interpret any other planet. If you are a begin-
ner, focus on the Sun as the basic life purpose and source of will with
regard to the zodiacal sign and house that it occupies, the house that
it rules, and any planets or asteroids that are conjunct with it. Then
scan to see if any other planets that square or oppose the Sun present
obstacles or challenges to the Sun's expression, and look for planets
that trine or sextile the Sun that may provide support. It is especially
important here to think about how to synthesize the meaning of the
Sun as the basic life purpose with the Ascendant ruler as the capacity of the personality to accomplish life goals that are motivated by
a core need.

If you are at an intermediate or advanced level and feel confident
of your process, begin to incorporate an analysis of the planet based
on its condition. This is the goal that you eventually want to reach.
But concentrate on first things first, until they become second nature
to you. Otherwise, you will become confused and build your readings
on a shaky foundation.

And finally, our discussion of the Sun raises a challenging philosophical issue that we will address more fully in our discussion on
counseling. It is our operating hypothesis here that everyone has a
life purpose, which, if expressed, brings a sense of meaning to the
life. But how do you interpret charts in which it is more difficult to
express that purpose, or in which the outcomes of the purpose result
in unfavorable reactions from others? How, as an astrological counselor, do you deal with a client whose chart reflects the likelihood
of a life containing obstacles, setbacks, lack of focus, or unrealized
potential? These are questions you have to consider when interact-
ing with clients.

Bill's core essence is shaped by the Sun in Scorpio in the twelfth house. Behind the exuberant, extroverted, social persona designated by the Sagittarian Ascendant is an individual who is intensely private, with deep penetrating insights that pierce beneath the surface of whatever he encounters—hidden agendas, strong passions, and intense attachment to others. The twelfth-house Sun can connote the suffering that arises from a sense of existential alienation, the call for selfless service to others, and a quest to illuminate what is hidden. A relentless investigation of the subconscious psychological forces that drive him and others is a source of both inner power and self-torture.

The Sun rules the ninth house (Leo occupying the ninth), which is associated with religion, higher education, long-distance travel, and multicultural perspectives. Arising out his own suffering from feeling isolated and rejected by others (twelfth house), Bill's life purpose can be imagined as the application of spiritual teachings (Sun ruling the ninth house) for transformation of the self (Sun in Scorpio) and for the benefit of others (Sun in the twelfth house). The desire for solitude in order to contemplate the ineffable (Sun in the twelfth) is polarized by Uranus in the sixth house, which adds a rebellious and nonconformist dimension to the basic nature. Uranus can precipitate ongoing disruption as well as innovation in its attempt to be resourceful and consistent (Taurus) in the world of jobs, daily routines, and health crises (sixth house).

Because the Sun is in a cadent house, there is not a lot of vital force available to pursue its agenda, at least in terms of outer manifestation. From a psychological perspective, the real work of the soul purpose may take place on the inner levels. The problematic nature of the twelfth house to result in unfavorable outcomes can be understood as an encounter with difficult psychological material, making others, when confronted with it, resentful of the person who has brought it to consciousness. The Sun in the twelfth house can illuminate all that is hidden and suppressed. The Sun is not in any sign of its own rulership, and thus does not have access to its own resources. While the Sun receives some assistance from the trine from Jupiter, the Ascendant ruler, it is also hindered by the square from Mars, its dispositor. Thus, the capacity to express the life purpose may operate at a low level, take a back seat to other agendas, have difficulty manifesting, result in problematic experiences, or be deferred until later in life.

The Moon

The Moon is a general symbol of the body, in counterpoint to the Sun, which is a general symbol of the mind. In and of itself, the Moon signifies the ways in which the impressions of our early child-hood conditioning have imprinted the patterning of our bodies, our instincts, and our emotional responses to life—all pre-cognitive faculties. When we respond to situations based on our instincts and feelings, when we "act without thinking," these behaviors often can be traced back to what we experienced in early life when we were under our mother's influence. As such, the Moon colors what makes us feel nurtured and secure, how we express nurturing toward others, and how we cope with emotional stress in our lives. Like the ocean tides that are regulated by the lunar phases, the tides in our bodies, as the ebb and flow of our moods, are under the domain of the Moon. While the Moon continues to symbolize all these other qualities, when evaluating its role in terms of the life purpose, we must see it as pointing to how an individual brings the conceptual vision of the life intention, as depicted by the Sun, into the physical world by grounding it in the daily actions of everyday life.

House Considerations

The Moon's house placement signifies the area of life activities in which the person attempts to establish emotional intimacy, connection, and comfort, as well as the area where the purpose will be brought into daily life. The topical meanings of houses ruled by the Moon (whichever house is occupied by the sign of Cancer) also are factored into the kinds of activities that bring the purpose into everyday life. The Moon attempts to bring about the affairs of the house it rules by means of its activities in the house it occupies. The relative angularity and good/bad nature of the house that the Moon occupies address how much strength the Moon has to produce its effects and how favorable those outcomes will be in the life.

Sign Considerations

The zodiacal sign the Moon occupies describes the manner in which the life purpose is actualized. It also symbolizes the qualities that nurture the person's capacity to do so, as well as the qualities that the person needs in order to feel emotionally nurtured, comfortable, and safe. The Moon located in Cancer or Taurus points toward self-sufficiency and esteem in connection with the Moon's significations, and in its capacity to actualize the intentions designated by the Sun. A placement in Capricorn or Scorpio indicates challenges with securing emotional needs and implementing the purpose. The Moon's dispositor provides additional information about the resources available to the Moon from its host planet.

Aspect Considerations

First, look to see if the Moon is conjunct another planet, asteroid, fixed star, Fortune, or lunar node. The significations of these planetary bodies will contribute their own natures to the actualization of the life purpose in the daily activities. Any planets or asteroids that square or oppose the Moon produce a state of dynamic tension, because their own agendas are often at cross-purposes with the individual's attempt to actualize the purpose. Factor in help and hindrance from the benefic and malefic planets.

Solar and Lunar Considerations

The Moon is never retrograde. It can suffer the effects of being under the beams, which means that being born within a day before or after the New Moon, when the Moon's light cannot be seen on Earth, carries some diminishment of the Moon's effectiveness. However, this is ameliorated if the Moon is in Cancer or Taurus. Check the Moon's speed, whether it is waxing or waning, and whether it is making applications to other planets (within 13 degrees across sign boundaries) or is void-of-course.

Then make a judgment. How and where and with whom does the Moon apply the life intention symbolized by the Sun to the practicalities of the everyday world? To what extent does the Moon have the capacity to be effective in terms of its vital force, resources, and assistance received in ways that produce favorable outcomes for the individual?

Bill's emotional nature is shaped by the Moon in Aquarius in the third house. In juxtaposition to the passionate, intense, all-consuming nature of the Scorpio Sun, the Aquarian Moon is marked by emotional detachment, impersonality, and a desire to create social change motivated by altruism and humanitarianism. In terms of zodiacal signs, the Sun and Moon are configured by a square aspect, suggesting tension between the thinking and feeling parts of Bill's nature. He may experience conflict between what he feels and what he thinks. The hidden emotional material of the Scorpio Sun needs to surface into his conscious awareness so he can better understand the deep currents that inform his communications.

The Moon is located in the third house of communication, where there is an emotional need to talk about the feelings. The Moon rules the eighth house (Cancer occupies the eighth) associated with topics of death, benefits accrued from death, sexuality (in modern, though not in traditional, astrology), and the psychological unconsciousness. Bill establishes emotional intimacy through conversing about these topics. The Moon attempts to bring about the matters of the eighth house by means of its activities in the third. There may also be some connection between inheritances (Moon ruling the eighth) and siblings (Moon occupying the third), or close involvement with siblings concerning joint financial resources. The third house also signifies the local community, and the Moon in this place may nurture and be nurtured through involvement in community interactions.

The Moon has a close opposition to Pluto and Pallas, pointing to deep attachments with loved ones, the inner feminine (Moon) imaged as a powerful (Pluto) intelligent (Pallas) woman, and the attempt to nurture others (Moon) through the challenging (opposition) of belief systems (ninth house). The Moon also is conjoined by sign with Juno, one significator of marriage, and with Mars, the principle of assertion and conflict. Bill has an emotional need for freedom (Moon in Aquarius) within a committed relationship (Moon conjunct Juno), and his marriages may be fraught with struggles for power and control (Juno conjunct Mars), battling over different belief systems (blending in the opposition from Pluto in the ninth house) and styles of parenting (Mars rules the fifth house of children). The Moon with Mars in the third house may also signify conflict with siblings and partners.

The Moon is in a cadent, but good, house, and is not in any places of its own rulerships, suggesting that there is not as much drive to express its significations as outer events, although the ones that are expressed are generally favorable. Again, from a modern perspective, cadent planets can be interpreted as having an active inner life, and, in this case, the Moon is busy in the sphere of thinking, learning, reading, and conversing. The Moon receives some help from Venus sextiling it, but also considerable hindrance from the co-presence with Mars. The Moon's dispositor/domicile lord is Saturn, which is located in the fifth house of children and is ostensibly weak in the sign of its fall, retrograde, and conjunct the south node. Because Saturn is in mutual reception with Mars, it has a hidden strength in providing resources to the Moon, but communication with a partner with regard to children may, nevertheless, be tense and strained. The Moon has challenges in meeting its emotional needs and may encounter some conflict and resistance in any attempt to establish emotional intimacy.

The manner in which the intention of the Sun is anchored

into the world by the Moon is primarily through the dissemination of information (third house) in the local community that
is innovative, progressive, free-thinking, and humanitarian
(Aquarius).

Now let's distill and summarize the main ideas from our analysis of
the Ascendant and its ruler, the Sun, and the Moon into a statement
of what Bill's basic life purpose might be:

> The core need that motivates the soul is the quest for a more
> expansive vision of family and home structures; the life purpose
> is expressed through the incorporation of spiritual teachings that
> effect personal transformation and liberation, which is actualized
> through disseminating information about innovative develop-
> ments within community life. The cadent positions of the Sun and
> Moon suggest that the essential work of the life purpose occurs in
> the inner realm of thought and spiritual practice.

Let's see if our statement speaks to the themes of Bill's life. Early
in life, Bill gained a national reputation as a filmmaker document-
ing the New Age communes that flourished along the West Coast
between 1968 and 1972. Thirty years later, he produced a public-
television documentary recognizing innovative community projects
and interactions in communities throughout the state. Currently, he
has a business renovating and building co-operative housing units.
He has recently bought a large home for the purpose of creating an
intentional domestic community that values spiritual practice.

You can see just how far you can get in the delineation of a chart
by following the trail of these three primary places of life. They
can provide a basic framework for interpreting the natal chart. In
the process of looking at the web of relationships depicted in Bill's
chart by the Ascendant, its ruler, the Sun, and the Moon, you have
also touched upon a number of other planets that are configured to
these principle significators of the life force. You have elucidated the
major themes that have shaped this person's life experiences. The
underlying message of the chart has begun to emerge and should be
relatively well defined. However, there may still be parts of the chart

that you deemed significant in your overview that have not been addressed. You can expand upon these themes and fill in additional details by considering other factors listed in your overview. Depending on the time remaining in your session and the focus questions indicated by your client, you can move on to other significant factors in the chart.

STUDY GUIDELINES

- Examine all the factors involved for a delineation of the Sun and the Moon in your practice chart.
- Prepare a written analysis, following the example in Bill's chart. In parentheses, indicate what astrological factor you are examining for each statement you make. Mention any important transits and/or progressions to the Sun and the Moon, but defer the interpretation of these factors until the next chapter.
- End with a statement in which you reframe the material into a concise summary that addresses life purpose, integrating the main point of the Ascendant and its ruler, and the Sun and Moon. This should be no more than 100 words.

CHAPTER SIX

TIMING BY TRANSITS AND PROGRESSIONS

We have examined the natal chart, which depicts the positions of the planets at the birth moment, and interpreted it as a description of a person's character over the duration of his or her life. We've used it as an indicator pointing to the kinds of activities that will lead a person toward a sense of living a purposeful life. But the birth chart is also a map of a person's destiny, indicating when the various events promised in the natal chart will occur. From a modern perspective, timing factors can forecast opportunities for personal growth, as well as the nature of obstacles to be overcome in the process of self-improvement and development. Dane Rudhyar spoke of timing in astrology as a schedule for the unfoldment of the birth potential over time.

Generally, when people's lives are going well, they do not seek advice or counseling. But when things start going badly—difficulty with or loss of relationships, jobs, health, or belief systems—they become anxious, fearful, and insecure. At these times, they are more likely to seek insight or advice about what is happening and what the outcome is going to be. This is when many people come to an astrologer's consulting room. The timing of these critical periods of crisis and change can often be seen through the timing factors in astrological prediction. It was astrology's claim to be able to predict the future that contributed to it becoming the premiere system of divination in the ancient world. In fact, historically, one of the main questions posed to astrologers is: What is going to happen next?

From a traditional perspective, timing factors predict the rise and fall of favorable and unfavorable periods in life. In addition, they indicate when specific events like marriage, the birth of children, health crises, or professional promotions will occur. Some of these events can be fortunate, others unfortunate. From a modern perspective, timing factors show periods of transition and change in our lives, where opportunities exist for growth by releasing and transforming the old so the new can emerge and take shape.

It is precisely at these times of crisis that people are most likely to take a hard look at their lives and question whether they are doing the right thing for themselves. They often are pushed into wondering if there may be other directions or paths that will give them greater happiness and fulfillment. This is where the motifs of crisis indicated by timing factors in the chart and concerns about meaningful life directions intersect. Clients are vulnerable, open, and receptive, and often want to consider the essential meaning of their lives when they come into the consulting room, because of the eruption of situations that threaten to disrupt and shatter their lives as they know them.

Modern astrology has a plethora of different timing mechanisms. Transits, secondary and tertiary progressions, solar-arc and primary directions, eclipses, and Solar Returns top the list of timing techniques in the Western system. The revival of traditional astrology is bringing forward many additional techniques—profections, planetary periods and ascensional times, circumambulations, decennials, zodiacal releasing, and *firdaria*—that are not generally part of the modern technical corpus. A beginning student can be overwhelmed and confused about which timing method to use, when to use it, and how to determine a hierarchy of importance.

Hellenistic (time lords), Medieval/Arabic (*firdaria*), or Vedic (*dashas*) timing procedures make use of long-term planetary periods and sub-periods to determine the broad divisions of time under whose auspices the transits and progressions occur. The value of these general time periods is the capacity to view the long-term patterns of the life that are more inclusive than a snapshot of what is happening in just one year. However, modern Western astrology, for the most part, lacks methods to signify these general time periods.

Instead, modern astrology relies primarily on the outer-planet transits through the signs to discuss long-term effects, but these often speak more to generational and social influences than to individual events. It also looks to the critical aspects each planet makes to itself by transiting aspect in the course of its own cycle—for instance, the Saturn return every twenty-eight to thirty years, punctuated by the square and opposition to its natal position every seven years—to convey the meanings of particular events within an unfolding cycle. The secondary progressed lunation cycle can be used to sketch out eight distinct three- to four-year periods as the successive stages of a thirty-year cycle of development.

By and large, modern astrologers use primarily the transits of the outer planets and secondary progressions to the natal chart to forecast the major influences and events that are likely to occur in the year ahead.

MAJOR TIMING PROCEDURES

Following is a description of the major timing procedures used by both modern and traditional astrologers, and suggestions for how you can prioritize the various timing mechanisms at your disposal. The second part of this chapter focuses on what you can cover realistically in a one-hour session through the use of transits and progressions. In later chapters, we will discuss the progressed lunation cycle, annual profections, and the Solar Return chart. The remainder of the traditional techniques will not be covered in this book.

Progressed Lunation Cycle

Unless you use the traditional methods of planetary time-lord periods to gain a sense of long-term influences, begin with the progressed lunation cycle. Every thirty years, the occurrence of a progressed New Moon (the progressed Moon is conjunct the progressed Sun) initiates the emergence of some kind of new vision or aspiration that grows to maturation twenty-one years later, and is brought to conclusion and summation at the closure of the cycle. A person's progressed lunation phase indicates the current stage in this thirty-year process. Checking the degree of the progressed New Moon relative to the natal chart, the house in which it occurs, and conjunctions to natal planets gives important information about the meaning of the entire cycle. Some astrologers also look to the Sabian symbol of the progressed New Moon for a symbolic image that embodies the new direction. This method will be discussed in more detail in chapter 8.[1]

Outer-planet Transits

You can assess the meanings of the outer-planet transits (Jupiter, Saturn, Uranus, Neptune, Pluto) to personal planets and to the angles that are sensitive points. You can gain insight by using the progressed lunation cycle as a framework in which to evaluate individual transits. For example, a Pluto transit to the Moon during a New Moon phase has a directive completely different from when it occurs during the final Balsamic phase. The period of intensity for the individual is the strongest when transiting planets are approaching natal planets, gradually building up pressure that becomes most concentrated at the conjunction, and then dropping off in intensity as they separate. Their effect is especially strong when transiting planets retrograde back and forth over the natal planet. The passage of a transiting planet through a particular sign and house also has significance for the length of time that the planet is in the sign. Outer-planet transits to the outer planets have more of a generational than individual influence. If an outer-planet transit is not making an aspect to a natal planet or point, we won't dwell on it, aside from a quick mention of the house it is activating.

Inner-planet Transits

The inner-planet transits (Moon, Sun, Mercury, Venus, Mars) move so quickly that their effects are transitory, except when they make a station and retrograde over natal planets, which lengthens their periods of influence.

Eclipses

Eclipses occur around twice each year, and you should keep in mind the degrees of the solar eclipse. If a solar eclipse aspects a natal planet or angle, and especially by conjunction, opposition, or square (3-degree orb or less) in that order, it may have a strong impact on the significations of that planet for up to six months or more after the eclipse.

Secondary Progressions

When looking at secondary progressions, the inner planets generally have more impact than the outer. The sign and house of the progressed Moon are especially important, as the progressed Moon moves through all twelve signs around the chart every twenty-seven years. The progressed Moon has a three-month period of influence on a natal planet or point—1 degree approaching, 1 degree conjunct, 1 degree separating. When the progressed angles or inner planets are within a 1-degree orb of a natal planet or angle it may be significant. Also, when a progressed planet changes sign or the year in which it makes an ingress (enters) into the next sign, it is likely to precipitate a shift of emphasis in the person with regard to the significations of that planet, now in a different sign and house.

Solar-arc Directions

Some astrologers use solar-arc directions that entail moving each planet at the same rate as the Sun's progressed movement, which is about 1 degree per year, and note the conjunctions of solar-arc planets to natal planets and angles as signaling the occurrence of events associated with the nature of the planets involved.

Solar Return

If you want to investigate a particular year, the Solar Return chart can be useful (see chapter 12). To the extent that modern astrologers use both precessed and non-precessed returns, as well as natal and relocated returns, they end up with four possible Solar Return charts. This can be a confusing morass to sort through. I have come to appreciate the simplicity of the Hellenistic approach, in which the Solar Return chart is used primarily as a transit chart on a person's birthday, where the positions of the planets on the birthday relative to the natal chart have an influence for the entire year that runs from birthday to birthday. I no longer look at Solar Returns as independent charts (hardly ever, anyway).

Annual Lord of the Year

An adjunct to the Solar Return is the annual lord of the year by profections from the Ascendant. The condition of this planet, both in the natal chart and in the Solar Return chart, and its placement relative to the natal chart points to the general tone of the year. Transits by the annual profected time lord to other planets in the natal chart or transits to the annual profected time lord in the natal chart by other planets are especially activated and "hot." In addition, any planets occupying the house of the annual profection are likewise triggered in the natal chart and by transit (see chapter 12).

Lunar Return

If you want to investigate a particular month, use the Lunar Return in the same way outlined for the Solar Return above. You can also look to see if the progressed Moon is making any 1-degree aspects to the natal planets, and you can look at the monthly profected house and its lord. This is also the context in which to evaluate the inner-planet transits to the natal positions or to the topical house being investigated.

TRANSITS

Now let's look more closely at the use of transits and progressions for a one-hour consultation session.[2] Here you will learn to identify the most important timing activations, ones that are the easiest to recognize. In chapter 12, we will discuss the use of annual profections and the Solar Return chart.

Simply defined, transits are the current positions of the planets in the sky. The doctrine of transits proposes that, as the planets move through the various signs, they activate the qualities of those signs in accordance with their own natures. This is the basis of the predictions of mundane astrology as applied to world affairs—for example, Pluto in Sagittarius between 1982 and 2008 will precipitate upheavals and transformations (Pluto) in the area of religion and belief systems (Sagittarius), while Pluto's entrance into Capricorn in 2008 will signal similar upheavals and exposures in political institutions and business corporations.

At the level of individual birth charts, as transiting planets pass through the various zodiacal signs in the years after a birth, whatever house is occupied by that sign is activated by the transit of a planet moving through that sign. Thus, if Sagittarius occupies your seventh house of relationship, during the time when Pluto is in Sagittarius, you may expect upheaval and transformations in your marriage. If you have Sagittarius occupying your tenth house, the catharsis may occur in your career. If there are planets or any of the four angles of the Ascendant, Descendant, Midheaven, or IC in that sign, the closer the transiting planet approaches the natal planet or angle, the more intense the experience becomes. The significations of that planet itself, as well as the topics of the houses it rules, are activated by the force and nature of the transiting planet. This is why certain parts of our selves come to the forefront during certain times in our lives, and not at other times.

As you progress in your studies of astrology, you will naturally begin to keep track of which zodiacal sign each planet is passing through during the coming year, as well as the range of the specific degrees of the sign it will transverse. It is a good idea to pick up your ephemeris periodically or generate one on your computer program. Then browse a year or two ahead to get a sense of each planet's movement, its retrograde periods and stations, and its ingresses into different signs.

You must know how long each planet spends in a sign, which is a factor of its speed based upon its distance from the Sun. The inner planets, Mercury and Venus, which are closer to the Sun, make complete revolutions every year and thus, unless they turn retrograde, spend about one month in each sign. Mars has a two-year orbit, which gives it about two months in each sign, and the asteroids have approximately four-year orbits, giving them around four months in each sign. The outer planets are farther away. Jupiter's twelve-year orbit around the Sun gives it about one year in each sign; Saturn spends about two and a half years in each sign, Uranus seven years, Neptune fourteen years, and Pluto, due to the eccentricity of its orbit, between twelve and twenty-four years.

Thus you can see that the influence of inner planets through a sign is of short duration—here today, gone tomorrow. So unless a client wants information about a particular day or month, examining the transits of Mercury, Venus, the asteroids, and even Mars has a lower priority in assessing the major influences in the year ahead. By contrast, the slower-moving outer planets have a longer, and thus more concentrated, effect, and so those are the transits on which you should focus. The only exception to this is that, if Mercury, Venus, Mars, or a major asteroid is making a station due to its retrograde motion on the degree of a natal planet or angle, it deserves mention. However, from the perspective of traditional astrology, if one of these inner planets happens to be a time lord by any one of the various time-lord procedures, it will have a greater influence by transit during the period when it is a time lord.

Beginners often ask how close to a natal planet or angle a transiting planet has to be before the person begins to feel the effects of the transit. On the most general level, as soon as a transiting planet enters a sign, the entire sign is stimulated by its presence, and every planet occupying any degree of that sign becomes charged, because the sign itself is charged. Thus, when analyzing a birth chart for current timing influences, note which house is activated by each of the outer transiting planets, regardless of whether or not any planets occupy that sign. If Saturn is transiting the second house, you may predict a tightening and limiting of the finances. If Uranus is transiting the fourth house, a destabilization and change in a domestic situation may result. However, these comments need to be placed within the context of how long the transiting planet will be there.

If transiting Pluto is at the beginning degrees of a sign, its activation of that house may be for twelve to twenty years, and thus your comment pertains to only the most general level of influence. If Pluto is at the 27th degree of a sign, it may still activate that house for several more years, but if Jupiter is at the 27th degree of a sign, it will probably be out within a month.

In addition to transits activating the signs through which they pass, which in each person's chart may affect a different house, the transiting planets also have increasing impact on any natal planets in that sign the closer they approach them. Your next priority is to note if a transiting planet will conjunct a natal planet or angle, and then see if the transiting planet will make an opposition or square to some other natal planet, node, or angle. The so-called "hard aspects" of the conjunction, square, and opposition are usually more dramatic and external in their effects than the "soft aspects" of the sextile and trine. And transits by the outer planets to the luminaries (Sun and Moon), the inner planets (Mercury, Venus, Mars, major asteroids), and even Jupiter and Saturn are more personal and intense than to Uranus, Neptune, and Pluto, which, in turn, are more diffuse and generational in their impact on the life.

When the transiting planets are within 5 degrees of exact to the conjunction or aspect with a natal planet or angle, it is time to wake up and take notice. For the slower-moving planets such as Pluto, the exact hit may still be up to five years away, so use a smaller orb. But for the faster-moving planets such as Jupiter or Saturn, it may be a matter of weeks or months and a larger orb of approach is appropriate. If the aspect is or will become exact sometime in the coming year, be sure to mention it and then go into some detail. If it will become exact in the following year, mention it in passing, but don't necessarily go into a lengthy discussion and explanation unless your client has asked for a long-term overview of forthcoming trends.

Outer planets regularly have periods of retrograde motion each year. Tracking their movement in the sky, they seem to move backward for a period of time before resuming their forward motion. In the ephemeris, their zodiacal degree decreases when they are retrograde, and then begins to increase when the planet turns direct. They may, in fact, make three passes over a natal planet during that period of the time, which, in some cases, may last for several years. The first pass by direct motion can bring the situation into focus. When the transiting planet turns retrograde and makes a second pass, it often becomes impossible for the person to ignore the situation that has arisen and he or she may be forced to make some kind of readjustment. The third pass after the transiting planet has turned direct will often coincide with the completion of the change and the resolution.

Table 4, on the next page, shows the average duration of each of the outer-planet transits to a particular planet or angle, as well as the kind of energy that each transiting planet precipitates.

As a counselor, you can use variations of the above key phrases to explain to your client the kinds of influences that the various planets bring with them as they impact houses and natal planets in the natal chart. You want to give your clients the sense that there can be positive eventual outcomes to difficult periods of crisis and transition in their lives. But as an astrologer, you should be aware of the nature of the problems that each client is likely to encounter in the process, before you begin to spin. And be careful not to find yourself in the position of making predictions about a specific day when using transits, because, for a variety of reasons, events do not usually occur "on schedule" or at an exact time. Instead, discuss the event in a general time period.

From the traditional perspective, the transits of Mars and Saturn are problematic, bringing experiences of conflict and separations for Mars, and endings, failure, hardship, and denial for Saturn. The transit of Jupiter is generally seen in a very positive light, bringing success and honors and fortunate circumstances.

The ancients did not know about Uranus, Neptune, or Pluto, but the raw interpretation of these is that Uranus brings unexpected disruption of the status quo, instability, anxiety, restlessness, rebelliousness, and desire for escape from confinement—everything that urges liberation from any situation that has become too confining and prevents new growth. Neptune brings confusion, fear, deception, illusion, desire for escapism, vulnerability to substance addictions, lack of clarity, and gullibility—everything that makes you want to transcend the harshness and materialism of the finite corporeal world

Table 4. The Transiting Planets[3]

Planet	Planetary Period	Normal Transit Duration	Opportunity and Challenge
♂ Mars	2 years	1 month	The opportunity to take action and strive for what you want. In the process, conflict and strife may arise.
♃ Jupiter	12 years	3 months	The opportunity to expand your horizons and experience abundance. In the process, things may become excessive and exaggerated.
♄ Saturn	29 ½ years	18 months	The opportunity to focus, define, and manifest what you want. In the process, you may have to come out of denial and face reality.
♅ Uranus	84 years	2 years	The opportunity to free yourself from past limitations. In the process, existing structures may be shattered.
♆ Neptune	164 years	3 years	The opportunity to experience greater spiritual perspective and sensitivity. In the process, existing structures may be dissolved.
♇ Pluto	248 years	3 years	The opportunity to transform and regenerate an area of your life. In the process, existing structures may be destroyed.

and connect with some kind of ideal, romantic, compassionate world. Pluto brings upheavals, catharsis, rage, eruption of toxicity, destruction, obsession, confrontation with the abusive use of power over you by others, death, and the revelation of hidden secrets—everything that forces you to release old unconscious, self-destructive patterns that have kept you locked in unhappy ways of being.

Ancient astrologers sought to determine the kinds of events that were likely to occur for an individual and, using timing techniques, to predict when those events would occur, as well as the longer periods of fortunate and unfortunate times in the life. Psychological astrologers look at general trends. This approach tends to see everything as potentially favorable. It explores the meaning of what happens and the response to changing situations rather than the events themselves. More scientifically oriented astrologers try to ascertain exact days when specific events will occur. As a counseling astrologer, you must locate your own position on this spectrum. But more important, you must gauge the kind of approach your clients want and how comfortable they are with it, and then adjust the lens through which you filter the information accordingly.

At the most basic level, be aware that the only constant in life is the process of change. To change is to grow and live, and to cease changing is to stagnate and die. Thus, to the extent that transits symbolize the ongoing transitions and dynamic transformations of our lives, ultimately their purpose is to facilitate the continuous growth of the individual. But, in fact, sometimes bad things happen that don't contribute to our positive growth. This can make it difficult to find the silver lining in the cloud. In the end, you must be honest with yourself about what is going on with your client and what is or isn't likely to turn out well in the final accounting.

Interpreting Transits

There are a few basic guidelines that can help you correctly interpret transits. The first two are correlates of one another, based on the principle that a planet's capacity for either triggering or manifesting events by any timing procedure is directly related to its condition in the natal chart.

Transits, or for that matter any timing procedure, cannot produce any event that is not already promised as a possibility in the natal chart. You must first determine if a planet that is the significator of a certain topic is supported in the birth chart to produce an event, and if so, if that event is likely to be favorable or unfavorable for the individual. Thus, if all the significations for the topic of marriage are weak (see chapter 11), a Jupiter transit, progression, or time lord will not result in any kind of long-lasting marital union. This is a mistake that many astrologers make in their interpretations. A client asks: When am I going to meet that special someone to marry? And the astrologer responds: Oh, you are going to have a Jupiter transit entering the seventh house or conjunct Venus next year, and that looks like a very promising time for relationships. But you must first evaluate whether marriage is a topic that is even indicated in the natal chart before making any kind of prediction about when it will happen.

The correlate to this is that what a transiting or time-lord planet yields in any particular chart is directly related, not only to its own inherent nature (like change for Uranus or limitation for Saturn), but also to its condition in the natal chart. Thus a strong and favorable natal Jupiter will generally produce beneficial events by transit in accordance with the relative angularity of the house it is passing through; but a weak and maltreated natal Jupiter cannot give the full measure of its beneficence by transit.

A third guideline is that not every transit produces an event. As an astrologer, you will encounter situations in which, at one time, the transit of a planet over the Ascendant had dramatic effects, and yet, the next time the very same transit occurred, nothing happened. Or perhaps a Saturn transit over one person's Moon resulted in a terrible experience, but in another chart, the same transit went by almost unnoticed.

These guidelines for using a planet's natal condition as an indicator of what it has the capacity to produce only partially explain discrepancies between various times and various charts. Preliminary studies in Hellenistic astrology indicate that ancient astrologers held that, when a planet becomes a time lord, it is "turned on" for a certain period of time. During that period, it is more active in terms of the transits it makes to other planets, as well as in terms of transits made to it by other planets. This may be one explanation of why transits over angles and planets do not always manifest as outer events. This can be a particular problem when rectifying charts of an unknown birth time by working backward from the assumption that transits or directions over angles indicate significant life events. Experience shows that, even with a very secure birth time, this is simply not the case in every instance.

Here is a summary of simple guidelines for using transits in a one-hour consultation.

- Use only the transits of the outer planets, unless the inner planets are making stations.
- If you are a traditional astrologer, you may use inner-planet transits if they happen to be a time lord during the period being investigated and interpret them within the context of the inquiry specified by the particular time-lord procedure.
- Note what house each transiting planet is activating.
- Note if the transiting planet is making a conjunction, opposition, or square to a natal planet or angle.
- Know the speed of each planet, as this will tell you when the effects begin and how long they will be operative.
- Aspects by transiting planets to the inner natal planets and angles are more powerful and personal. Aspects by transiting planets to outer natal planets are part of a generational influence.
- Look to general trends, not specific dates.
- The power of a transiting planet and the nature of the events represented by a natal planet that is activated by a transit are dependent on what topics and significations those planets govern in the natal chart and on their condition.
- Not all transits produce outer events.

Let's imagine that Bill comes in for a reading near his birthday in November 2006. Look at the transits for the year ahead through the end of December 2007 (see figure 6 on page 75). Don't simply print out the transits from your computer program. Pick up an ephemeris and look through the pages as you read along. First get a sense of the timing of the transits; then interpret them.

> Transiting Jupiter enters Bill's first house on November 23, 2006 and stays until December 2007. At the end of January, it will conjoin Venus and Mercury and then the Ascendant

by the middle of February. Jupiter stations at 19 Sagittarius in April, then turns retrograde and makes a second pass over these points in May-June. It directs in August and makes the final pass in September-October, squaring its own natal position in December, right before leaving the sign. For all practical purposes, the Jupiter transit over the Ascendant and first-house planets is operative for most of 2007.

The transit of Pluto has been in the first house since its entry into Sagittarius in 1982. What is significant is that it will square natal Jupiter to the exact degree by February 2007 and continue to stimulate that point until November 2008. Because Jupiter is the ruler of the Ascendant and the strongest planet in the chart, this is significant.

The fact that Pluto has been squaring Neptune in the tenth house is not as important, as everybody in Bill's age group has had the same thing going on. However, because Neptune is connected to Jupiter, when Jupiter is activated, the tenth-house professional significations of Neptune are more likely to come into play at that time.

The transit of Neptune in Aquarius has been in the third house since 1998 and will remain there until 2012. During 2007, it activates 17 to 22 degrees of the sign. Bill does not have any planets at those degrees of Aquarius, Leo, or Scorpio; but Uranus is at 19 Taurus receiving the square. However, Uranus is generational, so don't pay too much attention to the Neptune transit, except to note that, in 2008, it will square the Sun. That is an important influence on the horizon.

Uranus in Pisces has been activating Bill's fourth house since April 2003 and will continue to do so until 2011. During 2007, it moves from 10 to 18 degrees of Pisces, and so will square Venus, Mercury, and the Ascendant/Descendant axis during the entire year, with the peak periods to the Ascendant in April, September, and January 2008.

In September 2007, Saturn finishes up its two-and-a-half-year sojourn through Leo, which occupies the ninth house in Bill's chart. At present, it is squaring his Sun at 24 Scorpio, making a station in December 2006 at 25 Leo, which then opposes

his Juno at 25 Aquarius. Saturn goes retrograde and squares
Uranus during the spring, and re-contacts the Sun, Juno, and
Mars in July-August, right before it enters Virgo.

Also note that the transit of Chiron will make a conjunction
to the Moon in January 2007.

Now, let's try to get a sense of what is happening as a whole before
beginning to delineate the individual transits and prioritize which
ones are most important. First, are any of the four most important
points in Bill's chart involved—the Sun, Moon, Ascendant, or
Ascendant ruler? Yes, three of the four, so you know it is a big year.
Saturn, the principle of limitation, is urging the Sun to focus on its
priorities in Bill's life goals so he can reap recognition for his endeavors. In a larger sense, any transit of Saturn to the Sun activates the
awareness of unrealized potential. It brings up the question: What
do I want to be when I grow up? At Bill's age, the question may be:
Have I accomplished my life goal?

Meanwhile, transiting Uranus, the principle of liberation, is
stimulating the Ascendant for radical change and transiting Jupiter
for personal growth and the dissemination of knowledge. Transiting
Pluto is intensifying and transforming the significations of Jupiter,
which rules both the first-house Ascendant (self) and the fourth
house (parents, home). All this suggests an image of a coil that is
being pressed down by Saturn, increasing the Uranian force with
which it will spring forth and free itself. Your main discussion of the
timing as signified by the transits, therefore, will focus on what is
happening to the Ascendant and its ruler, Jupiter, as well as to the
Sun. Jupiter moving through its own sign of Sagittarius generally
heralds a period of reward.

Transiting Saturn in the ninth house and squaring the Sun,
which is the ruler of the ninth, is pressuring Bill for deep thought
and realistic appraisal of his broader intellectual ideas, spiritual
beliefs, and perhaps interests in foreign matters—and calling for him
to manifest the expression of his purpose that encompasses these
far-ranging visions.

Transiting Jupiter in the first house provides opportunities for success in his personal ventures, and urges expanded travel, education,

and the putting forth of his own knowledge. It will activate Mercury, which points to growth in communication skills, and Venus, which bodes well for monetary, artistic, and romantic endeavors.

Transiting Uranus in the fourth house is creating restlessness in Bill's domestic situation, destabilizing the situations that have served as anchors. With its square of the Ascendant/Descendant axis, it urges his inner individuality to break through his socially conditioned persona and promote radical change in his outlook and interactions with others.

Transiting Pluto is in its last stretch of a long-term regeneration of his personality and physical body, which, in the most positive manifestation, builds a sense of personal power. Its last act will be the square of Jupiter, the Ascendant ruler and ruler of the fourth house of home and parents. He may expect that certain familial structures in his life will be destroyed and replaced by others. In the process, the strongest and best planet in his chart will be catalyzed to lead his philosophical visions to their destination.

PROGRESSIONS

Progressions are the second major timing procedure used by modern astrologers. While transits depict the actual changing positions of the planets in the sky, progressions operate on a more symbolic level. They measure the movements of the planets in the days after birth, and symbolically relate them to a larger period of time. Although there are several different kinds of progressions (primary, secondary, tertiary), we will discuss only secondary progressions here. We'll examine the positions of the progressed planets relative only to the natal chart, and we won't look at the progressed chart as an independent chart.

The fundamental premise of secondary progressions is a simple formula: One day of time equates to the passage of one year of time. If, for example, you are interested in the timing influences for the tenth year of a person's life, open your ephemeris to the month of a person's birth and count down ten days after birth. (The precise calculation is more involved than this, but this is the general principle). The positions of the planets on the tenth day after birth relative to the positions of the planets on the day of the birth give information about how the birth potential signified by each planet develops over time by incorporating the qualities of the signs it passes through and the planets it encounters along the way. The implications of this procedure are thought-provoking. It suggests that we live through the entirety of our lives in the days after birth. Each day is a mini-encapsulation of a corresponding year of life. The experiences of that day are a preview of that year, slowly unraveling the details of a twenty-four-hour microcosm into a 365-day year of actualization.

In essence, secondary progressions are the transits that we experience in the first few months of life that will have a progressive effect over the course of our lives. As such, they evoke experiences that have already been imprinted in our infantile pre-cognitive memories. According to astrologer Brian Clark, the movements of the progressed planets around the chart depict the maturation and psychological growth of various aspects of the psyche.[4] The timetable and plan for development is an outgrowth of the initial movements and contacts made by the planets to one another in the days immediately following birth.

Entire books have been written detailing the subtleties and intricacies of secondary and other types of progressions. We will stay focused on what you need to look for in a one-hour consultation that combines natal and current timing information. There are four main movements to watch for when investigating a particular year by this timing method:

- Progressed planets or angles making exact aspects to natal planets
- Progressed planets or angles changing signs
- Planets that are retrograde at birth turning direct by progression, or natal planets that are direct at birth turning retrograde by progression
- The sign, house, and aspects of the progressed Moon (in chapter 7, we'll look at the progressed Sun/Moon lunation phase)

Your ephemeris will show you that the faster-moving inner planets (Sun, Mercury, Venus, and Mars) will move through several complete signs in a three-month period, covering up to an entire quadrant of the chart, which equates to around ninety years of life. The Moon passes through an entire sign every month and, thus, through all the houses of the natal chart every twenty-eight to twenty-nine years. These inner planets will not only change signs, they are likely to conjoin and aspect a number of other planets. By contrast, the slower-moving outer planets may only move several degrees over the course of a progressed lifetime, and may not have much direct contact with other planets.

Thus, in contrast to transits, where you look primarily at the movements of the outer planets, in progressions, you focus on the movements of the inner planets. The outer-planet progressions are generally insignificant, with a few exceptions. The degree of the Midheaven progresses at the same rate as the Sun, about 1 degree per year, and the progressed positions of the other three angles change in accordance with that of the Midheaven. The progressed angles are important.

The Sun's daily movement provides the base measurement for this procedure. For the progressed Sun, Mercury, Venus, and the four angles, take note only when one of these planets is within 1 degree of a natal planet. One degree approaching represents the year before; an exact conjunction represents the year in question; 1 degree separating represents the year following. Use the same 1-degree rule for the progressed Moon, only in this case, 1 degree approaching is the month before, an exact conjunction is the month in question, and 1 degree separating is the month following. With progressed Mars, ½ degree (thirty minutes) approaching is the year before and ½ degree separating is the year after. For the major asteroids, use a ¼-degree (twenty-five minute) rule for determining significance for the year in question. The progressed position of the outer planets must be within a few minutes of exactness to a natal planet or angle to have any bearing that differs from the natal lifelong influence. Be aware, however, that if Mercury, Venus, Mars, or the major asteroids are near their station points, either direct or retrograde, they are moving extremely slowly, so that 1-degree orb may represent much more than one year. This is not applicable to the Sun and Moon, because neither of them is ever retrograde.

Look primarily for conjunctions, take note of oppositions, and only perhaps glance at the other aspects. When a progressed planet contacts a natal planet, both planets are impacted. The progressed planet incorporates the qualities of the natal planet into its own ongoing development, and the natal planet is stimulated to receive and respond to the promptings of the progressed planet. Also watch to see if a planet changes signs. If you are using the Whole Sign house system, the sign change will also correspond to a house change. A sign change often points to an entirely new, and perhaps unfamiliar, way of expressing the significations of that planet, as well as the environment in which those energies actualize in the daily experiences of life. The culture shock, so to speak, is apparent in the first year or two of the transition to a new sign and house. Then there is a gradual assimilation of the new way of being in the world, as it pertains to that planet.

The third factor to track in your scan of noteworthy timing is whether any planet makes a station by progression, turning retrograde or direct during the time period under investigation. In modern astrology, the primary meaning of retrograde planets is that the planet's function is reversed, repressed, or inhibited in some way. Psychologically, this can point to some kind of trauma that has frozen the expression of that planet's function. Alternatively, it can indicate that its sphere of influence is occurring in the inner life and world. In traditional astrology, a retrograde planet is understood both in terms of its extremely slow motion, making it less active, and in terms of its apparent backward motion, which points to its significations being recalled or taken back.

When planets change direction, they mark major times of reorientation and different approaches to the expression of their significations. In general, if a planet is retrograde at birth, when it turns direct, it indicates an externalization and speeding up of its processes. On the other hand, if a planet is direct at birth and turns retrograde at some point by progression, this indicates an internalizing and slowing down of its processes.

Mercury has about a three-week period of retrograde motion; so if someone is born with Mercury retrograde, at some point before he or she is twenty-four years old, Mercury will turn direct. Venus

spends about six weeks in retrograde motion. If someone is born with
Venus retrograde, it will turn direct sometime before they reach the
age of forty-three.

When looking at the progressed positions of Mercury, Venus,
and Mars, take note if they have reversed direction by progression
from that of their natal position. Verify if your computer program
indicates that this is the specific year in which a reversal of direction
took place. If not, go back to your ephemeris. If these planets are
receiving major activations by other timing methods, or if they are
rulers of topics about which the client has expressed concern, it is
advisable to determine at which age the reversal occurred.

The final factor to evaluate when using progressions is the movement of the progressed Moon. Because the Moon moves so quickly
in relation to the other planets, passing through each sign and house
every two and a half years, it is a barometer of the ongoing fluctua-
tion of the feelings in the inner life. The progressed Moon indicates
the best way to meet changing emotional needs and establish emotional security at various stages in the life. Again, the months when
it changes sign and house are important to note. The alternation
from a masculine fire or air sign to a feminine earth or water sign
sets the tempo for the alternation between feeling more extroverted
or introverted and more active or receptive in accordance with the
nature of the sign itself. The house position of the progressed Moon
shows in what area of life activities a person is particularly sensitive
emotionally, and where he or she is being urged to develop new ways
of responding.

The progressed Moon's rapid motion will cause it to make aspects
to many planets in the course of its movement. While all the aspects
have meaning, look primarily for the conjunctions. The contact of
the progressed Moon with a natal planet will bring a person's emotional sensitivity to bear on the significations of that planet, and
can often trigger underlying issues. But remember, while this contact
may be intense and perhaps have long-lasting after-effects, it is of
relatively short duration—for a period of several months only.

During the period November 2006 to December 2007 (see
figure 6 on page 75), besides a mention of the progressed

Moon, there are only two other progressions that are notewor-thy for Bill.

The Midheaven, by progression, is conjunct the natal Ascendant at 16 Sagittarius. The MC angle that represents Bill's status in the larger society based on his professional contributions is now in exact alignment with his personality, symbolized by the Ascendant leading his life to its destiny. Note that the Ascendant is under major activation this year, being conjoined by the transit of Jupiter and squared by the transit of Uranus. Thus you can surmise that this will be a very important year for Bill in moving his life toward his goals.

The progressed Sun at 2 Aquarius is opposing natal Pallas and Pluto at 2 Leo. The progressed Sun entered into Aquarius and the third house about two and a half years ago, indicating a major shift from second-house financial affairs to third-house mental interests. This year, the Sun opposes Pallas Athena, the asteroid associated with creative wisdom, and Pluto, the planet of depth transformation, both in the ninth house of broad ideas and foreign travel. The ongoing development of the content of the basic purpose as depicted by the Sun concerning higher wisdom teachings about spiritual transcendence is now being communicated in third-house networking endeavors in the local community.

The progressed Moon in Cancer passing through the eighth house over the next six months will move into a conjunc-tion with progressed Chiron and then natal Chiron. Also note that transiting Chiron is passing over the natal Moon, dupli-cating the same theme, and this is very significant. Chiron is wounding and healing; the Moon is a general significator of Bill's emotions and mother. It rules the eighth house of death, inheritances, and psychotherapy through which the progressed Moon is passing. Remember that Pluto, by transit, is squaring natal Jupiter—the Ascendant ruler and that of the parents. You may cautiously inquire about the health of Bill's parents, the management of his financial affairs, and perhaps be sensitive to the psychotherapeutic surfacing and healing of emotional wounds.

STUDY GUIDELINES

- Examine the major timing activations of the transits and progressions for your practice chart. Think about which are most important and why. Which ones will you target in your consultation? Do you see repetition of any themes?
- Prepare a written analysis for your practice chart. As an astrologer, you are asked to make predictions. Write down what you think may occur. Ethical considerations demand, however, that you not make definitive statements of impending death, divorce, or other catastrophic events, because neither you nor the system is infallible. Begin to differentiate between what you suspect may be the case and what it is appropriate to convey to your client. Then determine how you will do that.
- End with a statement in which you summarize the most important timing, and decide what you are actually going to tell your client (as opposed to what you actually think may happen). This should be no more than 100 words.

PART III

BUILDING THE STRUCTURE

CHAPTER SEVEN

THE LUNATION PHASES

Your framework now includes three of the five places of life: the Ascendant (and its ruler), and the two lights—the Sun and Moon. You have also factored into your delineation the major timing activations of the natal potential as indicated by transits and secondary progressions. Now you are ready to investigate the derivative factors of the two lights as they interact with one another—the lunation phases, the Lot of Fortune, pre-natal lunation, the lunar nodes, and the eclipses. The visual phenomena and the points of intersection that occur between the motions of the Sun and the Moon during their various cycles lend depth, shading, and nuance to the basic themes concerning life purpose that you have already uncovered. They form the second tier of factors to integrate into your interpretation, fleshing out the structure of the chart. We'll begin with the lunation cycle, which depicts the changing relationship between the Sun and the Moon for each night of the lunar month.

THE LUNATION CYCLE

The Moon circles the Earth each month and, from the point of view of the Earth, it reflects different amounts of the Sun's light at various points in its cycle. The cycle of the Moon's waxing and waning phases is called the lunation cycle, and the various lunation phases depict the changing distances between these two luminaries. In the lunation cycle, the Moon gradually increases in light as it separates from union with the Sun at its closest approach at the New Moon.

It reaches its maximum elongation from the Sun and greatest illumination at the Full Moon, and then gradually decreases in light as it returns to the Sun, disappearing from sight altogether shortly before their conjunction.

The Moon, with its repeating cycles of waxing and waning light, was an ancient symbol for the birth, growth, death, and renewal of all life forms. The lunar rhythm presented a creation (the New Moon), followed by growth (to Full Moon), and a diminution and death (the three moonless nights). The lunation cycle can be viewed as a prototype for the successive stages of the organic growth of all living things, illuminating the alternating forces of life and death as they flow through cyclical process.

Various cultures have subdivided this cycle into two hemispheres, three phases, four quarters, eight cross-quarters, eleven figures, and twenty-eight mansions. The twofold division yields the waxing hemisphere where the life-force energy symbolized by the Moon is increasing and the waning hemisphere where the life-force energy is decreasing. The threefold division consists of the New, Full, and Dark phases of the Moon embodied as the Triple Goddess in her aspects as Virgin, Mother, and Crone. The fourfold division as New, First Quarter, Full, and Last Quarter Moons mirrors the symbolic meanings of the four seasons, directions, cardinal points, and elements.

We will explore the eightfold division of phases—New, Crescent, First Quarter, Gibbous, Full, Disseminating, Last Quarter, and Balsamic—in greater depth in the remainder of this chapter. These eight phases, which mark the increasing and decreasing light of the lunar month, in some intrinsic manner correspond to the eight divisions of the increasing and decreasing light of the solar year, as marked by the solstices, equinoxes, and cross-quarter days that formed the basis of the Celtic seasonal festival calendar.

Other divisions of the lunation cycle include those by Hellenistic astrologer Vettius Valens, who described the eleven figures of the Moon (conjunction, rising, first crescent, first half, double-convex, whole, double-convex, second half, second crescent, setting), as well as the figure when the Moon first begins to wane.[1] Paulus Alexandrinus had his own variation of the eleven lunar figures.[2] An early medieval text in Latin discusses the qualities of the Moon on each of the twenty-eight days of the lunar month, although this refers to the electional use of the Moon for planting, building, conducting business, and so on. Indian astrology uses twenty-seven *nakshatras*, each associated with a particular deity; Chinese, Arabian, and Tibetan astrology used twenty-eight mansions based, not upon the Moon's phases, but on its orbital path through a series of fixed star constellations.

THE EIGHT LUNATION PHASES

We have seen that the Sun and the Moon each hold a pre-eminent place in the hierarchy of astrological delineation. The Sun signifies the soul and the intention for the life purpose; the Moon signifies the body and the means of actualizing the life purpose in the concrete world. The lunation phases are a display of the changing relationship between these two luminaries during the course of the Moon's monthly orbit around the Earth. Each lunation phase describes the kind of energy that is generated at each stage of the cyclical process.

We are each born during a particular lunar phase, and this natal lunation phase describes the kind of energy inherent in that stage of cyclical process we use to express and actualize the life purpose (see figure 7 on page 140). While Hellenistic astrologers were aware of the different qualities of the various lunar phases, it was Dane Rudhyar who first articulated the classification of the eight lunation phases as eight personality functions and types. Rudhyar used the image of a seed as a metaphor of how the eight phases depict the successive stages of the life process by which life forms unfold, fulfill, complete, and renew themselves. He then extrapolated from these meanings to eight human personality types that reflect the behavior of individuals born during each lunation phase.[3]

The process begins at the New Moon, when a seed containing a new vision infused with an intention germinates in the darkness. With the light of the waxing Crescent phase, the first tender shoots of this vision have struggled to push themselves above the ground.

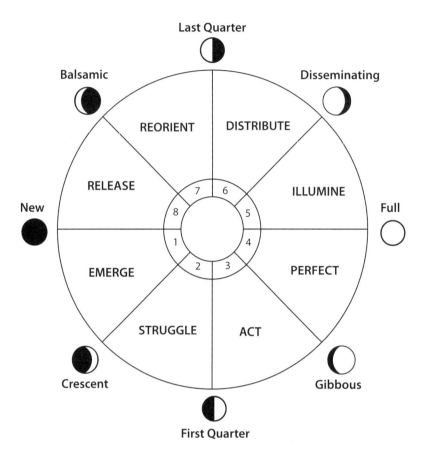

FIGURE 7. *Keywords for the eight lunation phases.*

During the First Quarter phase, the life force of the vision takes root by establishing itself; its stem and leaf structure give shape to a strong definite form.

The waxing Gibbous phase corresponds to the development of the buds with the promise and expectation of the flower that blooms during the Full Moon phase. Now halfway around the lunar cycle at the Full Moon, the vision is fully illuminated and infused with meaning and content. The waning Gibbous phase, also known as the Disseminating phase, corresponds to the fruition of the cycle, when the vision is acted upon and lived out through the lives of humanity, thereby fulfilling its purpose.

In the Last Quarter phase, the crop is harvested and what has been realized through the cycle is ingested and assimilated. Whatever fruit is left on the vine begins to wither and decompose. The essence of the vision is then distilled into a seed capsule that is buried underground during the final dark, or Balsamic, phase of the cycle, where it is nourished and prepared for rebirth. This germinal idea is subsequently released with the initiation of a new cycle.

It has been suggested that, in a model that accepts reincarnation, each person incarnates successively into each one of the eight lunation phases during one eight-fold cycle of experience in the development of a theme or lesson that extends over the duration of eight lifetimes. Thus the lunation phase, while clearly not indicative of the age of the soul as new or old, can be viewed as the stage of the soul's development in this life as commencing, culminating, or completing a thematic motif that began in previous lifetimes.

In a model that does not accept reincarnation, the stage of the plant's growth can be used as a metaphor for the purpose of an individual lifetime within a larger contextual organic process. For example, the life purpose of those born early in the cycle, however it is defined by the Sun and Moon, has to do with the generation and release of new visions; for those born in the middle of cycle, it has to do with the dissemination and distribution of what they have found meaningful; for those born late in the cycle, it has to do with the summing up and distillation of their wisdom.

New Moon Phase: Incarnate, Emerge, Project

(The Moon is 0-45° ahead of the Sun)

Like the seed germinating underground, this phase represents the emergence of the life into a new cycle of incarnations, or into the beginning stage of the development of a new theme or lesson. The soul has a youthful, innocent, and sometimes naïve quality and is eager and open to embrace new experiences and ideas, often plunging into them without any preconceived plan. The personality operates in a spontaneous and instinctive manner that can be very subjective. These people discover that the logical analytical approach to decision-making does not work very well; for them, the first impulses or thoughts that come to mind yield the best results. Some New Moon individuals can feel hesitant and shy about being in the world, while others feel compelled to push themselves forward and act in an overly self-involved manner. Both extremes are manifestations of the young personality trying to become aware of its identity and learning how to project itself.

For those born during the New Moon phase, the kind of energy that stands behind the expression and actualization of the life purpose as symbolized by the Sun and Moon is that of emergence, projecting a strong image upon the screen of the world, learning to inhabit the body with its new personality, and propelling their movements forward in an instinctive manner. They are here to respond to the call of new directions and to release the first intimations of new aspirations, even though they themselves may not always be aware of the long-term implications or outcomes of what they initiate.

Crescent Moon Phase: Overcome, Focus, Move Forward

(The Moon is 45-90° ahead of the Sun)

Like the young tender shoot of the plant that struggles against the force of gravity to push itself up through the dark soil so it can begin to derive its nutrients from the sunlight through the process of photosynthesis, those born during the Crescent phase experience their lives as a struggle against the forces of inertia. They must take charge of their bodies, focus their energies, and begin to relate to the dense physical environment of their world. In the process, they may encounter the resistance of forces from the past pulling them backward in the guise of family and loved ones who do not support or understand their impetus to move forward in their own direction. This resistance also manifests as a paralysis that results from their own fears of the unknown and unfamiliar, insecurities, lack of self-confidence, and habits and unconscious patterns carried over from the past. The antidote is to access the resources available in the immediate environment that will help to develop new talents, skills, and abilities. By adding new tools to their toolbox, they can gain the self-confidence to overcome the resistance from both outer and inner sources, break free of the past, and move forward. As they do so, many opportunities will open for them. The final challenge is to take advantage of the opportunities by acting on them.

For those born during the Crescent Moon phase, the kind of energy that stands behind the expression and actualization of the life purpose as symbolized by the Sun and Moon is that of struggling away from the inertia and dependency of past conditions and mobilizing their resources to assert themselves in forward-moving directions. These individuals are here to incorporate new talents into their repertoire of skills, to establish their fledging identities as viable independent life forces, and to develop self-reliance, faith in themselves, and the persistence necessary for the realization of the aspiration released at the New Moon phase.

First Quarter Moon Phase: Decide, Act, Build

(The Moon is 90-135° ahead of the Sun)

The plant now goes through a rapid-growth phase, establishing its root system and putting forth stems and leaves to support the flower and fruit yet to be developed. Those born during the First Quarter phase of the Moon likewise must root themselves into their world and build structures to support the realization of their aspirations. They are ready to test their growing strength, to reach out and shape, manage, and control their environment. In the process, they often encounter many external crises in which their own or others' structures and plans are challenged or fall apart and chaos ensues. They must learn how to harness the tremendous surge of energies released during these crises and, as quickly and efficiently as possible, solve the problems by taking direct action to build new structures so that they and everyone else can get on with their business. At these times, they may feel animated, energized, and excited as they embody the role of the hero who saves the day.

For those born during the First Quarter Moon phase, the kind of energy that stands behind the expression and actualization of the life purpose as symbolized by the Sun and Moon is that of learning how to anchor their life force in society, how to activate their personalities by taking strong direct action upon what they have decided to do, and how to exercise their will, repudiating anything that holds them back and constructing the foundations in the outer world that can facilitate the realization of their visions.

Gibbous Moon Phase: Evaluate, Analyze, Perfect

(The Moon is 135-180° ahead of the Sun)

Now the plant's buds come forth from the leaves, displaying the promise of what is yet to come. Those born during the Gibbous phase of the Moon likewise develop a growing awareness of the purpose behind the vision that has been released. They often carry a sense of anxious expectation that they are on the brink of a great revelation and feel the need to improve, refine, and perfect the structures that have already been built to be worthy vehicles for the expression of the vision. They do this by means of critical analysis, discovering what does not work and then adjusting and fixing it, so the forms can be functional and useful for their intended purpose. The drive for perfection also manifests as the drive for self-improvement by finding better ways of operating and better techniques for doing things or facilitating their personal growth. They desire to become as skillful as possible in their chosen field of expression.

For those born during the Gibbous Moon phase, the kind of energy that stands behind the expression and actualization of the life purpose as symbolized by the Sun and Moon is that of critical evaluation, with subsequent improvement, so they can contribute forms to society that are of value and practical use. Behind this outer expression resides a mind that is introspective and awaiting the full revelation of the vision that will infuse the structure they have perfected.

Full Moon Phase: Culminate, Illumine, Fulfill

(The Moon is 180-135° behind the Sun)

As the buds open, the flower blooms, turning itself toward the light. In a similar fashion, those born during the Full Moon phase open themselves up to others, who reflect back to them the full illumination of their vision. In the cyclical process, this is the phase where meaning is realized, and content is infused into the form that has been built. These people look for the ideal in all they encounter. They especially desire meaningful relationships with either one significant person or with a group of people who share their vision. It is through their interactions with others that they come to realize their own larger purpose. Thus, it is important for them to be fully conscious of how they relate to others. They must be willing to take responsibility for the consequences that their words, actions, and even thoughts have for others. Other people are crucial for the furtherance of their own purpose, not unlike the birds and bees that must pollinate the flower in order for the plant to bear fruit.

For those born during the Full Moon phase, the kind of energy that stands behind the expression and actualization of the life purpose as symbolized by the Sun and Moon is that of developing clarity in their thinking that guides their actions toward others in the formulation of conscious relationships. They are here to illuminate what is meaningful, on both a personal and collective level.

Disseminating Moon Phase: Distribute, Disseminate, Convey

(The Moon is 135-90° behind the Sun)

The apex of the plant's growth cycle occurs when the flower gives forth the ripened fruit that is ready to eat. In a similar manner, the lives of those born during the Disseminating Moon phase are the fruition of the seed impulse germinated at the New Moon. They are here to embody their vision fully and take it into the world in a way that can be assimilated by and of benefit to others. Like the word "disseminate," the keywords for this phase are about sharing, conveying, and communicating information that has been of personal value.

This can occur, not only in oral or written form, but also through the living out of beliefs. Some Native Americans taught that you must "walk your talk." To the extent that disseminating people have an important message they feel compelled to share and have a vehicle adequate to the task and a receptive audience, they feel as if their life is in the flow. When they are not impassioned about some idea or do not have a means by which to convey it, they may be overcome with a sense of meaninglessness, failure, or futility.

For those born during the Disseminating Moon phase, the kind of energy that stands behind the expression and actualization of the life purpose as symbolized by the Sun and Moon is that of synthesizing and disseminating information and ideas that they have found to be of personal value. They are here to teach and share their truths, fully immerse themselves in society, and, in the process, take in the feedback and wisdom of others.

Last Quarter Moon Phase: Reevaluate, Turn Away, Revise

(The Moon is 90-45° behind the Sun)

Now the crop has been harvested and whatever fruit is left on the vine begins to decompose, drawing its energy inward to create the seed for the next cycle. People born during the Last Quarter Moon phase likewise periodically find themselves faced with the necessity of letting go of obsolete forms that have fulfilled their purpose, and severing themselves from the parent plant. Dane Rudhyar called this phase a crisis in consciousness, because the crises that occur are not the physical crises of the outer world, but rather crises of thought in the inner mental realms. When these individuals realize that they no longer believe in the ideas they used to hold because they now know better, it is excruciatingly difficult to continue being the people that they used to be, since they no longer hold to the values of their former selves. They turn away from old accomplishments and begin to look for new ideas around which to reorganize their thinking. It is often difficult for them to externalize the change until they have first worked it through in their own minds. During this transition, they often continue to act in accordance with the old image, even though it is no longer a genuine reflection of their current authentic selves.

For those born during the Last Quarter Moon phase, the kind of energy that stands behind the expression and actualization of the life purpose as symbolized by the Sun and Moon is that of reevaluating beliefs, revising thinking, and reorienting around new creative possibilities. They are here to challenge and tear down societal structures that are antiquated and have outlived their usefulness.

Balsamic Moon Phase: Distill, Transform, Envision

(The Moon is 45-0° behind the Sun)

Now the seed falls to the ground and is buried in the dark soil until it re-germinates in a new cycle. People born during the dark Balsamic Moon phase, which is the final phase of the eight-fold lunation cycle, live a particularly karmic life as they straddle the past and the future, bringing closure to the old and preparing for the rebirth ahead. Their relationships are many, strong, poignant, and intense, as they must come to terms with and resolve old issues. They often feel out of synch with the rest of the world because they are ahead of their times, already envisioning what it will take the rest of us a number of years to realize. Many sense that they have a special calling or destiny, which, in fact, is the need to distill the wisdom they have gained into some kind of seed form that can be passed on to others as their legacy. These souls carry within themselves the sum total of the experiences from the previous seven lunation-phase lifetimes, which they bring to some kind of final synthesis as the preparation for the next round of incarnations.

For those born during the Balsamic Moon phase, the kind of energy that stands behind the expression and actualization of the life purpose as symbolized by the Sun and Moon is that of resolving and completing the past, making peace with those they encounter, and releasing seed ideas to assist the future.

The table on pages 148 and 149 contains summaries for the key meanings of each of the eight lunation phases. You'll find instructions for determining the lunation phase during which you were born in Appendix A.

Table 5. Indicators of the Stages of Development
in an Eight-fold Cycle[4]

Lunation Phase	Incarnating Soul's Purpose within a larger cyclical context	Flow of Solar-Lunar Energy
Phase 1 **New Moon** ● Moon ☽ 0-45° ahead of Sun ☉	Incarnate into a new being, emerge and project	Projecting the personality into new experiences in spontaneous, impulsive, and instinctive ways.
Phase 2 **Crescent Moon** ● Moon ☽ 45-90° ahead of Sun ☉	Claim possession of the body, struggle, focus, persevere, and move forward	Struggling away from the inertia and dependency of past conditions that seem to hold you back and mobilizing resources so you can move in a forward direction.
Phase 3 **First Quarter Moon** ◐ Moon ☽ 90-135° ahead of Sun ☉	Activate the personality, act and build	Taking direct action to manage the energy released from the many crises in life. Clearing away old structures to build new ones in order to create definite forms that can contain the life purpose.
Phase 4 **Gibbous Moon** ○ Moon ☽ 135-180° ahead of Sun ☉	Evaluate your expression, analyze and perfect	Analyzing self-expression in order to find better techniques for doing things or facilitating personal growth. Introspection as a quest for meaning.
Phase 5 **Full Moon** ○ Moon ☽ 180-135° behind Sun ☉	Clarify your purpose, illumine and fulfill	Searching for the ideal and infusing that meaning and content into life structures. Discovering objectivity and clarity about the life purpose through relationships.

Lunation Phase	Incarnating Soul's Purpose within a larger cyclical context	Flow of Solar-Lunar Energy
Phase 6 Disseminating Moon ☉ Moon ☽ 135-90° behind Sun ☉	Distribute values, disseminate and convey	Living out and embodying values. Sharing and communicating ideas that have been found valuable.
Phase 7 Last Quarter Moon ☽ Moon ☽ 90-45° behind Sun ☉	Revise your thinking, reevaluate, turn away and reorient	Going through internal crises by turning away from old patterns of behavior and attitudes so something new can germinate inside. Difficulty in externalizing the process until the change is complete.
Phase 8 Balsamic Moon ● Moon ☽ 45-0° behind Sun ☉	Mutate consciousness, distill and transform	Feeling "out of synch" with the majority. Distilling wisdom gleaned from entire cycle as a legacy to pass onto others. Completing karma and committing to the future, which brings transformation.

THE PROGRESSED LUNATION CYCLE

We are each born into one particular lunation phase and we resonate to those qualities over the duration of our lives. However, because of the timing system of secondary progressions, individuals experience the qualities of each of the other lunation phases as well. The movements of the progressed Sun and the progressed Moon have a thirty-year cycle from one progressed New Moon (progressed Sun conjunct progressed Moon) to another, and each progressed lunation phases lasts about three and a half to four years. They are the successive unfolding stages of one thirty-year cycle of the life purpose. Thus, we can see the lunation phases as a prototype for the development of any organic process, and use this as a lens through which to understand the nature of the life purpose as a stage of a cyclical process that is based on the interactive relationship between the positions of the two great luminaries, the Sun and the Moon. This pertains to both the purpose of the life as whole, as indicated by the natal phase, and to how this purpose unfolds over time, as indicated by the progressed lunation phase.

The progressed New Moon occurs approximately every thirty years, and the first phase of this thirty-year cycle lasts for about three and half to four years. During this time, there is often a clear-cut demarcation between the ending of an old way of life and the beginning of a major new cycle of activity. The keynote is the emergence of some new kind of vision or activity. At the progressed Crescent phase, the new direction begins to take shape. Individuals must develop perseverance and new skills that can assist them in overcoming fear and resistance so they can continue to move in a forward direction. The progressed First Quarter phase calls for the actualization of the new direction by taking action to build structures that can anchor it in the social world. At the progressed Gibbous phase, individuals must refine and perfect their skills and strive to master the techniques of their chosen vocations. Making the necessary adjustments ensures that the form will be a worthy vehicle for the expression of the vision.

During the progressed Full Moon phase, the seed intention germinated at the progressed New Moon flowers, and whatever was born then is now fully revealed. It is through clear, conscious, and meaningful interactions with others that individuals come to fully understand the larger purpose intended for what has been created over the previous fourteen years. It is difficult to sustain relationships or situations in the life that are not personally meaningful. During the progressed Disseminating phase, they move out into the world, link with others, and share the content of whatever was illuminated at the New Moon, embodying the beliefs into the life style. At the progressed Last Quarter phase, it is time to turn away from what has already been done, revise the thinking, and reorient the life.

The progressed Balsamic phase is the bridge between the ending of one cycle and the beginning of the next. Like the snake shedding its old skin, whatever has served its purpose in the life and is no longer of value for what is to come falls away. This is the time for the inner work of healing and regeneration, rest, introspection, and imagination. Some people are called to bring their life work to completion and pass on the baton to another. Some wait in the quiet stillness, dreaming dreams of the future that will be born at the next progressed New Moon.

INTEGRATING THE LUNATION PHASES

The obvious place in a chart reading for a discussion of the lunation phase is after you have examined the individual meanings of the Sun and the Moon. You can certainly place it there as a final synthesis of the luminaries. However, sometimes by this point, you are well into the main body of the session, and the insertion of this material may break the flow and continuity. I have successfully experimented with opening the consultation session with a discussion of the lunation phase, by both its natal and progressed phases.

There are several reasons for this, and they speak to the immediate establishment of credibility with the client. First, everyone has had a visual relationship with the phases of the Moon, and it does not involve much of a stretch of the imagination to consider that the lunar phase at birth has some relevance to the life. The eight natal lunation phases are grounded in the archetypal organic process, and this can provide a broad, but deep and illuminating, portrait of the life as a whole that is not predicated upon astrological language of signs and houses and aspects. When presented with the lunation phase material, clients almost always immediately recognize a central aspect of their personality and approach to life, which makes them more receptive to what follows. It also makes them more confident in your insight and skill as an astrological counselor.

The progressed lunation cycle is the only modern timing technique that looks at the general periods over the duration of the life. The understanding of where a person is at the present time relative to a longer thirty-year cycle that is not predicated upon the significations of one particular planet provides a frame of reference for the remainder of the reading. Deeper insights can be gained by evaluating the effects of other timing systems within this larger perspective. For example, a Saturn transit to the Sun that occurs during a progressed Full Moon phase has a totally different meaning from that same transit during a progressed New Moon phase. During the Full Moon phase, the emphasis is on defining your solar identity relative to others; in the New Moon phase, you define your identity in terms of releasing new visions that will shape the next thirty years of your life.

After you discuss the natal phase, inform clients about their progressed phase, giving the starting and ending dates. While this is meaningful information in and of itself, it is very powerful to place the current phase within the context of when the previous progressed New Moon phase began.

Since a new thirty-year cycle begins at the progressed New Moon, note that date. Look at the degree of the progressed New Moon and the house in which it falls in the natal chart, and also look to see if it conjoins any planets or asteroids. The house position will give information about the topic from which the new directions have emerged—whether it is livelihood (second house), relationship (seventh house), or profession (tenth house). If the progressed New Moon conjoins a planet or asteroid within several degrees, the significations of that planetary body will be involved in the new emerging direction. The Sabian symbol of the degree of the progressed New Moon can also provide insight into the spiritual impulse behind the emergent direction. You may want to ask your client if that time marked the end of an old cycle and the beginning of new directions, aspirations, hopes, dreams, or intentions, and what that was all about. Then you can discuss the current progressed lunation phase, and where your client is currently in the ongoing development of the seed vision that was released.

You should factor in:

- The dates of the previous progressed Balsamic phase: What ended?
- The dates of the previous progressed New Moon phase: What began?

- The dates of the current progressed lunation phase: How has the vision that emerged at the progressed New Moon developed up to this point, and what is now being called for in order to keep it moving along?

This information can then provide a platform and context for the remainder of the reading.

> Bill was born during the Crescent Moon phase, the second phase in the eight-fold sequence of lunation phases. Rudhyar characterized this phase with the keyword "struggle." The newly sprouted seedling, when it exhausts its food supply from the seed capsule, must struggle against the force of gravity to push itself upward through and above the earth in order to obtain its nutrients by photosynthesis from the Sun. Likewise, the individual born during this phase must struggle to establish the fledging identity as a viable force in its own right. The pull of the past—and especially the complex web of familial relationships and the conditioned patterns born of fears of failure, the future, the unknown, and inadequacy—can keep individuals tied to situations that, while providing security, do not support independence and striking out on their own. The keynote in this phase is one of self-actualization.
>
> Bill's life purpose as defined by the Sun and Moon is driven by a kind of energy whereby he experiences life as the struggle to overcome the resistance created by the pull of the past and by the density of the material world itself. He must develop new skills and abilities that give him the increasing confidence he needs to persevere in the forward momentum he needs to overcome obstacles and remain focused as he moves toward his visions, which are expressions of himself, apart from familial and cultural expectations.
>
> The previous progressed New Moon occurred in October 1992 at 19 degrees of Capricorn. This places the progressed New Moon in the second house of livelihood, opposing the natal position of Chiron. Bill said that, in November 1991, he

was laid off at the TV station where he worked, leaving him out of a job with a family to support. In October 1992, he was still struggling to find a way to make a living. By June of 1993, he had started his own business in digital video recording. He has since divorced and retired.

Currently, Bill is in a progressed Gibbous phase that will end in March 2008. In April 2007, the progressed Moon will conjoin natal Chiron and this may be a significant timing event. The progressed Gibbous phase will call upon him to refine and perfect his structure and his techniques of operation for the illumination of meaning at the upcoming progressed Full Moon. As we know, Bill has recently contracted to have prints made of films he made in the late 1960s about the counterculture revolution on the West Coast to submit to an international film festival.

STUDY GUIDELINES

- Determine the natal lunation phase for your practice chart and reflect on the extent to which the personality resonates to the astrological interpretations of that lunation phase. Write again your one-sentence interpretation of the basic life purpose, distilling the meanings of the Ascendant and its ruler, the Sun, and the Moon. Then add one more sentence explaining the kind of energy that is drawn upon in the expression and actualization of the life purpose, as defined by the lunation phase at birth.
- Determine the progressed lunation phase and the previous progressed New Moon phase. Write a paragraph detailing what new directions began at the progressed New Moon phase and what stage in the development of this larger cycle the client has reached. What are the challenges and opportunities? Consider the degree of the progressed New Moon and the house it activates in the natal chart. Does it conjoin any natal planet or asteroid? Also look at the Sabian symbol of that degree.

CHAPTER EIGHT

FORTUNE, LUNAR NODES, AND ECLIPSES

IN THE PREVIOUS CHAPTER, we examined the lunation phase, which indicates the kind of energy the Sun and Moon together utilize for the expression and application of the life purpose, within a model of cyclical process. In this chapter, we'll discuss other astrological factors that derive from the combinations and interactions of the Sun and Moon. These are the Lot of Fortune, the lunar nodes, and eclipses.

The Lot of Fortune is a mathematical analog of the Sun, Moon, and Ascendant. It indicates an area of life where accidental good fortune and happiness may come to us by means of luck or chance, rather than by our actions and intent. The lunar nodes are the points of intersection between the plane of the Moon's orbit with the plane of the Sun's apparent orbit around the Earth, called the ecliptic. They demarcate an axis of how past actions have led to current circumstances that provide opportunities for personal and spiritual growth. Eclipses are derived from the nodal relationship, so solar and lunar eclipses are actually a subset of the lunar nodes. A solar eclipse can occur when the Sun and Moon are conjunct at the New Moon; a lunar eclipse can occur when the Sun and Moon are opposed one another at the Full Moon. Eclipses point to strong intensifications of the energies involved.

THE LOT OF FORTUNE ⊗

The Lot of Fortune speaks to the role of chance, luck, and fate in the success of the life. It is more commonly known in modern astrology as the Part of Fortune, which comes from *pars*, the Latin translation of the Greek word *kleros*. In the world of the ancient astrologers, the Lot of Fortune was one of the most important points in the chart, equal in rank to the Ascendant, Sun, and Moon. It was considered one of the five places of life that were analyzed for length-of-life determinations. Its inclusion in the chart was one of the distinguishing innovations of Hellenistic astrology. Its calculation is dependant upon the exact degree of the Ascendant sign. The mathematics necessary for this were developed by the Alexandrian astrologer Hypsicles around 150 B.C.E.

The Lot of Fortune is the special lot of the Moon; the Lot of Spirit (also called the Lot of the *Daimon*) is the special lot of the Sun. Each of the other visible planets has its own special lot. These are collectively known as the seven Hermetic lots. Fortune, as the lot of the Moon, speaks to matters of the body, health, and wealth; Spirit, the lot of the Sun, addresses matters of the soul, profession, and actions. In fact, Hellenistic astrologers employed around ninety-six different lots—lots of marriage, children, treachery, injury, accusation—each of which gave additional information about any topic being investigated. Many of the lots are calculated differently, depending on whether the chart is for a day or night birth (see figures 8 and 9). Check to see if your computer software gives you the option of calculating lots. Here, we will discuss only the Lot of Fortune.

Calculating the Lot of Fortune

The Lot of Fortune is derived from the zodiacal degrees of the two lights, the Sun and Moon, along with that of the Ascendant. Ancient astrologers took the arc (the degree interval) between the Sun and Moon, and projected this arc from the Ascendant degree. Where it falls is the location of the lot. In a diurnal chart, the distance is taken from the Sun to the Moon in the zodiacal order of the signs; in a nocturnal chart, the distance is taken from the Moon to the Sun.[1]

It has become customary to write out arithmetic formulas for the construction of a lot using the celestial longitude of each planet or point in the chart. We will follow that practice here. Figures 8 and

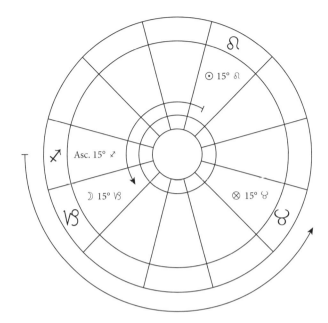

FIGURE 8. *Determination of the Lot of Fortune in a diurnal (day) chart*
    1. Diurnal day chart because the Sun is above the horizon.
    2. Take the distance from the Sun to the Moon in the direction of the
    order of the signs; from 15 Leo to 15 Capricorn is 150 degrees.
    3. Project 150 degrees from the Ascendant in the direction of the order
    of the signs; 15 Sagittarius plus 150 degrees equals 15 Taurus.

9 give diagrams that will help you understand the theoretical construct behind the calculation of lots.

The formula for the Lot of Fortune is:

• Day chart: Asc. + Moon – Sun
• Night chart: Asc. + Sun – Moon

Notice that the order of the Sun and the Moon is reversed for the
nocturnal lot. There is a tradition going back to Ptolemy in which
the Lot of Fortune in a night chart is calculated the same way as the
lot in a day chart. In fact, many modern software programs still do
this. However, it was the more common practice among Hellenistic

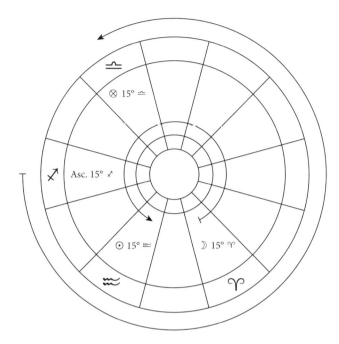

FIGURE 9. *Determination of the Lot of Fortune in a nocturnal (night) chart*

1. *Nocturnal night chart because the Sun is below the horizon.*
2. *Take the distance from the Moon to the Sun in the direction of the order of the signs; from 15 Aries to 15 Aquarius is 300 degrees.*
3. *Project 300 degrees from the Ascendant in the direction of the order of the signs; 15 Sagittarius plus 300 degrees equals 15 Libra.*

astrologers to reverse the formula for a night chart. Check the preferences in your software program to see how it calculates the Lot of Fortune and make any adjustments you want for nocturnal charts.

> Bill, born during the day with the Sun above the horizon, has a diurnal chart. Thus the number of degrees between his Sun at 24 Scorpio 23 and his Moon at 9 Aquarius 51 moving forward in the order of the signs is 75 degrees 28 minutes. If you add this number of degrees to the Ascendant at 16 Sagittarius 24, the Lot of Fortune falls out at 0 Pisces 52, which places it in the fourth house.

Interpreting the Lot of Fortune

In natal interpretation, the Lot of Fortune indicates an area of life where accidental good fortune and happiness may come by means of luck or chance, rather than by an individual's own actions and intent.

Lot, from the Greek word *kleros*, is related to the concept of fate. During the era when the doctrine of the lots was being developed in Ptolemaic Egypt, one of the meanings of *kleros* was an apportionment of land in a foreign country that was arbitrarily assigned to citizens. In the Greek literature of Homer and Hesiod, a person's allotment in life is arbitrarily doled out by the gods, either by Zeus or by the *Moirai*—the Three Fates. Fortune is associated with the Roman goddess Fortuna, known to the Greeks as Tyche, the personification of the principle of luck or chance. Poets describe how the capricious force of Tyche raises men and women up and strikes them down for no reason. To appease her unpredictable and uncontrollable elements, Tyche/Fortuna was widely worshipped in the Hellenistic era as the local guardian of the luck of a city. She is often depicted holding a cornucopia (horn of plenty) or the child Plutus (wealth) in the hope that she will protect and bless a locale. She is shown with wings, a rudder, and a ball as emblems of her variability. She is also shown striding upon the prow of a ship.

From the Hellenistic perspective, the Lot of Fortune, like all the other lots, thus carries the implication of fate as a random circumstance of chance and luck that befalls individuals despite their own efforts and actions. Lots attempt to quantify the amount of good luck an individual can expect with reference to various topics through the agency of chance. Individuals may thus be generally lucky or unlucky completely apart from their intrinsic integrity, intelligence, talent, and capacity for hard work, and this plays a considerable role in the overall success of the life.

In traditional astrology, the Lot of Fortune symbolizes worldly success and material prosperity—all that contributes to the happiness and financial welfare of the individual. In a more modern psychological context, Dane Rudhyar discussed the Lot of Fortune as a focal point for the expression of the power generated by the soli-lunar relationship (lunation phase). He spoke of it as the state of happiness that arises from an ease of function in which the life force can flow most naturally. It is the point that integrates the individual meanings of the Sun, Moon, and Ascendant, and, from this point of view, the Lot of Fortune can be understood as the place where the life purpose, as a combination of these three places of life, can be expressed most easily.

ANALYZING THE LOT OF FORTUNE

We are now ready to analyze the Lot of Fortune and interpret its meaning within the chart. This is a three-step process that examines the house location of the lot, its condition, and the condition of its lord.

In the most general sense, the house location of the Lot of Fortune indicates an area of life where a person benefits by gain in the things ruled by that house, and these gains occur due to the force of luck rather than effort. The house location of the Lot of Fortune also points to the area of life where the Ascendant motivation, the solar content, and the lunar application of the life purpose can be focused and integrated. This purpose can then find expression as a state of happiness, because the individual finds it easy to do what he or she is best equipped to do. This lends credence to the theory that we are most successful in doing what we enjoy, which is doing what comes naturally. But we all know that this state of grace is easier for some people to manage than others.

There are three factors that modify the condition of the Lot of Fortune.

- The relative angularity of the house location of the Lot of Fortune (angular, succedent, cadent)
- Whether the Lot of Fortune is under the Sun's beams
- Configurations to the Lot of Fortune by the benefic or malefic planets, especially when present in the same sign

The best placement for the Lot of Fortune is the angular signs/houses. The placement of the Lot of Fortune in the succedent signs/houses indicates a moderate amount of luck. Fortune in the cadent houses is considered to be rather unfortunate. If the Lot of Fortune is under the beams of the Sun, it is thought to have no power or efficacy. The Lot of Fortune witnessed by the benefic planets, Venus and Jupiter, portends gain and happiness through the topics of the house in which the lot is located, but witnessing by the malefic planets, Mars and Saturn, suggests loss, damage, and sorrows in connection with the significations of the house.

The final step in analyzing the Lot of Fortune is to examine its domicile lord. If the planet that is the domicile lord of Fortune is in the signs of its own rulership or exaltation, if it is in the angular and in the good/profitable houses, if it is witnessed by benefic planets, direct in motion, and not under the Sun's beams, these are all favorable indications for the person being able to take advantage of accidental good fortune. You should note that, if the Lot of Fortune is configured to its lord, this is a very important factor indicating whether the planetary agent of Fortune is connected to Fortune and thus able to take advantage of the luck it bestows. From a modern perspective, a well-placed Lot of Fortune and its lord contribute to the ease of the expression of the life purpose.

At what point in the delineation should you include a discussion of the Lot of Fortune? There are several possibilities. If the Lot of Fortune occupies the same sign as the Ascendant ruler, Sun, or Moon, or the first house, you can bring in the concept of accidental good fortune when you discuss these main significators of the chart. If the client brings a specific concern to the session, and the Lot of Fortune falls in the house that signifies the topic, (e.g., the fifth for children or the tenth for profession), that is another opportunity to enfold its meaning into the delineation concerning expectations of success. If you are developing a theme of life purpose looking to the Ascendant and its ruler, the Sun, the Moon, and the lunation phase, you can discuss the Lot of Fortune as the location where all these factors can be integrated.

> In Bill's chart, the Lot of Fortune occupies the sign Pisces and is placed in the fourth house. Thus accidental good fortune and gain may be expected from property, parents, and inheritance.

Fortune occupies an angular house, is not under the Sun's beams, and is co-present with the benefic Jupiter, all of which support the reception of good luck. The domicile lord of the Lot of Fortune is the benefic Jupiter, powerful in its own sign of Pisces, angular, and free from affliction by both malefics. Jupiter is present in the same house as Fortune, and thus can easily access the luck. Jupiter's weakness is its retrograde motion, which is the only drawback to a most powerful indicator of Bill being blessed by gods and capable of taking advantage of the many opportunities presented that portend good fortune.

Placing our discussion of the Lot of Fortune within the context of the place where the expression of the life purpose can occur most easily and grant the greatest happiness, you can posit that it is through participation in artistic or spiritual land-based communities, or the implementation of altruistic visions concerning domestic living environments, or other such combinations of the meanings of Pisces and the fourth house that Bill can integrate the impulses of his Ascendant, Sun, Moon, and Crescent lunation phase in terms of the living of a purposeful life.

THE LUNAR NODES

The lunar nodes are neither celestial bodies nor mathematical constructs, but rather points in space where the plane of the Moon's orbit intersects the ecliptic, which marks the apparent path of the Sun. Thus the lunar nodes symbolize the two points where the paths of the Sun and Moon cross one another. Eclipses occur at the New Moon or at the Full Moon when the plane of the Moon is in alignment with the plane of the ecliptic, and thus one of these bodies passes directly in front of the other, overshadowing and obscuring its light. Eclipses, therefore, symbolize the obstruction of the energies from either the Sun or the Moon.

The ecliptic defines the apparent annual path of the Sun as seen from Earth (either as the tropical zodiac marked by solstices and equinoxes, or as the sidereal zodiac marked by the constellations of the fixed stars). Most of the planets travel in orbits that are within

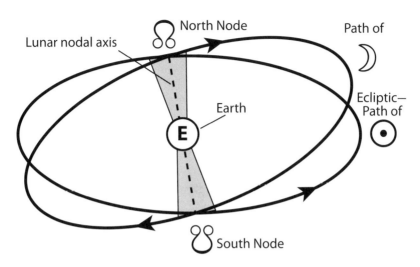

FIGURE 10. *The lunar nodes.*

15 degrees of celestial latitude north or south of the ecliptic. Thus their orbits are inclined at variable angles to the plane of the eclip-tic. The two points where the planes of the orbits of the planets intersect the plane of the orbit of the ecliptic are referred to as the nodes. Although there is some interpretive material in the astrologi-cal literature on the planetary nodes, in this lesson we will examine only the lunar nodes.

The Moon's orbit inclines at an average angle of 5 degrees 8 minutes to the ecliptic. The intersection of these two orbital planes forms an axis, and the points of intersection are called the nodes. The ascending or north node ☊ marks the point where the path of the Moon crosses the ecliptic from south to north latitude; the descending or south node ☋ is where the path of the Moon crosses the ecliptic from north to south latitude. The Moon spends half of its time traveling above the ecliptic plane in northern celestial latitudes and half of its time beneath the ecliptic plane in southern celestial latitudes. The zodiacal degrees of the mean ascending and descending nodes always occupy the same degree of opposing sets of signs, although the true nodes have slight variations from exactitude by opposition. In some cases, when using true node positions, one node can occupy the late degrees of one sign and the other node can occupy the early degrees of the opposing sign. The nodes move backward through the zodiacal signs at a rate of about 3 degrees a day; the nodal cycle has a period of 18.5996 years.

In modern astrology, the north lunar node is generally considered to be a symbol of the future direction of integration and spiritual growth, while the south lunar node points to the forces of past habit and unconscious conditioning that limit the development of potential. It is only in the 20th century, however, that the nodes have come to be associated with their present meanings.

The lunar nodes were mentioned in passing by Hellenistic astrologers, who called them *Anabibazo* and *Katabibazo*, which mean simply "to make go up" and "to make go down." They were not, however, given the importance they have today. Vettius Valens tells his readers that benefic planets conjoined to either of the nodes, but especially the ascending node, indicate success and reputation, but the malefic planets produce loss and accusations. In another section, Valens explains that the nodes break down the power of the zodiacal signs they occupy, as well as the power of their rulers.[2]

The nodes are first called the Dragon's Head and Dragon's Tail in the Sassanian Persian astrological literature of the fourth century C.E. These names were transmitted into the Hellenistic texts by the time of Rhetorius in the early seventh century C.E. Babylonian creation myth from the first millennium B.C.E. records the story of Marduk slaying the dragon Tiamat, whose head and tail subsequently formed the upper and lower hemispheres of the world. A variation of this tale appears in a Zoroastrian text on the *thema mundi*, the astrological chart of the creation of the world. Hindu mythology tells of the severing of a world dragon, whose head was called Rahu and whose tail was called Ketu. These were incorporated into astrological symbolism as the north and south node, where they assumed a rank equal to that of the planets. In contemporary Vedic interpretation, Rahu (north node) is associated with material or sensual gratification, while Ketu (south node) is linked with the powers of the unconscious, both as irrational fears and as wisdom and enlightenment.[3]

Medieval tradition saw the north node as benefic, having the nature of Venus and Jupiter and bringing honors and riches in accordance with the nature of the planet conjoined to it. It saw the south node as malefic, having the nature of Mars and Saturn and bringing poverty and afflictions in accordance with the character of the planet conjoined to it. The lunar nodes continued to be viewed in this way until the beginning of the 20th century in the Western tradition. To the extent that upward northward motion above the ecliptic plane as depicted by the north node is highly regarded in connection with the ascent of the spirit, and downward southward motion beneath the ecliptic plane as depicted by the south node is devalued as the descent of the soul into matter, we can argue for the historical association of good and bad with the north and south node.

In 1936, with the publication of Rudyhar's *The Astrology of Personality*, we see for the first time a more fully developed exposition on the meaning of the nodes from a psychological perspective. This perspective has shaped most of the subsequent literature on the topic. Rudhyar envisions the nodal axis as the directives of destiny along a line of stress between that from which the personality emerged and what it is meant to accomplish. He writes:

> If we should lie along the nodal axis, we would look into the future facing North and accept the past facing South. The North Node deals, therefore with the work to be done, the new accomplishment, the new faculty to be developed; and if we are willing to exert ourselves in that direction, from it we shall receive power in abundance. The South Node represents the work that has been done, the well-known accomplishment, the routine performance already gone through many times, perhaps—the easy way out. The opposition between, on one hand, self-integration, individuation, effort, the line of greatest connection through exertion; and on the other hand, self-undoing, automatism, inertia, the line of least resistance.[4]

When the themes of karma and reincarnation are superimposed upon the nodes, the south node comes to symbolize karma from past lives—usually, but not always, bad karma. By contrast, the north node is understood as the actions that lead to future incarnations, which, if conscious and well-motivated, can contribute to a favorable rebirth. It is not clear if Rudhyar was influenced in his reframing of the meanings of the nodes by his theosophical affiliations, which looked to the Hindu and Buddhist teachings of India and Tibet as their source of inspiration.

In *Finding Our Way Through the Dark*, I attempt to revision the negativity associated with the south node, wanting to give a more empowering and useful meaning to working with the nodal axis. Thus I suggest that the south node represents the sum total of our knowledge and wisdom from the past, which can be a foundation upon which to build new skills and capacities as indicated by the north node. It is only because we rely too much upon our innate abilities that we are led into problematic behavior. From a modern perspective, this offers an opportunity for counseling directives and a working definition of the nodes in delineation that might read as follows:

> The south node represents an innate talent or ability that may appear at an early age and arises effortlessly within us. However we may also be vulnerable to automatic fear-based behavior at the place of the south node that can cause us to stagnate, repeat unproductive behavior, and become limited in our growth. By contrast, the north node points to a future that is waiting to be actualized by the development of new attitudes and capacities that may create discomfort by pushing us to go beyond ourselves, but that results in great personal growth.

Eclipses

While this definition of the nodes can be very helpful in psychologically oriented astrological counseling and is not entirely inaccurate, it does not take into account the primary reason for the nodes traditionally having problematic significations. These significations derive from the intimate connection between the nodes and eclipses, which were considered to be ominous events indicative of calamity, disaster, and other unfortunate circumstances. The ancient astrologers called the nodes "the eclipsing places."

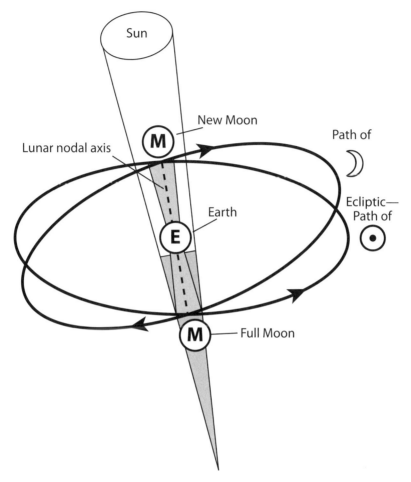

FIGURE 11. *Solar and lunar eclipses.*

Eclipses can occur only at a New Moon or a Full Moon when the Moon is also conjoined to one of the lunar nodes. When the Moon, in its monthly path, reaches the nodes, the plane of the Moon's orbit is aligned to that of the Sun and Earth. Solar eclipses occur at a New Moon when the Moon passes between the Sun and Earth, blocking out the solar rays from the perspective of an observer on Earth. When this event occurs at a Full Moon, the Earth passes between the Sun and the Moon, blocking the lunar rays and causing a lunar eclipse. These two alignments occur approximately every six months, when the Moon and the nodes are at the same celestial latitude and longitude at the time of the New or Full Moon.

In the ancient world, eclipses were looked upon with terror and awe, as the Sun or Moon suddenly and unexpectedly disappeared from the heavens. They were often viewed as portents of natural disasters, warfare, and danger to leaders. They were carefully observed and much effort was devoted to predicting their occurrence. There is substantial archaeo-astronomical scholarship suggesting that megalithic stone monuments like Stonehenge were designed to predict eclipses. Today, the interpretation of eclipses still carries traces of this negative connotation, but reframed as an influence that intensifies and stimulates, for good or bad, the points in the chart that are affected. Since the Sun and Moon are two places of life, when the light from one of these luminaries is temporarily obscured, it is natural to infer a cessation of the life force emanating from that celestial body. The ensuing struggle for survival, as when someone is being suffocated and deprived of air, describes the agitation that people may experience from the energies of an eclipse. This struggle propels them to extend themselves beyond their natural limitations, and can result in annihilation or in victory.

From a psychological perspective, when the light of the mind and consciousness (Sun) or the instinctive wisdom of the body and emotions (Moon) is blocked, something else that is normally held under restraint emerges unimpeded. Consider the analogy of robbers who prefer to do their work at night under the cover of darkness. Eclipses can allow us to access that which has been concealed or repressed—what Jung referred to as the shadow. This encounter with the hidden and rejected contents of the unconscious as it refers to either the solar mind or the lunar emotions can bring a person to integrate the unknown with the known, the dark with the light, the past with the future. This is the potential inherent in the encounter of the two lights perfectly aligned in conjunction or opposition at the places of the lunar nodes, with the opposing pole being the possibility of the breakdown or disintegration of the psyche.

Tibetan Buddhist spiritual traditions hold that the energies during eclipses are greatly magnified, and propose that the end results of the good or bad actions that are done during an eclipse have significantly larger-than-usual ramifications in the life.

Determining and Evaluating Eclipses in the Chart

There are three main considerations when interpreting eclipses in a natal chart for a single consultation session. The first relates to whether the person was born at the time of a solar or lunar eclipse. If you notice that the Moon is conjoined to either the north or south node (this will occur twice a month) *and* the Sun is conjoined to the Moon (New Moon) or opposite the Moon (Full Moon, and thus conjoined to the other node), you know that the person was born at the time of an eclipse. If the New Moon is within 15 degrees of a node, or if the Full Moon is within 9 degrees, eclipses must occur. A slightly larger orb—17 degrees for the Sun and 11 degrees for the Moon—indicates that an eclipse may have occurred; 5 degrees indicates a total or annular eclipse. The technical terms for these orbs are the major and minor ecliptic limits. Check your ephemeris for the exact dates of eclipses.

This is an important factor in delineation, and should be discussed in your interpretation of the Sun and Moon. The life will be especially intense, with the collective forces of the past and future presenting themselves in ways that bring the person to critical thresholds and turning points that could go in the direction of either greater or lesser integration. The sign and its domicile lord, house, and configurations of the eclipse point will be the same as that of the Sun or Moon and should be interpreted accordingly, unless the eclipse falls in an adjacent sign within 5 degrees of either luminary.

Some computer mapping programs contain an option for determining the path of an eclipse as its shadow sweeps over certain parts of the Earth where it is visible. Research indicates that these geographical places have particular import for the individual.

Second, you must consider the eclipses that will occur in the future. Eclipses occur several times each year, in pairs. If a solar eclipse happens, it will generally be preceded or followed by a lunar eclipse. As an astrologer, familiarize yourself with the eclipses that will occur in your client's chart in the coming year. When you are preparing the data for the timing activations in the chart, take notice if the eclipse will fall on the degree of a planet or angle within a 5-degree orb of conjunction. This is especially important.

Ancient astrologers were concerned if the eclipse activated the Sun, Moon, Ascendant, Midheaven, or one of the malefic planets, which were thought to be unfavorable influences. It is an open discussion among astrologers as to whether aspects other than the conjunction should be used, although I would not exclude a close opposition.

When evaluating what the eclipse may portend, look at the nature, condition, and location of the planet being aspected by the eclipse degree, as well as whether the benefic or malefic planets are witnessing the eclipse degree. The sensitivity and the duration of the effects of the eclipse can last for several years and, traditional astrology instructs, are triggered by the transit of Mars over that degree and consummated under the transit of Saturn. One rule of thumb used was that the effects of a solar eclipse lasted as many years as the eclipse lasted in hours, while the effects of a lunar eclipse lasted as many months as the eclipse lasted in hours.

The third consideration that can be used in a detailed study of eclipses is the prenatal eclipse—the solar and lunar eclipses that occurred before birth. There will be one, or possibly two, eclipses that occur within six months of the birth date. The degrees of these pre-natal eclipses remain as sensitive degrees in the chart for the duration of the lifetime. Transits and progressions by planets over these degrees often trigger events that would otherwise not be correlated to a timing activation. Again, the maps of the eclipse paths can provide much insight.

Pre-natal Lunation

The pre-natal lunation (PNL) is the final of the five places of life. You can use the pre-natal lunation in a more advanced analysis of the natal chart. The pre-natal lunation is the degree of the New or Full Moon before birth, whichever lunation is the closest. If a person is born during the waxing part of the lunation cycle, between the New and the Full Moon, the PNL is the zodiacal degree of the New Moon prior to birth. If a person is born during the waning part of the lunation cycle, between the Full and the New Moon, the PNL is the zodiacal degree of the Full Moon prior to birth. To the extent that the Sun signifies the soul and the Moon signifies the body, the pre-natal lunation represents the synergy between the body and the soul that occurs sometime in the month before birth. The degree of this lunation remains a sensitive point over the duration of the life. In Hellenistic astrology, it was used as a starting point for a time-lord procedure, and both Hellenistic and Medieval astrologers considered it in length-of-life considerations. Aside from this mention of the pre-natal lunation, we will defer further explanation of this point.

RECONCILING ASTROLOGY AND COUNSELING

Astrologers who are grounded in the historical tradition of nodes and eclipses consider that the nodes portend difficulties because they are the places where eclipses can occur. Eclipses block the life-giving qualities of the two luminaries, and thus open the way for life-destroying energies to propagate.

This is not helpful information, however, for a counselor to give a client in whose chart the nodes and eclipse points are emphasized. These clients may be struggling to hold the forces of the unconscious at bay, fighting to keep the past and the collective consciousness from overwhelming their psyches and blocking the movement that brings them into the present and reaching toward a beckoning future. In cases like these, it is the transformative potential of eclipses you must encourage. Even if it is unlikely, you should never completely exclude the possibility of grace entering a life and changing a determined course or direction.

Always remain fully aware of the dangers inherent in the nodes and eclipse points and lead your client to an understanding of how to take advantage of the best expression of the south-node energies to cultivate the possibilities implied by the north node. If the birth is an eclipse birth, the life force is especially fragile, but it is laden

with potential for massive breakthroughs that can liberate an individual from the density of conditioning by unconscious and collective forces. Eclipse degrees preceding and following the birth remain
sensitive over the course of the life and can provide insight into the
triggering of un-integrated aspects of the psyche. And eclipses by
transit over natal planets and angles can bring death and rebirth
experiences, intensifying the significations of those planets to reach
beyond their normal limits. When eclipses are witnessed favorably
by the benefic planets, they can also portend exceptional circumstances for good fortune, great accomplishments, significant and dramatic shifts in direction, and victory over odds.

> In Bill's chart, the north node is in Libra in the eleventh house
> and the south node is in Aries in the fifth house conjunct to
> Vesta and Saturn. From a traditional perspective, Saturn with the
> south node in the fifth house indicates difficulties, loss, rejec-
> tion by children or in love affairs, partially due to self-centered
> behavior in the pursuit of his own needs and agenda (Aries). As
> a counselor, you can encourage him to focus on the north node
> in Libra in the eleventh house, where he can develop friend-
> ships and participate in groups that share his ideals and visions
> in order to meet his intimacy needs, and where he will experi-
> ence collaborative efforts, strong consideration for others, and
> balanced interactions (Libra).
>
> As the Moon is not near either of the nodes, you can imme-
> diately eliminate the possibility that Bill was born during an
> eclipse. Your ephemeris shows that there was a total solar
> eclipse preceding his birth on October 12, 1939 at 18 Libra
> 37, and an annular solar eclipse after his birth on April 7, 1940
> at 17 Aries 52. If, in preparing for his reading, you notice that
> there are major transits to these points, consider this in your
> prognostication.
>
> On March 19, 2007, there is a partial solar eclipse at 28
> Pisces 07, and you immediately note that this will conjoin
> Bill's natal Jupiter, the Ascendant ruler, to the exact degree. The
> solar eclipse will further intensify and magnify the import of
> the events signified by Jupiter, which is also receiving square

aspects by transiting Pluto and Jupiter in this year. During this month, Bill bought a large house with the intention of creating an intentional spiritual community, which he says had been his life-long dream. His mother also had a stroke from which she recovered; he moved her next door to his new home so he could better attend to her needs. Note how the eclipse activation of Jupiter located in and ruling the fourth house brought about significant events concerned with both the parent and the home.

STUDY GUIDELINES

- Determine, analyze, and interpret the Lot of Fortune and its lord in your practice chart. Be sure to include a discussion of both the traditional and modern approaches to this point of integration of the Sun, Moon, and Ascendant.

- Compose an analysis of the north and south nodes of the Moon that factors in the sign and house placements of the nodes, as well as any planets conjoined to them.

- Check to see whether or not the person was born on an eclipse; determine the sensitive eclipse degrees preceding and following the birth; and note if the eclipses of the current year will affect any natal planets or angles.

CHAPTER NINE

MYTHIC ASTEROID ARCHETYPES

THE ASTEROIDS are thousands of small planetary bodies revolving around the Sun. Most of them travel in an orbital belt between Mars and Jupiter, having mean periods of about four years. Thus their positions in a chart are quite individual in contrast to the generational placements of the outer planets. However, some asteroids, known as "orbit crossers" (for example, Eros and Icarus), move from inside the asteroid belt to circle Venus and Mercury. These faster-moving bodies have orbital periods of less than four years. The orbits of other asteroids such as Hidalgo extend out toward the orbit of Saturn, and these slower-moving asteroids have longer orbital periods. In 1596, the prescient Johannes Kepler speculated on the existence of a planet between Mars and Jupiter (many contemporary and past astronomers regard the asteroids as the remains of a planet that exploded), yet the first asteroid was not discovered until December 31, 1800. By the end of the 19th century, over 1000 additional minor planets had been identified. Today, there are over 12,000 named and numbered asteroids.

The first asteroid to be discovered was named Ceres, after the Roman goddess of agriculture who was known to the Greeks as Demeter. This set the precedent for the next three asteroids discovered, which were also named for goddesses of classical antiquity—Pallas (Greek Athena), Juno (Greek Hera), and Vesta (Greek Hestia). In fact, of the 1000 asteroids discovered in the 19th century, more than 750 were named for goddesses from a variety of mythological traditions. Others were named for gods. When astronomers began to run out of mythic names, they started naming them after everything from ordinary people (John, Nancy, William, Barbara) to famous people (Einstein, Shakespeare), to geographical places (Dallas, Paris, Moscow, Arizona), to trees and flowers. They even named some after concepts (Academia, Karma, Beer, Lust, and Compassion).

It is only since 1973 that astrologers have had ephemeredes available for the study of the major asteroids, largely due to the efforts of Eleanor Bach. In 1981, practitioners such as Lee Lehman, Al Morrison, and Mark Pottenger began to calculate the positions of others and distribute these calculations to the community. It is very likely that there is an asteroid that has your own name and whose ephemeris you can obtain. While some tend to dismiss the asteroids as irrelevant and unnecessary clutter in the chart, remember that many astrologers in the 1930s refused to consider Pluto valid, because they had enough other planets to deal with.

To the extent that the asteroids are real planetary bodies orbiting in the solar system, and to the extent that the macrocosm of the heavens is reflected in the microcosm of the human being, they, like all celestial bodies, have correspondences to various aspects of human consciousness. Thus, it is of value to integrate their symbolism into the astrological chart. From an esoteric perspective, some suggest that the discovery of new planets external to us corresponds to an internal awakening in the human psyche of some aspect of consciousness represented by the symbolism associated with that planet. Social scientists foretell a quantum leap of consciousness, in which many dormant brain cells will become activated. Yet others see, in the discovery of hundreds of new bodies and their addition to the astrological pantheon, a mirror of the current explosion of information available to the human brain as the result of the Internet.

CERES ?, PALLAS ♀, JUNO ⚴, AND VESTA ⚶

These first four asteroids are considered especially significant, not only because of their early discovery, but also because their namesakes are among the most important of the classical goddesses. Ceres, Vesta, and Juno were the three sisters of Jupiter, Neptune, and Pluto, and thus are equivalent in rank to the leading Olympian gods. Pallas was the favorite daughter of Jupiter and tutelary goddess of Athens.

These four asteroid goddesses embody a large and comprehensive complex of symbolism and meanings.

If you look at the pantheon of planetary deities from an archetypal perspective, in the traditional ten-planet system, all but two planets represent masculine gods. Until recently, the Moon as mother and Venus as wife were the only two significators of the feminine, and most women were confined to these roles. The addition of four other powerful feminine planetary deities brings gender balance to the symbol system used for chart analysis, and thereby gives voice to many themes that express the feminine energies in human experience that were previously unacknowledged in traditional astrological symbolism. Since the discovery and astrological availability of the asteroid goddesses, many more aspects of the feminine principle have emerged in human behavior.

As you read the following summaries, note how the significations of the asteroids can be derived from their mythical biographies. The underlying premise of the mythic approach to chart analysis is that, when a celestial body is prominently placed in the skies at the moment of a person's birth, the mythological story of the eponymous god or goddess becomes a major theme in that person's life. The process of interpretation involves the telling of the story and the drawing of correlations between the mythical biography of the planetary deity and the themes that shape a person's life experiences. The story itself often overshadows the particulars of sign and house position, although these do indicate how and where the story plays itself out in a particular life. The rationale for this approach is the supposition that the mythological deities are the symbolic external expressions of the inner structures of the psyche. The astrology of the ancient Babylonian, Greek, and Indian cultures all had implicit, if not explicit, associations between the planets and the gods.[1]

Ceres ?

Ceres, known to the Greeks as Demeter, is the classical goddess of agriculture who worked unceasingly to bring food and nourishment to the people of the Earth. One of the most famous stories of antiquity tells of the ravishment and abduction of Persephone

(Latin Proserpina), Ceres' daughter, by Pluto, Lord of the Underworld, and of Ceres' subsequent grief and suffering as she wanders disconsolately over the Earth in search of her missing child. In her anger, she causes a famine, withholding production of all food, until her daughter is returned. Meanwhile, Persephone, in a symbolic act of rape, is tricked into eating pomegranate seeds, associated with sexual awareness, thus giving Pluto a claim over her.

A compromise is reached between Ceres and Pluto whereby Persephone spends part of each year in the underworld with Pluto caring for the souls of the dead, but returns each spring to her mother in the upper world after having initiated the dead into the rites of rebirth. For over 2000 years, this drama was celebrated regularly in ancient Greece as the initiation rites of the Eleusinian Mysteries.

In the human psyche, Ceres represents that aspect of our nature that longs to give birth, nourish, and sustain new life, as well as to nurture and be nurtured by others through the giving and receiving of unconditional love and acceptance. She represents the essential bonding or lack thereof that occurs between mother and child—a bonding centered on the giving of food as the expression of love. In our early experiences as children, this food/love may be freely given. In other instances, however, it is conditionally awarded, withheld as a form of punishment, or denied through neglect, causing the self-love and self-worth normally associated with Ceres to be undermined and undeveloped, and precipitating a host of psychological problems for the child and, later, the adult.

Psychological problems related to Ceres' symbolic withholding of food from herself and others in the midst of her grief include an obsessive relationship with food, a poor body image, and a range of eating disorders and food-related illnesses. In her grief, Ceres became totally immobilized. We, likewise, can be plunged into depths of depression and despair, making us incapable of daily functioning, of working and being productive.

The story of Ceres and Persephone is one of loss and return, death and rebirth. Ceres speaks to the complex mother-child relationship, and her mythos also contains the themes of physical or emotional loss, separation, abandonment, rejection, or estrangements that occur between parents and children, and, later in life, between other loved ones. As a symbol of attachment to what we have birthed or created, Ceres guides us to learning the lessons of letting go, as exemplified in the anguish we face when we need to share our children with others in cases of divorce or adoption.

Ceres' daughter, Persephone, was symbolically raped by Pluto, her mother's brother. This points to the fear that Ceres parents may have about protecting their children from harm—or the fact that they may have experienced incest or sexual abuse as children. In the desire of Ceres parents to keep their children safe, they can become overly controlling and restrictive. Their children may then struggle against the parental attachment in order to establish their own identities.

On a transpersonal level, Ceres, as the mother of the world, moves us to care about the homeless, the hungry, and the destruction of the Earth's resources. She urges us to take compassionate action, to provide for fundamental human needs, and to care for the body of the Earth that supports and sustains us. Not only did Ceres give birth to the living, in her aspect as Persephone, she received the souls of the dead back into her womb to prepare them for rebirth. Thus Ceres can also express as a vocation for hospice work, facilitating the life/death transition on the physical, as well as psychological, level.

Ceres teaches the wisdom that excessive attachment and possessiveness often result in eventual loss, and that sharing and letting go lead to reunion. She embodies the great truth of transformation—that from death comes new life.

Pallas Athena ⚴

Pallas was better known to the Greeks as Athena, the goddess of wisdom, who was said to have sprung full-grown, clad in a suit of gleaming war armor, from the crown of the head of her father, Jupiter (Zeus). She immediately took her place at his right hand. As patroness of Athens, she presided over military strategy during wartime and justice in peacetime. Idealized as Athena Parthenos, the virgin warrior queen, she was always accompanied by her great serpent, and she took no lovers or consorts. She walked easily and freely through the worlds of gods, heroes, and men as their colleague, advisor, equal, and friend.

Pallas Athena is mythically related to an ancient lineage of goddesses from the ancient Near East, Egypt, North Africa, and Crete who were associated with the serpent as a symbol of wisdom and healing. She affirmed this connection by placing the head of her dark sister, Gorgon Medusa, the serpent-haired queen of wisdom, on the center of her snake-fringed breastplate. In *kundalini* yoga, this serpent image is depicted coiled at the base of the spine, rising through the spinal canal, and emerging from the top of the head as cosmic illumination. This is a metaphor for the wisdom of Pallas Athena, who likewise emerged from the head of Jupiter.

Pallas Athena was unique among goddesses in that she held a position of power and respect in the eyes of the classical Greeks. Classical myths have Pallas Athena denouncing and denying her maternal origins as she arranged for the death of her sister, Medusa, and claiming that no mother gave her life. She upheld male supremacy in all things save marriage. The price that was asked and extracted of her for this power was the denial of her feminine nature. She severed her connection with her mother, her sister, the community of women, and her sexuality, and lost touch with her feminine qualities of softness and vulnerability.

In contemporary culture, women who are smart, powerful, strong, and accomplished are like Pallas in that they are not considered to be "real women." They are often pressured to make a choice between career and creative self-expression on one hand, and relationship and family on the other. Pallas Athena is epitomized by the girl in high school who is applauded for her victory on the debate team, but not asked to the prom. In Pallas Athena's symbolism, we carry the wounds of our severed feminine encased in our armor, and instead act with a kind of cold, ruthless, calculating, expedient strategy to further our ambitions. Healing in her realm entails looking deep within to remember the feminine roots of power, strength, creativity, and wisdom.

Pallas Athena also points to all the issues women face in their relationships with their fathers and father-like figures, which began with their own birth as their father's favorite daughter. Pallas portrays the ways in which women emulate men, seek their approval, want to interact in their world, and give them power over their lives. However, Pallas Athena's earlier matriarchal mythology places her as warrior/wisdom queen in Northern Africa, long before the arrival of the god Jupiter into Greece. This theme suggests the importance for women of acknowledging their own strength and wisdom nature rather than projecting it onto an external male authority.

Pallas Athena's serpent symbolism also connects her to the healing arts. One of her epithets is Hygeia, goddess of miraculous cures. She represents the power of mind in curing disease, and her armor and shield are likened to our immune system warding off attacks. Because Pallas Athena is a woman dressed in a warrior's clothes, she also speaks to calling up and expressing the masculine within women, or the feminine within men. This movement toward androgyny balances and integrates the polarities within the self and reclaims our contra-sexual identity.

In the chart, Pallas Athena represents the part of our nature that feels the urge to utilize our creative sexual energy to give birth to children of our minds—our mental and artistic progeny. She represents our capacity for clear thinking and creative wisdom, and speaks to our desire to strive for excellence and accomplishment in our chosen field of expression. Pallas shows how we use our creative intelligence to give birth to mind, art, truth, and worldly power.

Juno ⚵

Juno, known to the Greeks as Hera, is the goddess of marriage. She is wedded to Jupiter (Greek Zeus), supreme king of heaven and Earth, and, as such, becomes his Queen. However, in the mythical literature of an earlier time, Juno, long before her meeting with Jupiter, was one of the primary great goddesses in her own right. As the only goddess who is his equal, Juno is chosen by Jupiter to initiate/inaugurate the rites of legal, monogamous marriage. As the First Lady, she became but a titular figurehead and was repeatedly deceived, betrayed, and humiliated by her husband's many infidelities. In the myths, Juno is subsequently portrayed as a jealous, manipulative, vindictive, vengeful, and malcontent wife who, after tempestuous fights, periodically leaves her husband. However, she always returns to try to resolve the difficulties.

In the human psyche, Juno represents that aspect of our nature that feels the urge to unite with another person to build a future together through the vehicle of committed relationship. This partnership is sustained over time through a formal and binding commitment, whether it be a worldly or spiritual bond. Juno speaks to our desire to connect with a mate who is our true equal on all levels—psychologically, emotionally, mentally, and spiritually.

When we do not receive intimacy, depth, equality, honesty, respect, and fulfillment in our unions, Juno speaks to our emotions of disappointment, despair, anger, and rage, which can overwhelm us. This is especially true when we have given up a great deal—career, family, home, or religion—to enter the relationship. Juno makes us confront the issues of fidelity and infidelity, trust and deception, betrayal and revenge, or forgiveness, domination, and submission. In her domain, we find ourselves in power struggles for equality as we attempt to balance and integrate ourselves with others and learn to transform selfish desire into cooperative union.

Within a context of separation and return, Juno encourages us to take the vow of "for better or worse, in sickness and health, till death us do part." She is the wisdom that conscious relationship is a path to spiritual enlightenment and the knowledge that we must be in relationship to learn how to perfect the form.

In the birth chart, Juno represents our capacity for meaningful committed relationship, as well as the ways in which we express our disappointment over broken unions. These relationships are predominantly romantic in nature, but may assume other forms, such as business, professional, and creative partnerships. In today's world, she is also a symbol for the plight of battered and powerless wives and minorities; the psychological complexes of love-addiction and co-dependency; the rise in the divorce rate as people are driven to release un-meaningful relationships; and the redefinition of traditional relationships in the face of feminism and gay and lesbian coupling.

Vesta ⚶

Vesta, known to the Greeks as Hestia, is the temple priestess who presided over the vestal virgins of Rome. The vestals' lives were dedicated to spiritual service, and they were responsible for keeping the sacred flame that ensured the safety of the Roman Empire burning. If they violated their oaths of chastity, they were punished by a public whipping, and then buried alive. Vesta became the prototype of the Medieval nun. Several thousand years earlier, in the ancient Near East, the predecessors of these priestesses, who likewise tended the sacred flame, also engaged in sacred sexual rites in order to bring healing and fertility into the lives of people and to the land that nourished them.

Originally, the word "virgin" meant, not chaste, but rather unmarried. These priestesses thus represented an aspect of the feminine nature that is whole and complete in itself. In the transition from the old goddess religions to those of the solar gods, sexuality was divorced from spirituality. With the advent of the new gods, if a woman wanted to follow a spiritual path, she had to remain chaste—a virgin in the new sense of the word. In earlier times, priestesses, as representatives of the Goddess, could enter into a state of spiritual transcendence through sexual union with an outer partner in a manner that did not call for marriage or commitment. In patriarchal culture, however, the now-chaste Greek priestesses became the brides of the god Apollo and the Christian nuns the brides of Christ. Ecstatic illumination was experienced as the descent of the spirit of the god into the person of the priestess—an inner union often described by mystics.

In the human psyche, Vesta represents that part of our nature that feels the urge to experience our sexual energy in a sacred manner. This may occur in several different ways. Most of us are very much a product of the social mores of our culture. So we tend to internalize our sexual energy. We may devote ourselves to a spiritual, religious, or meditative path, following in the footsteps of priestesses and priests, nuns and monks, in contemporary settings. We may experience this union with the self as a process of psychological integration that is part of our life-long therapeutic work. In Vesta's realm, it is the quality of inner work that focuses or clarifies and energizes our circuitry. This then enables us to follow a vocation or calling to be of service in the world—a vision that arises from the whole and self-contained core of our being.

Vesta, as virgin nature, speaks to the importance of the relationship people have with themselves, which may lead to a single lifestyle in which they do not partner. Or if they do marry, they may not be comfortable with the total surrender asked for in the merging with another. In Vesta's realm, you may find your most satisfactory sexual encounters in communion with yourself. You, in a sense, may be your own best lover.

Those who hearken back to the earliest strata of Vesta memories may periodically find themselves in sexual encounters with others who pass briefly through their lives, or to whom they are not married or committed. These unions are often marked by a sense that something special, healing, and sacred has transpired. However, because our society has no context in which to validate sexual unions that do not lead to committed relationships, they are often left with a sense of shame, guilt, and insufficiency. Through an understanding of the inherent nature of Vesta's virgins, for whom sexuality and spirituality were unified, they can free themselves from their fears, guilt, shame, inhibitions, and restrictions in the expression of their sexuality.

In the birth chart, Vesta shows how we use our sexual energy to deepen our relationship to ourselves, integrating and regenerating on inner levels so we can focus and dedicate ourselves to our work in the outer world.

THE MAJOR ASTEROIDS IN THE CHART

While each of them means something, certain asteroids are more prominent in some charts than in others. Asteroids that occupy significant places in the chart will play more of a role in shaping the life experiences, and so are useful for recognizing the major themes of a life. When giving a one-hour consultation, focus on what is most important and put the other material aside for later when you may do a more in-depth analysis.

How do you determine the significance of an asteroid in the birth chart? There are four major criteria, which I will give in descending order of importance. The orbs that I suggest are for the four major asteroids only. For the thousands of others, your orbs may be much smaller.

1. **High:** Look to see if Ceres, Pallas, Juno, or Vesta is conjunct or opposite the Sun or Moon, or conjunct the ruler of the Ascendant, or if it is conjunct one of the four angles. The Ascendant and Midheaven degrees are more important than the Descendant or IC degrees. Use an orb of 10 degrees or a somewhat smaller orb of not more than 5 degrees if you need to cross sign boundaries. Location in any of these positions gives an asteroid a high significance rating, because these are the most powerful points in the chart. The asteroid adds its influence to the significations of the planet or point it conjoins.

2. **Moderate:** Note if an asteroid is square either of the luminaries or if it is conjunct or opposite an inner planet. This gives an asteroid moderately high significance. A moderate rating denotes an asteroid that is conjoined to the lunar nodes, and a moderately low rating indicates an asteroid that is conjunct or opposite one of the outer planets. Use an orb of not more than 5 degrees for these considerations.

3. **Low:** Check to see if an asteroid completes a major aspect pattern (T-square or grand trine) or if it is trine or sextile the luminaries or Ascendant ruler. Use an orb of not more than 4 degrees. This significance, although low, may still be relevant in some instances. An angular house placement, especially in the first or tenth houses, also gives an otherwise stray asteroid some importance.

4. **Nil:** If an asteroid is not connected to any important planets or points in the chart, it may not play a major role in the life. In a complete chart delineation, of course, it has meaning. But for a one-hour consultation, it is probably not the most important thing to discuss. Also be aware that, although an asteroid may not be prominent in the natal chart, if it is receiving an outer-

planet transit, its symbolism will become activated for the duration of the transit.

Once you have determined that a particular asteroid is important in
the chart, combine its meaning with the planet or angle contacted,
and finally modify its expression by sign and house placements, as
well as any other aspects it may be making. When interpreting a
chart from the mythic perspective, the story of the archetype itself
may make a much stronger impression on a client than a keyword
synthesis of an asteroid in a sign or a house, because it may relate
more closely to his or her experiences.

> In Bill's chart, Ceres is not conjunct the angles; not conjunct,
> square, or opposite the luminaries; not conjunct the ruler of
> the Ascendant; not part of a T-square or grand trine. But Ceres
> is angular in the tenth house, giving it a moderately low rating
> of prominence. Later, however, you will note that the asteroid
> Demeter (the Greek equivalent for the Roman Ceres) is partile
> conjoined to the MC degree, which boosts the importance of
> this archetype.
>
> Pallas has an opposition to the Moon and is partile conjunct
> Pluto, which gives it a moderately high rating of prominence.
> Juno is square the Sun by close orb and conjunct the Moon by
> sign, in close conjunction to Mars. Thus Juno gets a very high
> rating of prominence. Vesta is not conjunct the angles, and not
> conjunct, square, or opposite the Sun, Moon, or Ascendant
> ruler. Conjoined to Saturn and south node, Vesta gets a moder-
> ate rating of prominence.
>
> Therefore Juno and Pallas are most significant, followed by
> Ceres and Vesta, both moderately strong. Emphasize to Bill the
> importance of Juno in the analysis of the Sun, and Pallas in the
> analysis of the Moon. Depending on time and requested focus,
> you may pass over the other two.
>
> Pallas shows how we use our creative intelligence to give
> birth to mind, art, truth, and worldly power. This goddess of
> wisdom and artistic potential in the creative sign of Leo in the

ninth house of wide-ranging multicultural perspectives and of spirituality is configured to the Moon and Pluto. This suggests that part of Bill's demonstration of life purpose involves the power of his ideas, expressed artistically to transform the larger world.

Juno is the archetype of the wife and the principle of committed relationships. The close square to the Sun indicates that, while the need to develop good communication in solid relationships that support individuality are a major part of Bill's life purpose, they are also fraught with conflict and competition (Mars conjunction) and stress (square to the Sun). The Moon's connection to Juno emphasizes the emotional need for intimate personal relating; but the altruistic and impersonal ideals of Aquarius are not always compatible with the Scorpio need for total bonding, closeness, and merging with another.

Twelve Thousand More Asteroids

Since the introduction of the asteroids to the astrological community between 1973 and 1981, a number of contemporary astrologers have begun to incorporate the symbolism of Ceres, Pallas, Juno, and Vesta, as well as Chiron (1977), into their chart analysis, although there is still considerable skepticism and resistance. The thought of including the thousands of others, however, is simply too mind-boggling for most astrologers. And yet, in my twenty-five years of working with the minor planets, I have repeatedly seen how amazingly accurate these can be in detailing the specifics of people and places and mythic themes in an individual's life.

Following are some striking examples from the charts of celebrities that illustrate this point. Prince Charles, for instance, has the asteroids Camilla and Parks conjunct his Venus within 15 minutes of arc. The name of his life-long love and now wife is Camilla Parker. Bill Clinton has the asteroids Paula, Monica, Asmodeus (the Persian demon god of lust), and William opposite his Moon, and the asteroid Hillary conjunct his Moon as well as the asteroid Hilaritas conjunct his IC, the ground and anchor of the chart. Jacqueline Kennedy Onassis has the asteroids John and Aristotle, the names of her two husbands, opposite her Moon (within 1 degree), which, as one of the significators of marriage, is itself conjunct the asteroid Abunduntia, the Roman goddess of abundance. Her final life partner, Maurice Tempelsman, is indicated by the asteroids Maury and Temple, both on the degree of her Midheaven.

When looking for a philosophical justification for the inclusion of all the asteroids in the corpus of astrological symbolism, consider the hierarchal structure of the cosmos of late antiquity. In the writings of the ancient Greek philosophers, the planets and stars were viewed as the visible gods. However, between the divine realm and the human realm were thousands of *daimons*, intermediary spirits who bridged these two realms. Some philosophers wrote of the daimon as the conscience or guiding spirit. In the Hermetic writings, certain daimons were associated with each planet, carrying out the orders of that planetary god. The thousands of asteroids may be the counterparts of a class of celestial beings for which the ancients had accounted, but that were invisible—as were the asteroids before the discovery of the telescope.

To include the asteroids in your readings in any meaningful way, you must organize them thematically and have a methodology for determining their significance within an individual chart. Remember that perhaps only a dozen or so of the 12,000 asteroids will actually be relevant to a particular chart. Both Mark Pottenger's *CCRS Asteroid Program* and David and Fei Cochrane's *Kepler Cosmic Patterns* asteroid add-on module can generate the positions of all 12,000 plus for a given birth date. These programs also allow you to create custom lists. Appendix B gives a list of around 250 asteroids that I have chosen—either for their mythological significance or their representation of concepts. They can be sorted in the printout either zodiacally, beginning with 0 Aries and ending with 29 Pisces, or alphabetically. Appendix B also contains information on Web sites that will generate the positions of individual asteroids in your own chart as well as other resource material.

When I am doing an in-depth study of a particular chart, I generate the entire list alphabetically and pull out names and places that are meaningful to that person. But for the bulk of my ongoing chart consultations, I use the smaller zodiacal sort. I run down the list, pulling out and entering by hand into the basic chart certain mythic asteroids that I think are universally important, as well as those that are conjunct the four angles, the two luminaries, the ruler of the Ascendant, and anything else that strikes me as interesting. The *Kepler Cosmic Patterns* software allows you to add the chosen asteroids onto the chart directly. I look for personal names, places, concepts, and mythic figures. However, it is highly unlikely that I will interpret all these asteroids. What I look for is the emergence of certain themes to guide me in my choices for additional entries.

Appendix B contains a list of about 250 asteroids arranged in a zodiacal sort for the time and date of Bill's birth. From that list I have selected certain asteroids to place in his chart that are located close to the degrees of his Ascendant, Ascendant ruler, Sun, and Moon.

Another way to organize the asteroids is thematically—associating those that relate to healing, divination, sexuality, or relationship, as well as the clusters that are mythically related to each of the four major asteroids. For example, if you see that Ceres is prominent, check for the asteroid Demeter, which is the Greek version of her name. While these are two different asteroids, their archetypal meanings are similar. In the myth, Ceres' daughter is Persephone; the Latin form of this name is Proserpina. So you can add these two asteroids to the chart. Finally, look to Pluto, who abducted Persephone and was Ceres' major antagonist, and study the relationship between all of these bodies. When certain deities are related mythically and their planetary namesakes are all either prominent in the chart or closely configured to one another, the mythic theme becomes especially emphasized in that person's life.

It is true that, the more that you know about mythology and which deities belong to each culture and have relationships with one another, the more vivid your use of the many asteroids becomes. For example, in the event chart of the fatal plane crash of John F. Kennedy, Jr., the Ascendant was flanked by the asteroids Oceana and Anubis, the Egyptian dog-headed god who guided souls to the underworld. The asteroid Icarus, the youth who flew too close to the Sun and drowned in the sea below, was conjunct to the ruler of the Ascendant, and the asteroid Daedalus, the inventor-father of Icarus, was conjunct the Moon. There are many excellent books on world mythologies that can help you become familiar with the narrative stories of myths. You may also want to obtain a dictionary of gods and goddesses.

> In Bill's natal chart, the Sun is conjoined to Siva and Hidalgo. Hidalgo is the name of a 19th-century Spanish priest-turned-revolutionary who was martyred and immortalized as the Father of Mexican Independence. When this asteroid is prominent in the chart, it may indicate a connection with Latin-speaking countries, fighting for one's beliefs, standing up for the rights of others, or advocating for the underdog. Siva, also known as the Hindu god Shiva, is the god of ecstasy and transformation, connected to the Greek Dionysus. The prominence of this asteroid in Bill's chart may indicate a powerful urge to exult in strong emotion, ecstasy, sexual intensity, spiritual transcendence, breaking taboos, and pushing beyond barriers.
>
> Bill has the Moon conjoined Psyche and Irene. Psyche was a mortal princess who, in her quest for reunion with her lover Eros, mastered heroic tasks given her by a wrathful Aphrodite. She was later transformed into a goddess. In Bill's chart, Psyche may represent psychic sensitivity to the minds and feelings of another, which can lead to the yearning for a soul-mate union. Irene is a personal name, and he may have an important encounter with someone named Irene.
>
> Finally, Bill's Midheaven is conjoined to Demeter, whose mythic motifs are similar to those of Ceres. And we have already discussed the asteroids Amicita and Fraternitas conjoined to Venus, Mercury, and the Ascendant, and the asteroid Utopia conjoined to the Ascendant ruler Jupiter.

STUDY GUIDELINES

- Examine each of the four major asteroids in your practice chart and rate their importance: high, moderately high, moderate, moderately low, and nil. State your reasons for your judgment.
- To what extent is the theme represented by the asteroids that are significantly placed a major component of that person's

life experience? Give a brief astrological delineation of the asteroid(s) chosen.

- Chose one minor asteroid that is prominent in the chart and research its meaning. If it is a mythic asteroid, what do you think is the psychological principle behind the mythic biography? Ask the owner of the chart if this meaning is relevant in his or her life.

CHAPTER TEN

ASPECTS PATTERNS

SO FAR, we have discussed the most important individual factors in the birth chart that contribute to discerning the life purpose. However, planets do not operate only in isolation as they guide us toward the fulfillment of our life purpose; they also operate in combination. Planets have complex relationships with one another that can be harmonious and supportive, or difficult and obstructive. In astrology, the ways in which a planet connects with other planets is known as the doctrine of aspects. Viewing the chart as a map of the psyche, the lines formed by the web of interrelated aspects that connect the planets can be seen as analogous to a wiring diagram of the mind or the neural circuits of the body.

The doctrine of aspects has gone through considerable change since it was first formulated during the Hellenistic era. At that time, the only five aspects that were considered were the sextile, square, trine, opposition, and conjunction, which was called a co-presence. The modern quincunx and semi-sextile were not viewed as aspects; they were called aversions and indicated that planets had no relationship to one another at all. In many considerations, aspects were determined by whole sign rather than by degree, but the closer planets were to exact, the more active the relationship between the planets was thought to be. There was a special relationship between planets that were within a 3-degree range of application to another (or 13 degrees for the Moon) and able to cross sign boundaries (out-of-sign aspects). This more narrow range may have been the condition for the blending of the individual planetary meanings that is the standard today for any modern aspect interpretation. Especially important was the witnessing of a planet by a benefic or malefic planet. This was credited with either enhancing or preventing its capacity to bring about the matters it represented in ways that were favorable for the person.

In the Arabic/Medieval tradition, aspects were determined by *moiety*. Each planet was assigned a certain number of degrees based on its heliacal visibility—how far from the Sun a planet had to be before it was visible. Each planet had a different moiety, and if the arc of separation between two planets was less than or equal to the average of the sum of their moieties, they were considered to be in aspect to one another. Thus, if the moiety of Venus was 13 degrees and that of Saturn was 7 degrees, their average was 10 degrees. If, in a particular chart, Venus was at 1 Leo and Saturn was at 9 Libra, their orb of separation within the sextile aspect was 8 degrees (within that 10-degree range), and hence they were considered to be in aspect with one another. Note how this differs from the modern orb of 6 degrees for a sextile aspect.

During the Renaissance, there was a movement to reform astrological methodology. Johannes Kepler dismissed the validity of planets in signs and houses, and looked only to their aspects. In the process of this inquiry, he came up with many minor aspects—for example, the quintile, septile, and novile—that subsequently have become part of the modern tradition. Contemporary practice utilizes a multitude of different aspects that are determined by orb of separation from exactitude, based on each individual kind of aspect (such as 6 degrees for sextiles, 8 degrees for squares and trines, etc.), regardless of the planets' moiety or sign position.

Depending on the kind of astrology you practice, you must decide what model you will use to determine aspects and be aware of the variations in the historical tradition. Regardless of the model, however, planets that are in aspect to one another indicate that the planets are linked in some particular way. Modern practice blends the significations of the planets involved and calls their interaction easy/flowing if they are linked by a trine or sextile. It calls the interaction difficult/challenging if they are linked by a square or opposition. This is essentially similar to traditional interpretation. Ancient astrology also had a set of criteria that deemed one planet dominant—that is, doing something *to* the other planet, which then reacted in turn. This subtlety is generally not used in modern aspect interpretation.

When you look at an individual aspect between two planets, first factor in the meaning of each planet's basic nature, its modification by sign, the significations of the house it occupies, and the significations of the topical meanings of the houses that it rules. Then consider the meaning of both planets in combination with one another. Finally, analyze the kind of interaction that exists between them. In some cases, it is appropriate to blend the meanings of the planets—for instance, Mercury sextile Venus indicates a "smooth talker." But in other cases, you may want to interpret the aspect as one planet assisting or hindering the other—for instance, benefic Venus helping Mercury to accomplish its own significations.

This is an important step in the synthesis of the chart as a whole, especially when one of the planets involved is one of the key significators of the nativity. When analyzing the Sun, Moon, and Ascendant ruler, note which other planets are connected to these three places of life, and then factor in their influence when making your judgment. This is one of the times in the consultation session when you integrate the influences of the other planets—when they are connected to the three main planets in the chart. Another is when you are analyzing a specific topic—for example, relationship or career—in which case you focus on the planetary ruler of the topical house under investigation.

Aspect patterns in which three or more planets are linked reveal the broader themes of the chart, and the remainder of this chapter will be devoted to a discussion of these patterns. In my experience, the most significant aspect patterns are stelliums, T-squares, grand squares, and grand trines.

A stellium is comprised of three or more planets in the same sign. Imagine the situation as three roommates sharing a single room in a household. They may get along and learn how to accommodate each others' needs and agendas, or they may all be jockeying for the limited space and interfering with each others' plans. Ancient authors spoke of planets occupying the same house/sign as a co-min-gling of their natures. Planets in a stellium may act as a unit, bring-ing emphasis, focus, and concentration to the affairs of the house they occupy. However, if the planets are inharmoniously disposed toward one another, the result may be confusion, conflicting agen-das, imbalance in the topic that the house signifies, or overemphasis on the qualities of the sign in which the planets are located.

T-squares are comprised of two or more planets in opposition, with each one in a square configuration to the same third planet. Because the square and opposition aspects are generally inharmoni-ous, difficult, challenging, and destructive, planetary energies bound up in this configuration generate a tremendous amount of tension and stress. Two planets with conflicting and opposing agendas, pull-ing the individual in opposing directions while a third planet that squares the other two is at cross-purposes with both of them is not a harmonious condition. The individual may feel torn asunder and locked in a vice grip at the same time. Yet, like water held back by a dam, a huge amount of potential energy is being amassed. Thus the potential of a T-square is like that of a generator that can fuel the ambitions to accomplish a task. Many successful people who have overcome great obstacles in the achievement of their success have T-squares, as this is a configuration that produces the energy to accomplish work if it can be properly harnessed.

Grand squares are a variation of the T-square in which four or more planets are all square to one another, with two sets of opposi-tions. The energies of the grand square, or grand cross as it is some-times called, are an intensification of those of the T-square, with even less maneuvering room to resolve the dilemmas presented by the life. Individuals may feel boxed in or trapped by life experiences, seeing no way out of circumstances that seem beyond their control to change. They may feel as if they are carrying the burdens of oth-ers, sometimes even the weight of the world; this may lead them to struggle against resignation and despair. There are tremendous pressures upon them as they attempt to hold together a number of diverse commitments and responsibilities. People whose charts con-tain a grand square are called to develop great strength of will and determination. In order to relieve the inner pressure and tension, they must learn how to utilize their concentrated internal energies for outer productivity. In the process, great things may be realized and brought into manifestation.

Grand trines involve three or more planets, each in a trine relationship to both of the other two. The simple trine is the most harmonious and helpful aspect, so three interrelated trines give tremendous creative energy that is easy to access and express. Some astrologers posit that a grand trine represents an innate talent or gift that has been carried over from other lifetimes, because it can emerge at an early age and seem almost effortless. The energies flow, opportunities abound, and the results are good. In some cases, the grand trine can be counterproductive, however, since the lack of internal pressure can cause certain individuals to lose their motivation to do anything productive with their gifts, remaining full of unrealized potential.

Some astrologers also consider the Yod (two quincunxes joined by a sextile, often referred to as the Finger of Fate or Finger of God) and a host of other patterns such as the Kite, Mystic Rectangle, and Star of David. For the purposes of a one-hour consultation, however, focusing on these rather than the first four mentioned can take you off track into scenic detours. While they may be of interest and have meaning, they can divert you from the essential themes of the chart. In longer in-depth or ongoing sessions, it is certainly reasonable to explore these finer shadings of the chart's meaning.

There is dissension among astrologers as to whether the nodes, lots, and angles should be considered as part of an aspect pattern. Some see that the tension built up in T-squares and grand squares can be released via a trine or sextile from one of the planets involved in this configuration to some other planet. Be aware that ancient astrological texts did not mention aspect patterns at all, although there were special delineations for three planets in the same sign.

DELINEATING ASPECT PATTERNS

Not every aspect pattern will be equally potent in an individual's life. There are several criteria you can use to determine whether an aspect pattern is more or less prominent. Here are some guidelines to follow when you consider aspects:

- An aspect pattern is operative by sign; however, the closer to exact degrees the planets are, the more active are the manifestations of the events that the pattern signifies.
- Aspect patterns involving planets in angular houses will be more prominent as the manifestations of outer events in the lives of the individuals.
- Aspect patterns involving the Sun, Moon, or Ascendant ruler are more likely to tie into the basic life theme.
- Aspect patterns involving the personal inner planets tend to be more personally significant, in contrast to aspect patterns involving only the outer planets, which are more generational than individual.

Before creating an interpretation of an aspect pattern, pay careful attention to the significations of the houses, planets, and signs involved.

- Look at the houses involved. If there is a T-square between planets in the first, seventh, and tenth houses, you know right away that tension is going to be present in the areas of self-identity vs. relationship, and how that polarity impacts the career. For your own studies, create a short sentence for each combination of houses involved in T-squares such as the one above.
- Look at the planets involved. Create a short sentence of just the planetary archetypes.
- Blend the influence of the sign with the planet, and then place them in their respective houses, also noting what houses, and thus topics, those planets rule.
- Once you have established the where, who, and how of this pattern, create a more flowing, detailed, and psychologically perceptive delineation.

If you use Whole Sign houses and aspects by sign rather than by degree as your default systems, the aspect patterns are more true to form in terms of the natural relationships that exist between the various signs and houses.

The essence of the conjunction aspect is a co-mingling of the natures of the various planets. Since stelliums connect three or more planets in the same sign and house, they therefore point to areas of concentrated activity. Depending on the nature of the planets involved and their individual conditions, stelliums may function to augment or decrease the significations of that area of life. But for good or ill, the topics of the house and the qualities of the sign that contain the stellium will be emphasized in the person's life.

The essence of the trine aspect is affirmation and support, and grand trine patterns connect planets in the same element. Thus the grand trine will link the three or more planets that occupy all of the fire, earth, air, or water signs in a manner that facilitates a harmonious and supportive interaction of the significations and topics represented by the individual planets and the houses involved. Because all the planets occupy the same element, a theme is immediately suggested that emphasizes the nature of the element: freedom and vital energy with the fire signs; material security and competence in the physical world with the earth signs; communication and intellectual activity with the air signs; emotional sensitivity and nurture with the water signs.

The grand trine can occupy the following sets of houses: first, fifth, and ninth (identity, creativity, higher wisdom); second, sixth, and tenth (resources, work/illness, profession); third, seventh, and eleventh (siblings, partners, friends/associates); or fourth, eighth, and twelfth (parents/home, death/its benefits, afflictions/transcendence). Note that each of these sets contains one angular, one succedent, and one cadent house. If you understand the meanings of these sets of houses in combination—in terms of their topical significations, their relative angularity, and their relative good/bad condition with regard to configuration to the Ascendant—the delineation begins to become transparent. For example, a grand water trine linking the third, seventh, and eleventh houses—all "good" houses—suggests a theme affirming emotional nurture and support (water) in the area of peer relationships between siblings, partners, and friends.

The square and opposition aspects indicate negation or challenge, and T-squares or grand squares connect planets in the same modality. Thus the T-square or grand square link planets that occupy either the cardinal, fixed, or mutable signs in a manner that accentuates some kind of conflict, struggle, or tension between the significations and topics represented by the individual planets and the houses involved. Because all the planets occupy the same modality, a theme is immediately suggested that emphasizes action and external crisis for the cardinal signs, stability and rigidity for the fixed signs, or change and indecisiveness for the mutable signs.

The T-square and grand-square patterns also configure sets of houses that are either angular (first, fourth, seventh, and tenth), succedent (second, fifth, eighth, and eleventh) or cadent (third, sixth, ninth, or twelfth), and this information indicates the amount of dynamic energy behind the planets to produce outer events. Thus the most externally potent combination involves planets in cardinal signs and angular houses, while planets in cadent houses have less force for manifesting externally, or they may be more likely to constellate internal processes. If, for example, the T-square is an opposition between the second and eighth houses, polarized by mutual squares to the eleventh, you know that these succedent houses indicate a moderate level of dynamic activity, and that the issue revolves around personal money vs. a partner's money as it affects group affiliations. Furthermore, if the planets are in fixed signs, the individual will tend to be rigid and controlling around these issues, while if in mutable signs, the individual will tend to be more flexible, or even changeable and flip-flopping about. Finally, the individual planets and the houses they rule flesh out the details.

For instance, the major aspect patterns in Bill's chart are:

1. Stellium: Moon, Mars, and Juno in the third house.
2. T-square: Angular T-square in mutable signs; Neptune/Ceres opposite Jupiter, both square Venus and Mercury. The opposition from Jupiter to Neptune is tight, while the squares to Venus and Mercury are by sign, not by degree.
3. Grand square: Cadent grand square in fixed signs; Sun opposite Uranus both square to Moon, Mars, and Juno, which are

opposite Pluto and Pallas. This also by sign, but not by tight by degree.

4. Grand trines: Water signs in houses four, eight, and twelve; Sun, Jupiter, Chiron. This is by sign and by degree. Fire signs in houses one, five, and nine; Venus and Mercury/Vesta and Saturn/Pallas and Pluto. This is by sign, but is not close by degree.

How do you determine which of these is most important? If you look to the key significators of the chart—Sun, Moon, and Jupiter (Asc. ruler)—you see that they are involved in all the patterns except that of the grand trine in fire signs, so that doesn't help you much. But the mutable T-square is in the angular houses, which indicates great dynamic activity and involves Jupiter, the Ascendant ruler. This may help you make a reasonable determination. If I were interpreting this chart, the first planets I would mention are Venus and Mercury, because they occupy the first house. Then I'd point out Jupiter as the Ascendant ruler, and Jupiter's square configuration to them and the opposition to Neptune. That pattern would most likely assume primacy for both those reasons. Since the Sun is linked to Jupiter by a close trine, I might next bring in the Sun/Jupiter/Chiron grand trine briefly, but would tend to focus more on the Sun's grand T-square, as it pulls in the Moon.

In Bill's chart, the mutable T-square in the angular houses is significant. Fourth-house family matters and tenth-house professional concerns create a major dynamic tension with the first-house sense of identity. You can posit that Bill's sense of identity and effectiveness as an individual may be continually shaped by stressful situations in connection with his family and his career. In other words, Bill's sense of personal accomplishment is defined by his ability to provide for his family through success in his profession and actions in the larger world. Because the pattern entails planets in mutable signs, his identity, family situation, and career all go through a number of changes. He may experiment with different options trying to make things work better, or he may be unclear himself about just who he is and what he wants to do in the world to support the home foundation.

Looking at the planets involved, Mercury's placement echoes this theme as it rules the seventh house of relationship and the tenth house of career, and is in its detriment in Sagittarius. Thus it may be difficult for Bill to find a career that is effective; this may translate into a sense of personal powerlessness and, consequently, a lack of support and respect from a partner. Venus' rulership of the sixth house of job reinforces the theme that this is a work-related issue, and the square configuration between Venus/Mercury and Neptune suggests that Bill's talents may lay in the field of the arts and cinematography. In fact, we already know he achieved some recognition as a filmmaker early in life making documentaries (note Ceres' placement in the tenth house—goddess associated with "going back to the land"). After marriage, Bill had his own business with a TV production studio, but neither of these occupations generated abundant financial revenue. Jupiter in the fourth house is the strongest planet in this configuration, because it is placed in its own sign of rulership, Pisces. In a very general sense, as the ruler of the Ascendant, its placement points to the topic that drives the soul and leads to a successfully lived life. Bill's participation in a construction renovation business whose vision is to create an intentional community thus provides a solid foundation for the successful achievement of his goals and financial well being.

In a session with Bill, you can acknowledge his artistic talents in the career arena, but also indicate that they may not lead to ongoing professional and financial success. Encourage Bill rather to focus his energies on working with fourth-house matters—family, land, homes, etc.—as this may be a more fruitful area for gaining a sense of accomplishment, and may be a source of revenue that can support the pursuit of his artistic ventures.

STUDY GUIDELINES

- Determine and list the aspect patterns in your practice chart. Rate them in their order of importance and explain why.
- Choose the most important ones, and prepare delineations for each. Synthesize the meanings of the individual planets in their respective signs and the nature of the pattern in which they are involved, but also look at the grouping of the houses, their relative angularity, and whether they are good or bad houses, as well as the element or modality that contains the planets in question. Be sure to note if one of the planets is a key significator of the chart, or if it conjoins one of the angles by close-degree orb.
- If you arrive at a conclusion that is less than glowing, think about suggestions for how the person can use the difficult energy constructively.

CHAPTER ELEVEN

ANALYZING RELATIONSHIP AND VOCATION

THERE ARE TWO major components to the natal portion of a complete astrological reading. The first entails a broad general discussion of the individual's personality and the purpose of his or her life, with an articulation of the major themes of the chart. The second involves a more detailed focus on particular issues. Before beginning a session, ask your client if he or she has any specific questions, and make sure that you leave enough time to address these concerns. The most frequent topics on which clients ask for clarification and guidance are relationship, career, and health. In this chapter, we'll discuss how to evaluate relationship and career, and give a few guidelines about health.

The modern approach to chart interpretation looks at the chart as a whole. To a certain extent, this tendency spills over into the evaluation of a particular topic as well, reflecting the assumption that everything in the chart contributes to who we are. Ultimately, this is true. But it can also be difficult to discern just where to look in the chart for clear and specific information about a particular concern. Traditional astrologers look first to the house that signifies the topic under investigation.

The word "topic" comes from the Greek word *topos*, which means "place." This was the technical term used for the concept of an astrological house. Just as we look to the topography of a landscape to locate various geographical features, ancient astrologers looked to the twelve astrological houses as the locations of the various topics, or departments of life. Their analysis of topics, therefore, begins with the location of the house that signifies the matter under consideration. The essential and most distilled meanings of the twelve astrological houses are:

- First house: the body, character, physical appearance, personality
- Second house: livelihood, finances, material possessions
- Third house: siblings, neighbors, communications, short journeys
- Fourth house: home, hearth, parents, land
- Fifth house: children, creativity, romance, sexuality, pleasurable pursuits, games of fortune
- Sixth house: illness and health, accidents, jobs, servitude
- Seventh house: marriage, sexual unions, partnerships
- Eighth house: death and benefits gained from death, lawsuits, joint resources, depth psychology, the occult
- Ninth house: foreign travel, long journeys, higher education, religion, philosophy
- Tenth house: profession, actions in the world, honors, reputation
- Eleventh house: friends, organizations, gain from patronage, social activities and activism
- Twelfth house: enemies, afflictions, suffering, loss, karma, transcendence, the mysteries

Many ancient astrological texts devoted chapters to an analysis of the topics pertaining to each house, with interpretations varying from one author to another. In a discussion of marriage, Valens presents a relevant procedure that examines the planet Venus, the seventh house and the lord of that house, and the lot of marriage.[1] From this, we can extrapolate a general procedure for the investigation of any topic that involves a specific planet associated with that topic, a house that signifies the topic, and a lot that pertains to it.

1. Each topic has one or more planets that are its general significators, such as Venus for marriage, Mars for siblings, Jupiter for children, the Sun for the father in a diurnal chart and Saturn for the father in a nocturnal chart, Venus for the mother in a diurnal chart and the Moon for the mother in a nocturnal chart.

Because this same planet can be used in every chart, the indications to which it points are the most general.

2. Each topic is located within the provenance of a particular house—the seventh for marriage, the fifth for children, the fourth for parents, etc. The planets that occupy a house, as well as the planet that is the lord of it, are investigated. The planets that occupy a house have an impact on what takes place in that area of life, but it is the house's planetary ruler that has the ultimate authority to render judgment about how the matters will turn out in the final analysis. Imagine a restaurant where the employees are likened to the planets located in the house. The quality of the chefs and the wait staff (planets located in the house) most certainly affect the operations of the establishment, but it is the owner of the restaurant (ruler of the house) who has the ultimate say in deciding the major policies.

3. Each topic has one or more lots that address the matter, and the lot and its planetary ruler are both important.

Ancient astrologers looked at the relative strength and condition of these factors governing a topic. They then decided whether or not the topic would eventuate in the person's life, and, if so, whether the planet would produce fortunate or unfortunate results. The major criteria to which the significators of the topic were subject were configuration with the benefic or malefic planets, the strength of their sign rulerships, direct or retrograde motion, being under the beams of the Sun, and the relative angularity of the house they occupied. If most of the significators were free from affliction from the malefics, direct in motion, in signs of their rulership or exaltation, and in angular or succedent and good houses, the eventuation of that topic would likely have a beneficial outcome.

This perspective stands in sharp contrast to the approach of many modern astrologers, who may not first consider whether the manifestation of a topic is supported by the chart before beginning to discuss it. Counseling protocol advises against telling a client that marriage or children or profession are unlikely to be realized or prove to be the cause of misfortune. However, this approach can provide useful and important background information for guiding the counseling session. Here, we will follow traditional guidelines, but interpret them in a modern context and add the insights of more contemporary approaches.

ANALYZING RELATIONSHIPS

Some of the most common inquiries that clients bring to their sessions are about relationships, but the questions are often unfocused. People ask astrologers to tell them about relationships, but often what they really mean is: When am I going to meet that special someone? Is my partner being unfaithful to me? Will this current relationship last? Are we headed for a break-up? Is there someone better for me out there? What kind of person would be a good match for me? Am I compatible with so and so? Will I ever get married (again)?

After years of doing relationship analysis, I have come to realize that the important question is: What do I need in a relationship that will make me happy and satisfied, and can this potential/current partner actually provide that? The correlate to this is: What does my potential/current partner need from a relationship in order to make him or her happy, and can I in reality provide that? The real inquiry that underlies both of these questions is: What is my capacity to do relationships well and do I have the inner resources to sustain interactions with others? Identifying the factors associated with these questions is more useful than telling someone that his Moon is trine her Venus, so they will feel comfortable and find pleasure together, even though this may be a true statement. We can be compatible with all kinds of people with whom we cannot have successful relationships. The starting place for all these inquiries, however, is to assess if marriage is even a possibility for the person, or if the timing factors point to this event occurring at an appropriate age.

Beyond the question of whether the chart supports the topic of a relationship that will bring good fortune to the person, however, there is the issue of fate or karma. Relationships will occur for people who have problematic indicators and troubled synastry (comparing two charts for compatibility), because the unconscious forces of the collective past are usually stronger than those of immediate good judgment. Sometimes, we have unions with others whose larger purpose has nothing to do with our individual happiness. From an Eastern spiritual point of view, we are here to work out unresolved karma from the past that is aptly described by difficult chart contacts.

Before you can discuss these deeper matters, however, you have to know the baseline from which the individual is operating. Here, I will first present a procedure for a traditional analysis of the topic of marriage that you can use primarily for your own information. Then I will offer suggestions from the perspective of a modern counseling session

A Traditional Approach to Analyzing Relationship

One factor in analyzing relationship is the planetary significator. Look first to the condition of Venus as a general indication of marriage for both women and men. Some texts differentiate between looking at Venus for men and Mars for women as significators of sexual union, and the Moon for men and the Sun for women as significators of legal marriage.

- If Venus is in a sign of its rulership or exaltation, and well-placed by house, not afflicted by configurations with malefic planets, direct in motion and not under the beams, this person will more likely be capable of having beneficial relationships and ease in relating.
- If Venus is in detriment or fall, placed in a difficult house, poorly aspected by the malefics, retrograde in motion or under the beams, this person may have difficulty entering into or maintaining relationships, or may be involved in relationships that are not beneficial.
- Remember that, unless Taurus or Libra occupies the seventh house, Venus also signifies topics other than relationship, and thus can give only very general kinds of indications in the matter of marriage

Another factor in analyzing relationship is the house significator. To explore this, look to the seventh house of marriage and its ruler.

- Planets occupying the seventh house show what influences are brought to relationship matters. The benefics in good condition bring happiness and prosperity to relationship; the malefics in poor condition can bring strife, rejection, and unfortunate circumstances to marriage. Difficulties may also arise if the malefic planets square or oppose the seventh house. Planets occupying the seventh house generally rule other houses; as such, they use relationships as the means by which to bring the topics they rule to realization.

- The planet that rules the seventh house is the specific significator of relationship matters and has the ultimate authority in bringing about this topic. The house placement of the ruler of the seventh indicates what the person seeks from marriage—if the ruler of seventh house is in the fourth, a home and home life; if the ruler of the seventh house is in the fifth, children; if the ruler of the seventh house is in the second, financial security; etc. The condition of the ruler indicates the extent to which individuals will be successful in creating and maintaining good relationships, as well the likelihood of their specific needs in relationships being fulfilled by a partner in a positive manner. Aspects to the seventh-house ruler by the benefics or malefics can help or hinder its functioning in ways that are fortunate or unfortunate for the individual.

The last factor in analyzing relationship is the lot significator. Here, look to the Lot of Marriage. You will encounter a number of different calculations for the Lot of Marriage by various authors. Valens uses the formula of Asc. + Venus – Jupiter for a day birth, and the Asc. + Jupiter – Venus for a night birth. Other astrologers have set forth alternate formulas. You may want to experiment. Look to see if the lot is angular, succedent or cadent, under the beams, or witnessed by the malefics or benefics and judge accordingly. Then look to the ruler of the lot and apply the usual criteria.

A Modern Approach to Analyzing Relationship

When counseling clients from the modern perspective, look to the sign of Venus to describe the manner in which they express their sexuality and magnetism, their approach to relationship, and what they find attractive in a mate. The house placement of Venus can point to the arena in which sexual/relational encounters and issues will eventually constellate. Difficult aspects to Venus from Mars may indicate that issues of conflict and domination arise, and difficult aspects from Saturn point to issues of restriction or inhibition of the sexual/romantic impulses. But remember, this is a very general kind of statement, because Venus may rule other topics as well, unless the sign Taurus or Libra occupies the seventh house.

The addition of the asteroid Juno to the astrological pantheon allows you to interpret Venus as the principle of sexual attraction and Juno as the principle of commitment in marriage. If Venus and Juno are in incompatible signs, the qualities that stir the attraction instincts may not be ones the person can live with day after day. Venus in Sagittarius may be attracted to the exciting free-spirited world traveler, but Juno in Cancer wants the mate to show up at dinner every night. You can evaluate Juno by sign, house, and aspect to derive information about what is necessary for ongoing commitment and what else in the chart has the capacity to thwart it. A prominent Juno in the chart indicates that relationship is a very important theme and concern in the life.

Look to the qualities of the sign on the Descendant by element and sign as indicative of what is being sought in a partner or from partnership. The attributes of the element and sign occupying the seventh house represent the needs that the person seeks to have met from partnership. Fire signs need freedom and power; air signs need communication and relating; earth signs need physical and material security; water signs need emotional safety and presence. Aries occupying the seventh house points to the need for autonomy in relationships, Taurus to the need for material security, Gemini to the need for mental communication, etc.

The house placement of the ruler of the seventh house indicates what the person is seeking from marriage in order to be satisfied. For one person, it may be children (ruler of seventh house in fifth house), for another a home (ruler in fourth house), and for yet another, a best friend (ruler in eleventh house). The condition of the ruler gives information about the person's relative capacity for successful relationships. Again, check the aspects to see if other planets support or curtail the capacity to function well in relationship and what other agendas they represent that the individual must heed.

Modern psychological theory also suggests that the sign on the Descendant is the place of projection for the non-integrated parts of an individual's psyche, and may describe the qualities by which he or she is attracted to others in order to experience the unconscious aspects of the self. For example, a person with Libra rising who is naturally skilled in compromise will have Aries on the Descendant, seeking out forceful partners in order to learn how to be more assertive.

You can examine asteroids whose mythic themes constellate around love and relationship—Psyche, Eros, Aphrodite, Amor, Sappho, Cupido, Hera, Lilith, Vesta, Lust, and Pecker. If they fall in prominent places in the chart, they can give more detailed information. Also, the personal-name asteroids can be very illuminating in confirming the importance of being drawn to individuals who carry that name.

You can present the traditional analysis to the client or use it for your own information to give you a solid baseline that can inform how you present the analysis to the client within the modern context. If you are concerned that the traditional approach is too deterministic and limits the free will of the evolving self, you can use this information as a guide for pinpointing the areas where psychological counseling and right action can transform difficult unconscious patterns.

You will most likely have conflicting testimonies from the above analysis, as we humans are very complex creatures, especially when it comes to love, sex, marriage, and commitment. Look to see if all the indicators are favorable or if all of them are unfavorable. This will give you an idea of whether to encourage the client in pursuit of relationships, or whether to encourage the development of other parts of the life. This is not to say that clients in relationships should not actualize their individual paths. If some testimonies are favorable and others unfavorable, relationship will be a mix of good and bad, or relationship will occur but be varied, difficult, or transitory, as is the case for many people. However, you should be able to identify just where the problems will emerge.

Ultimately, our capacity for creating successful relationships is more a matter of our own charts rather than our synastry with others. Someone who has well-situated relationship significators will naturally be attracted to and merge with those who also are well suited to creating and maintaining positive relationships. On the other hand, someone who has poorly situated relationship significators will more likely be attracted to those who are unsuited for intimacy and commitment, and to unions that do not come to anything or do not turn out well. However, the synastry between two charts can describe the specifics of the good or bad interactions that do take place in any relationship. Relationships whose main purpose is the resolution of difficult karmic patterns may be indicated by key planets that are closely connected by challenging synastry contacts, such as Venus in one chart opposed to Saturn in another. Generally, it is not appropriate for you to make definitive statements to clients about whether or not to marry or divorce based on a comparison of the charts. Couples come together for all kinds of reasons, and you may not be aware of the larger scheme of things. Where an astrologer is most effective is in explaining the dynamics of the interactions and the range of options, based on a careful analysis of the variables.

Astrologers are often concerned with whether good synastry over-rides poor natal relationship patterns, and whether a good electional marriage chart over-rides bad synastry between a couple. In the course of your astrological career, you will have to mull over and consider these questions based on your own experiences in counseling others in this area.

In Bill's chart, Venus is in Sagittarius in the first house. Venus is placed in a strong, angular, and good house, free from affliction by the malefics, direct in motion, not under the beams, and in her own bounds. While Venus is not in the signs of its domicile or exaltation, her domicile lord, Jupiter, in its own sign, Sagittarius, gives much support. These are all good indicators.

Others see Bill as a kind of "Renaissance man," well educated and well traveled. He is attracted to women with whom he can share intellectual interests and outdoor physical adventures (Venus in Sagittarius). With Venus in the first house, his sexuality and charm are right up front and he is happiest when he is in love.

Gemini occupies the seventh house of marriage, and he needs a relationship that supports the free expression of his ideas and someone with whom he can make a mental connection and who will listen and respond to him. No planets occupy the seventh house, and the house itself is not afflicted by squares or oppositions from the malefics.

Mercury, the ruler of the seventh house, occupies the first house, conjoined to Venus. Talking and conversation turn Bill on. Because the ruler of the seventh is located in an angular house, the topic of relationships is extremely important to him and much of his life energies are directed toward them. His own identity becomes more solid when he can function as a partner in relationship to another. In fact, with the ruler of the seventh in the first, he may want a partner to put him and their relationship as first priority. Because Mercury is in detriment in Sagittarius, he may have difficulty sustaining partnership, or it may be that his mates cannot sustain that kind of ongoing intensity and focus, much to his disappointment. However, Mercury is not hindered by the malefics, is helped by a bonifying conjunction with Venus, is direct in motion, not under the beams, receives a lunar application, and is strong in the first; thus the topic of relationship is relatively well supported. Therefore, good relationships are presented, but are challenged in their staying power due to Mercury in the sign of its detriment.

Because Mercury and Venus are in T-square by sign with planets in the fourth and tenth houses, issues around providing a home and having a career create tension in Bill's efforts to enter and maintain relationships as his primary agenda. With squares from both Jupiter and Neptune, his expectations of relationship may be inflated and idealistic.

The Lot of Marriage falls at 0 Virgo 32 in the tenth house. The lot is angular, not under the beams, and free from harm by Mars and Saturn, which are both in aversion to the sign Virgo. These are all excellent indicators for the eventuation of marriage, and it suggests that the marriage partner is linked in some way with professional endeavors or joint efforts in the social world. The ruler of the Virgo lot is Mercury, which is also the ruler of the seventh house. Therefore, the same considerations described above apply.

Juno is in Aquarius in the third house, closely conjunct to Mars and widely conjoined to the Moon. The Juno/Moon connection reinforces Bill's emotional need for relationship, and, in an air sign and the third house, echoes the theme of mental interaction. If you consider the projection theme, Bill may be attracted to women who are independent and free spirits (Aquarius), yet, with the conjunction to Mars, experience conflict and power struggles when divergent points of view are expressed, especially highlighted by the ninth-house opposition by sign from Pluto and Pallas. As Mars is the ruler of the fifth house of children and sexuality, much of the conflict may center on disagreements over these topics.

Overall, relationship is indicated, as, aside from Mars/Juno, there are no severe harmful influences to Venus and Mercury, who are both strong by their first-house placement. The issue of relationship will be very important in Bill's life. However, his relationships may not be all that he had hoped for. As a counselor, you can discuss the motif of projection and how the kind of women to whom he is attracted—intellectual, free-spirited, independent (Venus in Sagittarius, Juno in Aquarius, Gemini on the Descendant)—are likely to have vibrant lives of their own and may not want to merge their lives with another in pursuit of a joint vision or collaborative endeavor.

ANALYZING CAREER

The tenth house is associated with the topic of profession. The Greek word most commonly used to describe this house is *praxis*, which means "action" or "what one does." It is the area of life that speaks to the question: So, what do you do? This house is also associated with honors, reputation, and social standing. To the modern way of thinking, the ancient astrological texts are confusing and difficult to understand in their analysis of profession. This may be due partially to the different way the notion of profession was interpreted in the ancient world as compared to today.

In ancient times, high social status, as indicated by the tenth house, did not derive from a profession. In fact, those who were part of the upper class did not work to make a living. Manual work was something the poorer people did. What today are considered high-status professions—medicine and law—were looked on as trade skills in the world in which ancient astrology was formulated. For the ancients, *praxis* meant rather what someone did *with* his or her life—what we would today call a vocation. Thus it is difficult to draw direct analogies between the Hellenistic techniques for assessing profession and their modern counterparts. But traditional astrologers such as Ptolemy, Paulus, and Hephaistio nonetheless have important insights to share about *praxis*.

Ptolemy, in his discussion of how to locate the planet that governs *praxis*, discusses the importance of the planet that has made its morning appearance closest to the Sun or occupies the tenth house, especially when the Moon is applying to it. If there are no planets in either of the above conditions, he advises looking to the planet that rules the tenth house, although such natives are generally inactive.[2] I take this last statement to mean that the ruler of the tenth is a weaker indicator of the matter of profession than a planet that has made a morning appearance or occupies the tenth house. Ptolemy and Paulus also discuss the significance of Mercury, Venus, and Mars and their signs for determining the quality of action. Paulus, like Dorotheus, mentions the importance of the placement of these planets in the angular or succedent houses, with the tenth, second, and sixth houses being most preferred.[3]

Keeping all of this in mind as background, let's try to set forth a model we can use to analyze the topic of career. In the contemporary world, this often means answering the question: What am I going to do with my life that will give me a social identity and make money to support my livelihood?

The first thing to clarify when discussing the topic of career is the difference between "vocation," as the expression of how we want to be recognized by society for our actions, and "job," as something we do to make money. For some people, these are the same; for others, they are different. For example, someone who answers "I'm a musician" when asked "What do you do?" may actually work as a waiter to earn money for survival. You have to discern whether the tenth-house vocation just gives social identity or is also the source of the second-house finances, and whether the tenth-house vocation is the same activity as the sixth-house daily employment. For some people, there will be a connection between career, money, and job; for others, these topics are not connected.

Generally, the tenth, second, and sixth houses indicate the chart signature for the topics of career, money, and job. Just as you looked to the seventh house to evaluate the topic of marriage, you will assess these houses to determine to what extent individuals will be successful in their endeavors to produce a meaningful career, sufficient money, and beneficial working conditions. Look to the planets occupying these houses, as well as the planets ruling them. The nature of the planet tells you what kinds of activities can be performed, and the condition of the planet tells you the extent to which the endeavor will be successful. However, as a counseling astrologer, be careful not to promise fame and fortune if it is not indicated. At the same time, be careful not to tell clients they will be ineffective in their career efforts. There is a fine line between describing what someone's vocational aptitudes are and knowing how successful someone will be in realizing them. And the soul purpose may be something altogether different from a career. Here are some general guidelines for analyzing career.

- The tenth house, called *praxis,* describes our actions in the world, what we do, our status, and our role in society.
- The second house, called *bios,* describes our livelihoods, how we make the money to support our existence in the physical world.
- The sixth house used to be the house of slaves and servants, but is now the house of jobs, employees, and daily work habits and environments. The ancients called this the House of Evil Fortune, perhaps signifying the state of servitude resulting from having to work for others.

Unlike the topic of marriage, there is no single planet that is the general indicator of profession, although Jupiter is associated with honors and reputation. Ptolemy used Venus, Mercury, and Mars as rulers of the tenth house, and the signs they occupy to designate different kinds of career activities. And while there are lots for livelihood, reputation, praxis, and honor, there is no Hellenistic Lot of Profession.[4]

General Considerations for Analyzing Career

Here are guidelines to follow in the analysis of the topics of career, income, and employment. As with the topic of relationship, we will follow a traditional approach, but reframe it within a modern context.

- Look to the element of the signs that occupy the tenth, second, and sixth houses to see if the topics of career, money, and job are driven by a need for freedom and power, by communication of ideas, by physical security, or by emotional safety (fire, air, earth, and water signs occupying these houses). In the Whole Sign system, all three of these houses will be driven by the same elemental need. Then look to the quality of the individual sign for more specific information.
- In accordance with the ancient authors, look to see if there is a planet making a morning rising relative to the Sun (keep to the visible planets and make sure that they are not under the beams),

or if there is a planet that occupies the tenth house. This may be one of the strongest indicators of profession, vocation, status, and reputation. The nature of the planet will correspond to the kinds of activities that take place within the career.

- Check to see if the tenth house is being afflicted by squares or oppositions from Mars or Saturn. If so, there may be obstacles or difficulties.

- If there are no planets making a morning appearance or occupying the tenth house, consider the planet that is the domicile lord of the tenth house. The career will have something to do with the topic of the house in which it is located. Analyze the domicile lord by location and condition. For example, if Leo occupies the tenth house and the Sun is located in the fifth, the career will have something to do with the topic of children or artistic creativity or accidental good fortune, as in speculative activities.

- Examine the second and sixth houses in a similar manner. Begin by looking at the planets occupying these houses to see how much activity (number of planets) and what kind of activity (nature of planets) is being expended in these areas. Note if Venus and Jupiter are providing beneficial assistance or if Mars and Saturn are creating difficulties. If Mars and Saturn are in good condition, they will help; if Venus and Jupiter are in poor condition, they can't do too much good.

- Examine the placement of the ruler of each of these houses. Its house location will indicate in what area of life the career, money, or job will be sought; its condition will indicate the relative success of this endeavor.

- See if these three rulers are configured to one another and by what kind of aspects. If they are linked by trine and sextile, they are working together cooperatively for the achievement of the goal; if they are linked by square or opposition, they may be functioning at cross-purposes; if they are not connected at all, it may indicate that there is no connection between the person's vocation, daily employment, and earning potential.

- Look to asteroids conjunct to the Midheaven degree or to the rulers of these three houses for more specific information.

• You may want to experiment with the various lots of action (praxis).

In Bill's chart, the earth signs occupy the tenth, second, and sixth houses, indicating that the topics of career, making money, and daily employment are motivated by a drive for physical and financial security. No one of the classical planets is making a morning rising relative to the Sun. Neptune, the planet of fine arts, illusion, spirituality, and healing, occupies the tenth house, along with the asteroid Ceres, which is connected with nurturing and the land. Begin by positing that the career and reputation incorporate activities signified by these two planets. The tenth house is not afflicted by any squares or oppositions from Mars or Saturn.

Because the sign Virgo occupies the tenth house, look to the placement of its ruler, Mercury, for additional information. This planet of communication occupies the first house in the visionary and expansive sign of Sagittarius, while also being in detriment. You can speculate the career involves some kind of self-propelled (first-house) visionary communication (Mercury in Sagittarius) that also entails the attributes of the fine arts or healing expressed with technical proficiency (Neptune in Virgo) and land-based nurturing (Ceres in Virgo).

We know that Bill made film documentaries and, later in life, made a documentary about cooperative community activities. Here, you can see how Neptune supplied the film and television significations and Ceres supplied the topic of communes and communities, while Mercury in Sagittarius shaped it into media communications. However, the detriment status of Mercury deterred the achievement of long-lasting success and extensive recognition.

An evaluation of the second house of livelihood indicates that it is devoid of planets, and its domicile lord, a retrograde Saturn, is in its fall in Aries in the fifth house of children and creative expression. The ruler is also conjunct the south node and Vesta. Bill's responsibilities as a parent are the primary motivator for earning a living, but he has not made very much money from his artistic endeavors. However, also note that Saturn is in mutual reception to Mars gaining in power. So, despite the difficulties, he has managed some accomplishment in and recognition for his artistic endeavors.

Uranus, the planet of individuality and rebelliousness, occupies the sixth house of daily employment, which has made it challenging for Bill to work for others. With Uranus' opposition to the Sun, Bill is a highly individualistic personality who is rebellious to any kind of external authority, especially from an employer. The ruler of the sixth house, Venus, is in the first house of self. The conjunction of the rulers of the tenth and sixth houses, which are located in the first, denotes a person who must work for himself. However, Bill has always enjoyed working in a cooperative fashion with those who are artistically talented and competent. The rulers of these houses are all configured in a harmonious manner; Mercury is conjoined to Venus and both are trine to Saturn. Thus there is a good connection between the topics of profession, earnings from livelihood, and jobs.

ANALYZING HEALTH

While it is a question of utmost concern to clients, you must be acutely aware, as an astrologer, of the dangers of playing physician. Although you may be tempted to diagnose and prescribe, don't; it is illegal. Furthermore, you do not have the medical training to do this. You can make general statements as to the overall health and vitality of a client's body, the body parts that are most vulnerable to illness, and timing for potential health crises and their resolutions. But clients will want to know what is really wrong with them, whether their physicians have diagnosed them correctly, and when is a propitious time for a surgical procedure. Steer clear of these questions, as well as those concerning medications and the advisability and outcomes of operations. Do not share insights that may cause a client to question the judgment of a physician. If a client has doubts about a diagnosis, encourage him or her to get a second opinion. It is not that astrology cannot provide clear insights into these questions; it is simply that, if you, as an astrologer, err in your judgment and a client listens to you instead of a physician, the consequences can be devastating for both of you.

Here are several general guidelines for evaluating the topic of health.

- The Moon is a general significator for matters of the body. The sign of the Moon points to the region of the body that is most vulnerable, and afflictions to the Moon from the malefic planets in the natal chart indicate a problem with that body part.
- The sixth house and its ruler are significators for the topics of illness and accidents. If the ruler is in a bad condition and location, there may be chronic problems. If the malefics occupy the sixth house, there may also be difficulties with maintaining good health. Timing activations to sixth-house planets or to its ruler may indicate periods of health crisis.
- The first house and its ruler are indicators for the topic of vitality. How strong is the basic constitution to withstand bouts of illness and make good recoveries?
- Some astrologers set up electional charts for surgeries that have already been advised by a physician. There are a number of guidelines to follow, including that the Moon should not occupy a sign that governs the part of the body being operated on. Try to keep the Moon free of conjunctions, squares, and oppositions with Mars and Saturn. The astrological lore also advises against surgeries occurring at the New or Full Moon, due to the danger of excessive blood loss during these times.

STUDY GUIDELINES

- Examine the topic of relationship and career in your practice chart. Prepare written delineations for these topics, following the procedures set forth.
- Then write out two statements. In the first, make notes to yourself as an astrologer about how likely and how fortunate the out-

come of these topics will be for the client. If you see problems in the topics of relationship or vocation, write a second statement in which you outline the problem. Include ways in which the problem may be addressed or give alternative directions to pursue.

- Think about how you will proceed if your client really wants to be married and the indicators are not favorable, or if the client is desperate to find a successful career, but prospects of that are unlikely.

CHAPTER TWELVE

Timing by Solar Returns and Annual Profections

In the previous chapter, we saw how transits and progressions can indicate the kinds of events and issues that will be activated at a particular time in a person's life. The influences of the slower-moving outer-planet transits can last for several years, but within that span of time, there can be yearly fluctuations of better and more difficult periods. Many clients want to know what the current year or the year ahead holds for them. The Solar Return chart is another timing method you can use to investigate the nature, potentials, and challenges of a particular year.

The Solar Return is cast every year around the birthday, when the Sun returns to the same degree and minute at which it was located at birth, providing a snapshot of the coming year. Because the year has 365¼ days, this return can occur the day before, the same day, or the day after the birth date. The positions of the planets at the time of the Sun's annual return give indications about the likelihood of the realization of the natal potential during the coming year.

The question to ask in analyzing the Solar Return is whether the events indicated in the natal chart as possibilities are likely to eventuate during a particular year that runs from birthday to birthday. How do the positions of the planets at the time of the Return support or negate the realization of that natal potential? Remember that the Solar Return chart cannot indicate the occurrence of anything that is not already indicated as likely in the natal chart.

In modern astrology, there are four possible combinations for constructing the Solar Return chart, each depending on variables of location and precession. Here, we will use the natal location, as opposed to the relocation at the moment of the return. We will also use the exact degree and minute of the Sun as it was in the natal chart, as opposed to the precessed degree position. Thus, natal location and non-precessed Sun are our defaults.

The Solar Return chart is most often viewed by modern astrologers as an independent chart. Prognostication of the year ahead is based primarily on this chart, without necessarily making reference to the natal chart. One of the main problems with this approach is that there are four different possible charts, depending on the options used for location and precession. It is a stretch to consider that all four charts will give valid, clear, and non-contradictory indications.

Traditional astrologers had a different approach to the interpretation of the Solar Return. They saw the positions of the Solar Return planets primarily as transits to the natal chart on the birthday, rather than as an independent chart. However, the interpretations of these Solar Return transits on the birthday itself influence the nature of the entire year. The Solar Return Ascendant and its lord were also important factors in the evaluation of the year. This method was used in conjunction with another timing technique called annual profections that focuses on a particular planet as the annual profected time lord in the natal chart.

A time lord, called a *chronocrator* in Greek (literally a "ruler of time"), is a planet that governs the life for a certain period of time. Traditional astrology used a number of timing procedures that have been lost to modern practice (circumambulations, zodiacal releasing, decennials, and *firdaria*) and each timing system generated its own time-lord sequences. When a planet becomes a time lord, it is "turned-on" for a period of time that varies according to each procedure. Whatever that planet signifies in the natal chart is most likely to be realized during the period when it is activated. In the timing system of annual profections, the annual profected time lord has a period of one year in which to bring about the matters it represents. The time-lord method of profections was used in conjunction with the Solar Return chart to obtain a picture of a specific year.

Profections are a simple and powerful timing procedure that was used by many Hellenistic, Arabic, and Medieval astrologers to investigate the events and nature of a particular year, with subdivisions of months and days. The most basic version of the procedure entails moving from one sign to the next, house by house, and taking the domicile lords of these successive houses as the time lord. When this movement takes place every year, we call them annual profections. Beginning with the Ascendant, the ascending sign moves to the next house in the chart on each birthday. The sign occupying each successive house in turn becomes the ascending sign for the year, and the topics that are signified by the profected house become highlighted during that year.

For the first year of a person's life, the Ascendant itself is the sign of the profection. When the person turns one year old, the ascending sign "profects," moving on to the second house of the birth chart. Then the ascending sign profects to the third house, and so on. After twelve years, the cycle repeats itself from the Ascendant, so that starting at the twelfth, twenty-fourth, thirty-sixth, forty-eighth, sixtieth, and seventy-second birthdays, the sign of the profection is co-incident with the natal Ascendant. Thus each year, various topics become highlighted in some way in orderly sequence around the chart—second-house livelihood, third-house siblings, fourth-house home and parents, fifth-house children, sixth-house illness, seventh-house marriage, etc. Any natal planets located in that house or any Solar Return transiting planets configured to that house play a role in the interpretation of the year.

Furthermore, the domicile lord (ruler) of the profected sign becomes the annual profected time lord. The annual profected lord of the year is the planet responsible for the general activities and conditions of a person's life within a particular year that runs from birthday to birthday. Whatever that planet signifies in the natal chart in terms of the house it occupies and the houses it rules, it has the opportunity to realize those significations during the year when it is time lord. Thus an evaluation of its condition in the natal chart is an important factor in prognosticating what to expect during the year in which it is the annual profected time lord.

In reflecting upon this procedure, it is clear that the pattern indi-

cated by the annual profected sign and the natal placement of its lord
repeats every twelve years. Yet, every twelfth year is not identical
to the previous cycle in the specific details of the projected events.
These qualitative differences were determined by the ancient astrologers by identifying the annual profected time lord as the planet
that has the authority to handle the affairs of the life for that year
and bring about its own events. This planet's condition at the time
of the Solar Return, as well as its location and configurations relative to the natal chart, are critical to how capable it will be of doing
things successfully. This, in turn, affects what in fact is likely to be
accomplished and realized by the individual.

The Hellenistic astrologers all discuss the primary role that
the annual profected time lord plays in the evaluation of the Solar
Return chart. The annual profected time lord was considered the
most important planet in the Solar Return chart, because it has governance over the affairs of the year. Hephaisto tells us to investigate
how the lord of the year is situated, both in the natal chart and in
the transit chart at the time of the Solar Return, with regard to its
"mixture, position, and phase."[1] This means we must look to its condition by sign rulership, its house location relative to the natal chart,
whether it is under the beams of the Sun or retrograde, and if it is
being witnessed by benefic or malefic planets.

If the annual profected time lord in the Solar Return chart occupies a sign in which it has rulership, is located in an angular or succedent and good house relative to the natal chart, can witness the
house of the annual profection as well as its own natal position, is
direct in motion and not under the beams, and is well configured by
benefic planets in good condition, you can expect that the year will
be good and the events it signifies will be accomplished with fortunate outcomes. But if the annual profected time lord in the Solar
Return chart occupies a sign of its fall or detriment, is located in a
cadent or bad house position, cannot witness the house of the annual
profection or its own natal position, is retrograde, under the beams,
or configured to the malefic planets in poor condition, it indicates a
problematic or uneventful year.

In addition, because this planet is "turned on," the transits it
makes to other planets will be intensified and the transits made to it

in the natal chart will point to very significant events and motifs for the year. Use Bill's chart to locate the profected sign and the annual time lord for a particular year, and its role in the Solar Return chart. In addition, note if the domicile lord of the Ascendant of the Solar Return chart is in a good or bad place in the natal chart and how it is configured with the annual lord of the year, both natally and by transit at the time of the Solar Return.

> In Bill's chart, the natal Ascendant is Sagittarius, and thus the annual profected time lord of his first year of life was Jupiter, the lord of Sagittarius. The sign of the profection of his second year of life was Capricorn, the sign occupying the second house; the annual profected time lord was Saturn, the lord of Capricorn. Now investigate the year that began on Bill's sixty-sixth birthday (November 17, 2005). To find the profected sign for the year he turned sixty-six, count from the natal Ascendant as sixty years old. Counting in a clockwise direction, sixty-six falls in the seventh house. The topical meaning of the seventh house will thus be highlighted in some way for this year.
>
> The seventh house signifies marriage. The sign Gemini occupies the seventh house, and the domicile lord of Gemini is Mercury, who then becomes the annual profected time lord, governing the affairs of that year. The topic of relationship will probably be important, since Mercury, its lord, is intensified, activated, and turned on, and thus has the opportunity this year to bring about its significations. Start with a natal analysis of Mercury, in terms of its capacity to bring about and sustain relationships. If the topic of relationships is not indicated or supported in the natal chart, then no timing procedure, whether it be transit, progression, or Solar Return, can make marriage occur. In the previous chapter, we determined that, for Bill, Mercury is strong by placement in the powerful first house, bonified by a conjunction with Venus, and not afflicted by either Mars or Saturn. Thus, Mercury promises relationship and this is a major theme in the life. However, because Mercury in Sagittarius is in detriment, not having access to its own resources, there may be a difficulty in sustaining unions.

Bill's Natal Chart
November 17, 1939
8:30 am MST +7:00
Seneca, NE
42°N02'36" 100°W49'57"

Bill's Solar Return
November 16, 2005 (±1 sec)
8:41:58 am MST +7:00
Seneca, NE
42°N02'36" 100°W49'57"

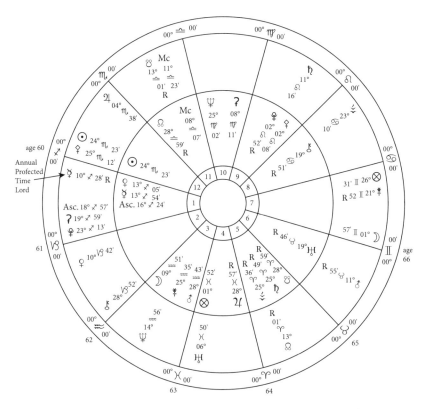

The Natal Chart is the inner wheel, the Solar Return is the outer.

FIGURE 12. *The natal and Solar Return charts for 2005.*
In 2005, Bill turned 66 years old.
At age 66, the 7th house is the annual profected house.
The annual profected time lord is Mercury, the ruler of the 7th house.
In the Solar Return chart, Mercury is located at 10 Sagittarius 28
retrograde, activating the 1st house in the natal chart.

Now examine Mercury in the Solar Return chart and, through an analysis of its condition at the time of the Return, determine if it is sufficiently powerful to bring about its significations and, if so, whether the outcome will be fortunate. In the Solar Return for 2005, Mercury occupies the sign of Sagittarius, is retrograde, and occupies the first house of the natal chart. Because the angular first house is the strongest house, and because Mercury is configured to its natal position (both are co-present in the same sign) and is able to witness the seventh house as the annual profected house, Bill may expect a relationship to eventuate. However, Solar Return Mercury's detriment in Sagittarius (as in the natal chart) suggests a difficulty in sustaining the relationship, and its retrograde motion points to a reversal in status—what is given will be taken away. Solar Return Mercury is not afflicted by the malefics (conjunct, opposed, or squared by Mars or Saturn), nor is it helped by the benefics (conjunction, trine, or sextile from Venus or Jupiter) in the Solar Return chart.

The Ascendant of the Solar Return is Sagittarius, the same as his natal Ascendant, and Jupiter is the domicile lord. In the Solar Return, Jupiter occupies the cadent and bad twelfth house relative to the natal chart, is not in any positions of its own rulerships, and is opposed by Mars and squared by Saturn. While Mercury, the annual profected time lord, and Jupiter, the domicile lord of the Solar Return Ascendant, are configured by square in the natal chart, they are in aversion with no connection at all in the Solar Return chart. This indicates some difficulties around the motif of loss and suffering in satisfactorily bringing about the matter of relationship this year. Because the condition of both Mercury and Jupiter in the Solar Return chart are worse than their condition in the natal chart, we can say that this year will not be as successful in the matter of relationship relative to the baseline established by the natal potential.

Within a week of his birthday in November, Bill entered a new and very passionate and intense relationship with someone who embodied his "ideal"; by springtime, it was over.

Further study of the Solar Return entails looking to see if any Solar Return planets make close conjunctions to natal planets or natal angles. If so, these contacts will precipitate significant events. From a modern perspective, you can also say that a Solar Return planet falling in a natal house seeks its expression during that year through the topics indicated by that house. Thus during this year, natal Venus seeks expression through second-house livelihood matters; natal Moon seeks expression through seventh-house relationship matters, and so on.

MONTHLY PROFECTIONS

A more in-depth study of profections can give you indications on a monthly and daily basis. In a seventh-house yearly profection, the seventh house governs the first month following the birthday—in Bill's case, November 17 to December 17. The eighth house governs the following month—December 17 to January 17, etc., with each of the lords governing the time for that month under the auspices of Mercury as the year lord. You can use monthly profections and the lord of that house to track which house is activated month by month and how those affairs will turn out. You can also look to see when the monthly profection arrives at the natal house location of the planet that is the annual time lord. Often, it is during that month that the effects of how the time lord is functioning in the life become fully apparent.

In Bill's case, the yearly profection is the seventh house, beginning on November 17. Counting one house per month, on May 17, the monthly profection reaches the first house, where natal Mercury, the annual time lord, is located. It is during the month from May 17 to June 16 that it becomes clear just what Mercury has been able to bring about in terms of relationship. And around that time, it was obvious that the relationship was over.

Thus the Solar Return chart is used to study the potentials of a given year. The most important planet to study in the chart is the annual profected time lord. This is the planet whose significations in the natal chart have the opportunity to be realized during the Solar Return year in accordance with its condition and its location relative to the natal chart at the time of the Return. The domicile lord of the Solar Return Ascendant is another important planet to evaluate. Remember that the Solar Return chart cannot indicate anything taking place that is not already indicated as a possibility in the natal chart. A well-situated annual time lord at the time of the Return can bring opportunity and gain, while a poorly situated annual time lord can lead to loss and reversals in fortune, but these conditions are temporary and will not supersede the natal indications for the duration of the life.

STUDY GUIDELINES

- For your practice chart, determine the yearly profected sign/house and the annual profected time lord. What area of life is being highlighted? Give a brief interpretation of what the annual time-lord planet signifies in the natal chart and its condition in the natal chart.
- Calculate the Solar Return chart for this birthday year, placing the Solar Return planets in a bi-wheel around the natal chart. Give an analysis of the condition and position of the annual profected time lord in the Solar Return and also relative to the natal chart.
- Check to see what other planets may be occupying or witnessing the yearly profected sign/house.
- Examine the position and condition of the domicile lord of the Solar Return Ascendant and its configuration to the annual profected time lord.
- Determine if any Solar Return planets are making close contacts to natal planets and angles.
- Make a prognostication about the kind of year it will be and the extent to which the annual profected time lord can bring about its significations.

CHAPTER THIRTEEN

THE FINISHED STRUCTURE

WE HAVE DISCUSSED many of the individual components of astrological analysis, all of which contribute in some way to a description of the nature of life purpose and to the timing of its unfoldment. Now let's review what we have covered and consider how to assemble the information and present it in a coherent and orderly manner. Ultimately, each astrologer must find his or her own voice and procedure, but you can look at this model as a starting point from which you can make your own adaptations.

There are many ways to approach the reading of a chart. Here, we have attempted to answer the question: According to my chart, how am I supposed to be living my life? In choosing this perspective, however, you have to be careful not to ignore other subsidiary issues about which the client may also be concerned. Be sure that you address these as well. How do you fit in all the material? Where do you start the reading? And where do you go next?

It always helps to have a plan. For the most part, you should follow that same plan for each reading, especially the first time you do a reading for a client or the first time you read a particular client's chart. Some astrologers prefer to work more spontaneously, jumping in at whatever point calls them most strongly. For most beginning students who are just learning how to synthesize and organize a reading, however, this is too unstructured an approach. For the many who do not have benefit of seasoned experience, it creates confusion and undermines self-confidence, resulting in sessions that are scattered and unfocused. What ends up being discussed may not be what is most important about the chart.

Table 6. Proposed Schedule for a One-hour Consultation

Segment	Time for Segment	Total Time elapsed
Initial questions and interview	5 minutes	5 minutes
Lunation phase, natal and progressed	10 minutes	15 minutes
Ascendant and its ruler	10 minutes	25 minutes
Sun, Moon, and focused questions	15 minutes	40 minutes
Other timing not already discussed	10 minutes	50 minutes
Other client questions	5 minutes	55 minutes
Summary and closure	5 minutes	60 minutes

Each session—even each one-hour session—is different. The exact length of the session may vary from client to client, depending on the variables of the chart and the needs of the client. Be sure that, by the end of the session, you have covered all the important points that you planned to discuss. Hold the fine line between being responsive to the client and maintaining control of the session. If the client comes to you as an astrologer, he or she may have expectations that you will give information for which you are being paid. On the other hand, if the client comes to you as a therapist/astrologer, he or she may want the opportunity to do most of the talking. Locate where on this spectrum you are most comfortable working, and always honor the desires and needs of your clients.

As you look over the following outline, you will notice that most of the session time is devoted to a discussion of the lunation phase, Ascendant, Sun, and Moon. This is because the thesis of this book is that the most important themes in the life are indicated by the interrelationship of these factors.

You have obtained the birth data and verified its source, scheduled the appointment, and prepared all the charts. You may have an idea of the client's questions or you may wait until the session begins to ask what has brought the person to you and what his or her concerns are. In the initial interview, you also get a sense of the level at which you should give the reading—in terms of both the complexity

of the astrological terminology and the client's own level of com-
prehension, awareness, and personal development. You must establish rapport and compassion, extract the pertinent information, and
prevent an overly talkative client from going on and on about the
details of his or her life and problems for the next fifteen minutes.
You have only five minutes for this initial portion of the session.

You may begin the formal reading of the chart with a short statement that simply tells the client what the Sun, Moon, and rising
signs are. Almost everyone is familiar with their Sun sign, and this
affirms immediately that the client knows something about astrology. Many have at least heard the terms Moon sign and rising sign
in casual conversation. If the client already knows this information,
it is another affirmation; if not, the client will often like to learn
it right at the beginning of the session. You can then explain that
many astrologers consider the Sun, Moon, and rising sign the three
most important significators of the personality, and that you will discuss each one in turn over the course of the session. However, there
is one more very important factor to add to this triad, and that is the
relationship between the Sun and Moon at the time of the client's
birth, which is called the lunation phase.

Point out that the Moon circles the Earth each month, and the
various Moon phases reflect this changing relationship between the
two lights in the sky. In astrology, this is called the lunation cycle,
and it is divided into eight distinct phases. Explain that each person
is born during a particular phase of the Moon's cycle, and that the
Moon was in a particular phase at birth. Each month, this phase
reoccurs for several days. During that time, the person will be especially sensitized emotionally, as symbolized by the Moon, and these
feelings will come closer to the surface of conscious awareness, as
symbolized by the Sun, particularly with regard to the meaning or
lack of meaning in his or her life. Illustrate how you locate the natal
Moon phase each month by reference to an astrological calendar or
by looking at the weather page of the daily newspaper.

Because everyone has a regular and direct visual experience of the
phases of the Moon, we all have a visceral sense that the Moon has
something to do with our personality. Thus, you are beginning the

session with information that is accessible and tangible to everyone, and this makes your clients feel as if they are starting off the exploration of their lives on firm ground. You can then give an explanation of the interpretation of their natal lunation phase. Again, because there is little or no astrological jargon involved, clients can receive the information easily. This establishes an immediate sense that you, the astrologer, are telling them something that they can understand and relate to, and that makes sense in terms of their own life experiences. Clients are then more receptive to receiving what follows.

After a discussion of the natal lunation phase, move on to the progressed lunation phase. Explain that, while each person is born into one particular phase, due to a timing system in astrology called secondary progressions, everyone goes through the qualities of each of the other phases as well. One phase follows another in approximately four-year periods in the sequential development of a thirty-year cycle that unfolds in accordance with the nature of each phase in a cyclical process. Tell clients when this thirty-year cycle began at the previous progressed New Moon and in what phase they currently are by progression. This gives them a broad view of their lives over a long period of time and indicates what qualities they are being called upon to express at this time. You have no more than ten minutes for both the natal and progressed lunation phases.

We have already presented the full interpretations of the natal and progressed lunation phases for Bill's chart, but let's distill this information somewhat and re-present it so you can see the flow between these two sections and those that follow.

Bill was born during a Crescent Moon phase, and his life is characterized by a struggle to establish his own identity apart from familial, social, and cultural expectations. By accessing the resources available in his immediate environment, he can develop new talents, skills, and abilities that give him the means by which to move beyond the old and familiar into new uncharted territory that stimulates his curiosity. Cultivating focus and perseverance can help keep him progressing in a forward direction, and his final challenge is to take advantage of the many opportunities that present themselves by taking action upon them.

By progression, Bill is almost halfway through a thirty-year cycle that began in October 1992, when the progressed New Moon heralding the beginning of a new cycle and the release of a new vision occurred in his second house of livelihood. He ceased working for others and began working for himself, putting his video and computer skills into creative endeavors. Currently near the end of the progressed Gibbous phase (October 2004 to March 2008), he has been refining and perfecting his techniques of operation, and becoming as skillful as he can be in his chosen field of expression. He has been called to do the "finishing work" on the structure he has been building since 1992. He has assembled all of his early films and made new prints of them, using the latest state-of-the-art technology. He has also completed the renovation of the building that houses the intentional household. In March 2008, he enters the progressed Full Moon phase, halfway around the thirty-year cycle. Over the next four years, the content of his vision becomes infused in the form he has built. It will be through his conscious relationships with other people that he illuminates his larger meaning in his life.

Once you have discussed the natal and progressed lunation phases, giving clients a snapshot of their stage of development within a model of cyclical process, you are ready to begin a discussion of the chart proper. The Ascendant marks the moment of our birth; thus this is a good place to start the reading. Describe the ascending sign as the personality characteristics of the outer image that are projected to the world at large, and speak to the psychological need that stands behind the expression of those qualities. It is appropriate at this time to mention any planets or major asteroids that occupy the first house or are within a 3-degree orb of the Ascendant degree crossing sign boundaries. Also note if there are any minor asteroids within a 3-degree orb of the Ascendant. Using Whole Sign houses, for the most part those planets and asteroids will be located in the same sign as the Ascendant, so whatever you have said about the

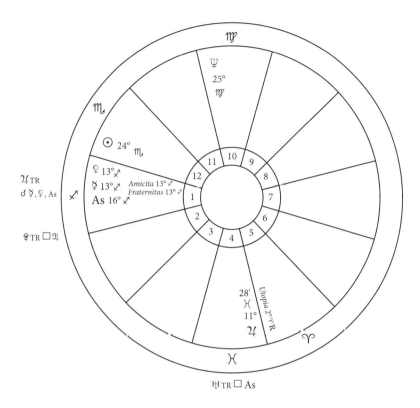

FIGURE 13. *Main factors to consider in the delineation of the Ascendant in Bill's chart.*

Ascendant sign applies to their signs as well. However, it will scatter and diffuse the discussion if you begin to talk about the aspects being made to the first-house planets at this point, so defer that for now.

Describe the ascending sign by element, referring to the basic drive that motivates the life, and discuss the first house as the helm of the ship where the steering mechanism of the life journey is located. Planets in the first house have their hands on the rudder and their agendas are front and center as the life moves forward. However, it is the planet that rules the Ascendant that is likened to the steersman of the ship, who gives the orders that guide the life toward its destination. This brings you to a discussion of the planet that is the Ascendant ruler. Describe this planet according to its own nature, giving an archetypal image if possible—Venus the lover, Mercury the communicator, or Mars the warrior. Explain that the house in which it is located is the topic that steers the life—relationship, children, profession, etc. Look to see if this planet is configured (conjoined, sextile, square, trine, or opposed) to the Ascendant by whole sign. This is indicative of a line of vision and communication between the steersman and the helm.

Examine the condition of this planet to determine how capable it is of doing its job in a manner that will bring about fortunate results for the client, looking to its sect status, sign rulerships, house location, and its speed, direction, and visibility as derived from its relationship to the Sun. You can factor in any aspects made to the Ascendant ruler by other planets at this time as an affirmation or negation of the calls the steersman makes. Include all the planets, and the four main asteroids and Chiron if you want to. Consider them by Whole Sign aspects, but know that the closer they are to exact orb, the more active the influences will be. Pay special attention to help and assistance by conjunction, sextile, or trines from Venus and Jupiter, or hindrance and negation by conjunction, square, or opposition from Mars or Saturn as aiding or hurting a planet's capacity to express its favorable significations. In the process of observing the influences from other planets, you will explain the significations of those planets and bring them into your reading.

If the lunar nodes or the Lot of Fortune occupy the first house or the same house as the Ascendant ruler, discuss their influences. If there happens to be a major outer-planet transit activating the Ascendant or its ruling planet, expand on what that means for the current time period.

> Bill projects an expansive, idealistic, and philosophically questing personality that arises from a desire to explore the horizons of his mind and world (Sagittarius Ascendant). He is seen as both communicative and charming (Mercury and Venus in the first house). He is motivated by a drive for power and influence (fire sign) in manifesting his Utopian ideals (Jupiter as ruler of the Ascendant and conjunct the asteroid Utopia). The topics of land and home (Jupiter in the fourth house) steer his life toward

its intended destination in a manner that is compassionate and that arises from spiritual insight (Jupiter in Pisces). He has the necessary resources (Jupiter in its own domicile) and focus (Jupiter angular) to accomplish this intention, and the capacity to overcome the obstacles on the way (Jupiter configured to the Ascendant sign by square). The final outcome may eventuate in the latter part of his life (Jupiter retrograde). He can expect a substantial amount of accidental good fortune to arise from his ventures in real estate and relationships with his parents (Lot of Fortune in the fourth house with a well-situated domicile lord, Jupiter).

Neptune in Virgo in the tenth house opposing Jupiter is pulling Bill in the opposite direction, however, toward a professional career in the arts in which he can utilize his technical skills. Venus and Mercury in Sagittarius in the first house are working at cross-purposes with both Jupiter and Neptune, lobbying for a life of personal enrichment and development through travel, adventure, and learning, in which he has the opportunity to share his ideas and be in love (Mercury and Venus in Sagittarius). He finds it challenging to be in a relationship and simultaneously have the focus for artistically creative or work endeavors. The Sun in Scorpio in the twelfth house, which seeks deep introspection into the mysteries of life and spiritual transcendence, is sympathetic and helpful to Jupiter's aspirations, as it provides a source of meditative insight that can be incorporated into the Utopian vision.

In 2007, the transit of Jupiter passed over Venus, Mercury, and the Ascendant, bringing opportunities for travel, growth, and expansion. Bill studied French and brought his films to the Cannes Film Festival. Pluto by transit activated natal Jupiter by square, and this influence will continue through 2008, bringing endings, new beginnings, and transformation to both personal identity (Jupiter as Ascendant ruler) and matters of the home environment (Jupiter located in the fourth house). Bill purchased a large home, moved his aging mother next door, and began his intentional spiritual community.

You can see that, in the process of looking at the main aspects made to the Ascendant ruler, Jupiter, we have touched upon the significations of four other planets in the chart: Neptune, Mercury, Venus, and the Sun. Now you are ready to complete the delineations for the Sun and the Moon.

Examine the Sun to determine the areas of life that describe the content of the life purpose. This content will partake of the significations of both the house the Sun occupies and the house it rules, which will be whatever house contains the sign Leo. The Sun is trying to bring about the matters associated with the house it rules, but it does so by means of its activities in the house in which it is located. The sign in which the Sun is located not only indicates the mode and manner by which this comes about, but also acts as a filter that shapes the expression of the purpose in accordance with its own attributes. If the Lot of Fortune or the lunar nodes occupy the same sign and house as the Sun, bring them into the discussion. You have five minutes for this discussion.

In Bill's chart, the Sun in Scorpio rules the ninth house, and thus the matters it is trying to bring about are those connected with higher wisdom, philosophy, spirituality, multi-cultural motifs, and long-distance travel. It does so by immersion in twelfth-house activities that have to do with solitude, experiences of suffering and loss, purification of karmic actions or self-defeating unconscious patterns, selfless service, and the desire for transcendence and liberation. Scorpio is a feminine, watery, and fixed sign that speaks to the desire to penetrate the mysteries of life, as well to the intensity of the emotions. You can say that the content of Bill's basic life purpose as represented by the Sun is the learning and application of spiritual teachings (Sun ruling the ninth house) for self-transformation (Sun in Scorpio) that arises from his need to heal his own emotional suffering over losses and his desire to understand the transcendent nature of reality (twelfth house). This comes about in a slow and steady manner (feminine, fixed sign) that is contingent upon the actions of others (watery sign).

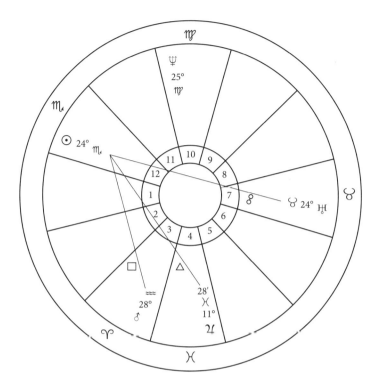

FIGURE 14. *Main factors to consider in the delineation
of the Sun in Bill's chart.*

Bill relates that, as a young person, he felt unrecognized and
socially rejected by his peers. As he grew older, these experiences made him sympathetic to the underdog and motivated
him to search for causes and relief of suffering through spiritual
teachings and practices.

Now, how capable is the Sun of actually bringing this
about? To find out, evaluate the planetary condition. The Sun
belongs to the sect in favor, and is the sect leader; thus it has
the authority and leadership to set the life agenda for bringing about favorable outcomes. The Sun does not occupy the
signs of its rulership or exaltation (nor of its detriment or fall).
So it does not have access to its own resources, but rather is

dependant on those of its domicile lord, Mars, to whom it is configured by a square. Mars is the Sun's host, but is working at cross-purposes with the Sun and tends to withhold its support. If support is given, there are obstacles thrown in the way. The Sun occupies and rules cadent houses. From a modern perspective, the cadency indicates that the life purpose will not manifest as outer dramatic events, but rather as inner processes.

Now consider which other planets are sympathetic or harsh to the Sun's desire to express the life purpose. The Sun is opposed by Uranus in Taurus in the sixth house, pulling Bill out of the contemplative realm into the world of busy, physical, tangible daily activities connected with jobs and employment. The Sun is also square by sign and degree with the asteroid Juno (committed relationships), which may also be working at cross-purposes with his meditation practice, and may be one possible cause of the suffering. The Sun is also squared by sign to the Moon, which is a general significator of family responsibilities and, in particular in his chart, of financial affairs with others (Moon ruler of the eighth) that compete with his inner work. It is the trine from Jupiter that gives the Sun the most support and affirmation.

Overall, you can make a judgment that the Sun is challenged in its aspiration to apply higher spiritual and philosophical teachings to Bill's life for personal transformation, alleviation of suffering, and service to others. And yet that is what he is here to do. The affirming trine from the strong benefic Ascendant ruler, Jupiter, points to eventual success in overcoming the obstacles.

Here we have touched on the significations of three additional planets—Mars, Moon, and Uranus—as well as one of the major asteroids, Juno. If there are any major outer-planet transits or upcoming eclipses activating the Sun, be sure to include timing prognostications at this point in the session. Now, let's focus on the Moon as the area of life where the content of the life purpose seeks application in the everyday world.

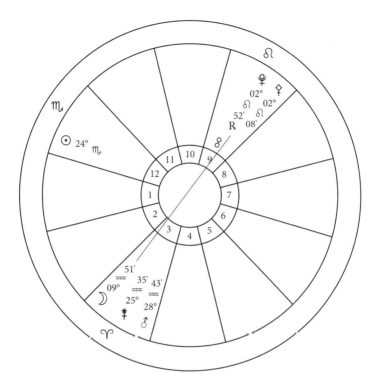

FIGURE 15. *Main factors to consider in the delineation of the Moon in Bill's chart.*

This application of the life purpose will partake of the significations of both the house that the Moon occupies and the house that it rules, which will be whatever house contains the sign Cancer. The Moon is trying to bring about the matters associated with the house it rules, but it does so by means of its activities in the house in which it is located. The sign in which the Moon is located not only indicates the mode and manner by which this comes about, but also acts as a filter that shapes the application of the purpose in accordance with its own attributes. If the Lot of Fortune or the lunar nodes occupy the same sign and house as the Moon, as well as any significant timing factors, bring them into the discussion. Again, you have about five minutes to devote to the Moon.

In Bill's chart, the Moon in Aquarius rules the eighth house, and thus the matters it is trying to bring about are concerned with death and dying, benefits gained from death (inheritances), financial ventures with the money of others (as opposed to that earned by his own labor), the psychological unconscious, and personal transformation (as extensions of death, the underworld, and rebirth). The Moon does so by immersion into third-house activities that pertain to siblings, his own neighborhood community, the nature of mind, and all kinds of communications involving media, networking, writing, and speaking. The Aquarius (masculine, fixed, airy) filter indicates that the application of the purpose is shaped by a humanitarian, progressive, and innovative vision that facilitates social change and can utilize the new technology. You can suggest that the application of Bill's life purpose entails taking the wisdom he has gained from his meditative practices and personal introspection (the content of the solar purpose) and disseminating information through various media (third house) concerning personal transformation and cooperative financial ventures (eighth house), with a vision to create progressive social change through the development of group consciousness (Aquarius).

The Moon is cadent and thus less than totally focused on its task, and it is located in a mildly good/profitable house. It is dependent on the resources of its domicile lord, Saturn, which, despite being in the sign of its fall, is made more powerful by its mutual reception with Mars. The Moon is assisted by the sextile from the benefic Venus, and hindered by co-presence with Mars. It is traveling with slower-than-average speed, and is thus less active, but it is increasing in light. You can conclude that the Moon has good aspirations and access to resources in order to bring about its intentions, but it suffers from being easily distracted or diverted. Bill may find that, sometimes, he is not able do as much or as well as he had hoped in accomplishing his aims. Nevertheless, he does have some visible success.

The Moon is influenced by the opposition from Pluto and Pallas, pulling him away from local community involvement into the larger world of foreign travel and higher wisdom teachings that both challenge and stimulate his own points of view. By sign, this axis forms a grand-square pattern with the Sun and Uranus. The Moon is also influenced by its co-presence with Juno, indicating an emotional need for intimate and committed relationships that function within a social and group context. The co-presence with Mars may point to emotional arguments and conflict with others. As Mars rules the fifth house of children and love affairs, responsibilities with children and turbulence in love affairs can be a cause of disruption.

As you completed the discussion of the Moon, you made reference to the influence and significations of two other planets—Pluto and Mars—and two of the four major asteroids, Pallas and Juno. You are now two-thirds of the way through your one-hour session and have fifteen to twenty minutes remaining. At this point, there are several different directions in which you can move.

This may be an appropriate time to pause and give a one- to two-sentence summary that integrates what you have said so far concerning the lunation phase, the Ascendant and its ruler, and the Sun and Moon. The ability to make a statement of the essential meaning of a chart in a hundred words is a valuable and an excellent skill for you to develop. This will be much appreciated by the client as a distillation of the most important points of the reading.

Bill has an expansive, intellectually questing nature that is motivated by a need for freedom and influence to bring a spiritual Utopian vision to matters pertaining to housing that facilitates cooperative living. His basic life purpose is the application of wisdom teachings for personal liberation and service to others. This is best accomplished in the world by the dissemination of progressive and innovative information about personal transformation within his own community. The energy that drives the expression and actualization of his larger purpose is that of pushing through resistance and persevering in his vision. (94 words)

This is also a good time to ask if the client has any questions or requires further clarification of what you have covered. Depending on the time remaining and whether the client's focus questions have been addressed, you may decide to cover the sections of the chart that have not yet been discussed. In our sample delineation of Bill's chart, this would be the fifth house of children, creativity, and romance. This area is important, as it contains the lunar nodal axis and the two planets that have not yet been discussed, Saturn and Vesta. However, you may need, instead, to move to the questions of vocation or relationship that brought the client to the session. In Bill's case, you would note that these two topics are both ruled by Mercury. During the last part of the session, it is important to discuss any current timing not yet mentioned that may concern the prognostications for the year ahead.

What I have been trying to illustrate here is how much of a chart can be covered and synthesized by following the sequence of natal and progressed lunation phase, Ascendant, Ascendant ruler, Sun, and Moon. The meanings of other planets or points and current timing are brought into the interpretation as they connect to these major significators of the chart. You can address relationship, vocation, health, money, children, parents, travel, homes, etc. earlier in the reading if the planets ruling these topics are one of the three main chart significators. Otherwise, you can discuss them later in the session, framed within the context of what the chart indicates as the main purpose of the life. If there is a major timing activation of a particular planet that you have not yet brought into your reading, be sure to include some words on the nature of the planet, the topics of the houses it rules, and the duration of the timing activation. When you speak about vocation or home life, look at the Midheaven or IC angles and to planets or asteroids conjunct the degrees of these angles.

Periodically, check to see how many minutes you have used and how many minutes are remaining in your session. This tells you if you have the leisure to develop more detail and explore tangents, or if you have to speed up, condense what you want to say, and remain focused. However, it is important not to be so rigid that you can't be responsive to the needs and desires of your client. You must be flexible enough to give the client the space to express strong emotional reactions or to disclose additional background information. Be sure to leave some time at the end of the session for any last-minute questions the client may have.

If it seems to you that there is more to cover than the time I've allowed, you can schedule your sessions for seventy-five or even ninety minutes. Many astrologers like to give themselves the additional time to go deeper into the chart and answer more client questions that may arise later in the session. Ultimately, pick a length of time that gives you the opportunity to do a thorough reading without feeling rushed. Since most astrologers tape their readings, your clients will be able to listen to the tape many times in order to absorb the information you have communicated.

STUDY GUIDELINES

- For your practice chart, make a list of the key points of your reading and the order in which you will present them.
- Give the reading to your "client" and time how long it takes you to cover each of your points. Assess where you are at the end of the hour.
- Ask your "client" for feedback.
- If necessary, spend some time reorganizing your plan, cutting it back or filling it out. Then give the reading a second time.

Part IV:

The Person
Who Lives in the Chart

CHAPTER FOURTEEN

ENCOUNTERING YOUR CLIENTS

Now THAT YOU have a procedure for uncovering the essential meaning of the birth chart and evaluating the capacity of each planet to bring about the matters it represents, you should feel fairly comfortable about your ability to look at a chart and decipher the symbols that reveal a portrait of a human life. The chart itself is a structure that supports a living person, pointing the way to the themes and events that are potentially available for experience in the course of the life. But the chart itself is *only* the structure; it is not the living, breathing, feeling human being that dwells inside the structure. It is one thing to assemble and display the vessel that contains us and provides us with the resources by which to shape our experiences, but quite another to acknowledge and relate to the person who inhabits it. After the structure has been built, someone must move into it. Let's now turn our attention to the person who lives in the chart and consider how best to relate to that person.

I was once told by my literary agent that, when my book was written and published, and copies of it were stacked in boxes in my garage, I would think that I had completed the monumental task of becoming an author. However, nothing could be farther from the truth. The real work was yet ahead—that of promoting, distributing, and selling the book. It is, likewise, not enough for you to have knowledge of astrology. You may know how to calculate a chart, or know the significations of all the planets, asteroids, signs, and houses. You may be versed in the variations of modern, traditional, or Vedic astrology. You may be able to interpret horary, electional, mundane,

business, and synastry charts, or have a dozen timing techniques at
your disposal. That's the easy part. The hard part is facing your clients and saying something meaningful about their lives.

In the original formulation of the discipline of astrology in
ancient Mesopotamia, astrologers belonged to a class of the priest-
hood. The act of interpreting the will of the planetary deities to the
kings of the land was a religious act that ensured that the kingdom
and its people were governed in accordance with divine intention.
Despite the attempts of successive cultures to take the soul out of the
planets and transform astrology into a secular discipline, astrologers
today remain as astrologers always have been—mediators between a
cosmic realm depicted by the positions of the celestial bodies at the
moment of a person's birth, and the earthly realm filled with conditions of human suffering and the universal desire for happiness.

While some people come to an astrological consultation out of
casual interest or curiosity, others want specific practical information about their business, health, or the recovery of missing items.
Many come because they are troubled or confused and are seeking
guidance. Once astrologers make the shift from dispensing objective
impersonal information to helping clients solve personal problems,
they assume the awesome mantle of responsibility that was traditionally donned primarily by the spiritual representatives of a society
who were thought to have a direct link to the divine realm.

PREPARING FOR A READING

You must have a full awareness of the role you take on as an astrologer and an appreciation of the responsibility for other people's lives
that this profession entails before you are ready to encounter your
clients. Very few modern astrologers would identify themselves as
spiritual counselors; yet the seers of old always prepared themselves
for the descent of divine inspiration to increase their clarity of mind
and connect them to a higher source. If you know that you have a
session at 1 P.M., you must "hold your energy" until that time. Ide-
ally, you don't want to engage in any conversations or activities that
drain and agitate you or fill your mind with disturbing thoughts and
emotions. However, we do not live in an ideal world, and many

astrologers schedule their sessions in the evenings, which makes taking care of daily business unavoidable. Nevertheless, it is important to cordon off a certain segment of your energy and save it for your readings.

The priestesses at Delphi are described as entering a state of ecstasy before giving oracular pronouncements. Ecstasy comes from the Greek word *ekstasis*, meaning "to stand outside of oneself." Then they entered into a state of enthusiasm—*enthusiasmos*—which in Greek means literally "having the god inside of you." In a similar manner, try to get all of your own "stuff" out of the way. As the time for your session approaches—you have all your charts prepared, your ephemeris at hand, your computer booted, your recorder hooked to the phone line, your consulting room picked up, and your water bottle or coffee cup filled—take a few moments to clear your mind. Take all your mundane problems, anger, irritations, and things-to-do lists, and set them aside temporarily. Visualize placing all that mental clutter on a high shelf in the coat closet. Once your inner space is cleared of your personal baggage, there is space for the presence of the transcendent. The ancients all concurred that divination, or the ability to foresee by supra-natural means, is a gift from the gods.

It is the spark of divine inspiration that distinguishes an enlivened reading from a flat recitation of analytically derived facts. This spark elevates dry facts into a lively, transformative, healing experience. Lighting a candle before the session is one way to acknowledge the source of the wisdom and request that the presence of the ineffable infuse your words. A correlate to this is that, having donned the mantle of an astrologer, the more skillful you are in the *techne* of your craft, the more worthy and functional a vessel you will be to receive the descent of the spirit.

What Do You Say . . . and How Much?

Unless you have received psychological training or credentials and see clients on an ongoing basis within the context of psychotherapy, chances are you will see your clients only once, or perhaps once every year for annual updates. Thus, assuming that you will see your clients only once, for perhaps a one- or one-and-a-half-hour session, how do you make the most effective use of the time allotted? And just how much can you actually convey in a one-hour session?

Just as there is a huge gulf between knowing the individual significations of each planet, sign, and house and synthesizing these meanings into statements about the life, there exists a gulf between knowing what a chart signifies in all its complexity from the dozens of techniques you have available in your toolbox, and knowing what you actually want to say to your client. As you gain experience interpreting charts, you will likely have many, many hours of material that you can discuss. However, in my experience, clients can only absorb information for about an hour—one hour and fifteen minutes at the maximum. You can continue to wax eloquent, but your clients will glaze over and no longer be able to absorb the meaning of your words.

I remember a humorous incident from my early days when my sessions sometimes lasted three to four hours. An emotionally exhausted client was inching his way to the door, desperate to get out and get relief from the scrutiny of his psyche. I was, figuratively, grabbing onto his leg, saying, "But wait, I still haven't told you about Mercury quincunx your Saturn." The point is that you must be able to distill from all that you perceive in a chart what is most important, both in the natal chart and in the current timing, and to organize and condense it into a concise session, while still allowing time for client questions and feedback.

There may be patterns and possible portents that you see that you may not think are appropriate for the discussion—sexual abuse, or upcoming transits that may be disastrous. You need to decide how to present this material, so that you do not infuse the client with a sense of shame, despair, or terror. If you look at a client's chart that has a difficult configuration—like Moon conjunct Saturn in Scorpio in the twelfth house receiving a Pluto transit—you may shudder and say to yourself, "Oh #*%!" But in the actual session, you have to take a deep breath and attempt to address the difficult signature in a manner that has some redeeming possibilities, while subtly conveying the cautions and warnings.

Should you give readings that are "all and only good and positive," or should you be honest about exactly what you see, no matter what it is? On one hand, clients in a state of malaise who come to you for guidance want to leave feeling somewhat healed, or at least with a perspective on or plan for what lies ahead that frames the possible difficult experiences within a larger context of growth toward their highest good. Some astrologers explicitly say that they discuss only positive things with their clients, because our thoughts create our reality. They do not want to set up a belief system in clients that predisposes their thinking toward manifesting the negative possibilities of the configuration in question. However, if you see clear indications for, let's say, major health problems, and don't inform clients to seek medical advice because you don't want to scare them or say anything bad, you end up being irresponsible. If your doctor doesn't tell you about the tumor that shows up on your x-ray because he doesn't want to encourage negative thinking and worry in you, is he doing you a favor? Of course, you should never predict a fatal health condition as inevitable; just guide your clients to appropriate follow up.

On the other hand, if a chart really depicts problematic themes and issues and a client has indeed had a difficult life, there will be a disconnect between the session content and his or her experience if you only give a glowing report of what is and what is possible. Clients may leave feeling even worse if your analysis of their charts leaves them with the sense that they have not actualized the best-case scenario of their chart indications set out by you as the picture of their life. Perhaps it is ultimately more compassionate to acknowledge the reality of the hardship of a client's life, and discuss just what may be possible within a limited range and what is not likely to occur.

This brings us to the very sensitive issue of how deep you can go into a client's psyche and still be respectful of boundaries. This will vary from person to person. You need to learn how to pick up cues from your clients' tone of voice, their demeanor, the kinds of information they give you, the kinds of questions they ask, and from their age and general background. Some clients are emotionally open—perhaps used to counseling and therapy sessions from other practitioners—and are desperate to understand something that has been the cause of much suffering. Here, you can go deep. But first, test the waters.

For example, if you suspect a client may have been subject to some kind of abuse as a child, ask if he or she is aware of any traumatic experiences in childhood in which circumstances conspired against expectations of being protected. Depending on the response, you can proceed farther or pull back. But never give a pronouncement on these kinds of topics as a definite statement of what is. If the client is not ready to accept or not capable of dealing with this kind of information, the results can be disastrous. It is irresponsible to stir up repressed emotional material in clients and then send them out the door with no resources by which they can process and integrate the implications of what has been surfaced.

Another way of handling this situation is to ask clients directly if they feel comfortable discussing this particular topic. If not, tell them that there are many other things in the chart to address. Again, take your lead from their responses. In this way, you allow clients to help you navigate around safe or unsafe waters. Sometimes, they may call back for another appointment to discuss something that they were simply not ready to acknowledge previously.

Are there certain topics that are taboo? For some people, yes, and for others, no. Sex, infidelity, abuse, bank-account figures, and religion are a few potentially dangerous subjects. You must learn to be a shrewd judge of what is permissible for each person. You must be willing to respect other peoples' values and sense of propriety. As an astrologer, your role is not to shock, badger, frighten, undermine, or liberate the client from a belief system and morality that you deem antiquated or ignorant. Always keep in mind that your clients are paying you to help them solve problems in a manner that does not destroy or challenge the world in which they live. When they leave your consulting room, they still have to go back to their lives. Certainly, suggestions for change, healing, and transformation are appropriate, but it is up to them to implement these suggestions in their own time and in their own way, and in a manner that is consistent with their own conscience and values.

So how do you, as an astrologer, decide what and how much you are going to say? How do you know what not to say or what you must reframe or spin? And finally, how do you make a quick assessment of your clients' level of emotional resilience, or how much truth they either want or can handle, without precipitating an eruption from the unconscious that you do not have the training to manage?

THE INITIAL INTERVIEW

In chapter 3, we discussed the importance of the initial interview, conducted in the first five minutes of the session. In this brief period, you must ask about your clients' previous astrological background, as this radically affects what you say to them. This puts you in touch with the level of simplicity or complexity with which you can frame the technical astrological terminology you use. For novices who are totally unfamiliar with the language of astrology, take the time to explain what you are doing in careful and straightforward terminology. Make sure that, by the time they leave the consultation session, you have discussed the basic meanings of the Sun, Moon, and Ascendant in a manner that they can grasp.

For example, I might say something like this to a first-time astrological client:

> We are now going to discuss your rising sign, which is also called the Ascendant. You may have heard both of these terms mentioned by your friends, and they refer to the same factor. The rising sign describes, first of all, your appearance, outer personality, and bearing. It is determined by the zodiacal sign that was rising, ascending, coming up over the eastern horizon at the exact moment of your birth and is calculated from the time of day that you were born. No matter what your Sun sign is, you can have any one of the twelve signs as your rising sign. The qualities of your personality as signified by your rising sign are . . .

Then I would elaborate about the factors connected to the Ascendant and its ruler.

However, for clients who have had annual readings for a number of years and are somewhat familiar with the language of astrology, even if they are not practitioners, the last thing you want to give is yet another rendition of the rising sign unless the Ascendant was receiving a major outer-planet transit at the time of the session. For these clients, quickly assess which parts of the chart they already understand and find out what they want to focus on for this session. Again, depending on how well these clients understand "astrologese," this will affect how much technical jargon you toss about and to what extent you explain it.

Finally, for clients conversant in the language—intermediate or advanced students, or even professionals—you can jump right in using technical shorthand and without any explanation of terms:

> Venus, in the twelfth house, debilitated in the sign of Virgo and square Mercury, its domicile lord, and ruling the second and ninth, will be receiving a transit from Jupiter over this next year, who happens to be your annual profected time lord beginning at the time of your Solar Return, and you may expect . . .

If you begin a reading like this for a first-time novice, the client will likely feel lost, confused, and frustrated.

You should pay attention to the speed and tempo of your clients' speech in this initial interview as well. Notice how long it takes them to process the information you give them. Try to match your rhythms to theirs for the most effective communication. Some clients have sharp quick minds and you can quickly deliver dense ideas in technical vocabulary. Others take in the meaning of words at a much slower rate. For them, slow down and pause frequently between phrases and concepts to allow them time to absorb the material.

As astrologers, we must remember the importance of putting the client first, and developing, using Rudhyar's terminology, a client-centered approach to consultations. The purpose of your sessions is not for you to show off how much knowledge you have and how accurately you can "nail a chart." Your purpose is to put the needs of your clients first, and to talk to them on a level they can understand—one that is neither too simplistic for the advanced client nor too sophisticated for the novice. My editor has repeatedly admonished me to identify my audience when writing. At first, this was a continual source of irritation to me. I wanted to say what I had to say just as it came flowing from my mind. I soon realized the wisdom of this advice, however. I realized that, even if I set down a profound exposition, if it wasn't intelligible to the audience for whom it was intended, there was no ultimate benefit for anyone. So identify your audience. Each time you encounter a new client, ask him or her point blank: What is the level of your previous astrological background? Then shape the manner in which you present the information accordingly.

As an astrologer, you need to know why your clients have come to you and what concerns they have in their lives about which they want insight and reflection. Some people see astrologers on a regular basis for their "yearly updates," and do not have any specific questions. It is of value to them to obtain a sense of the "weather" in store for them in the year ahead—they want clues about opportunities they may have or obstacles they may encounter. For repeat clients, ask them about what has occurred since you last spoke. For the many who come to you because some kind of crisis, change, or decision is before them about which they need insight and guidance, listen carefully and make a few notes to yourself about their expectations for the sessions and the questions they are bringing you. Then make sure that you address those situations.

If the client is inquiring about practical matters and outer events like a move or a job change, focus the session there. This kind of reading occurs at a very different level of intimacy than one that attempts to unravel sexual problems within a relationship. But, beyond your clients' specific questions, this initial interview informs you of whether they want a practical, psychological, or spiritual perspective from you in this particular session. An effective astrological counselor speaks to clients in a language, manner, level, and orientation that brings the greatest ease of understanding and focuses upon each client's stated concerns, whatever they happen to be.

Furthermore, the manner in which your clients describe themselves and the nature of their concerns tell you much about how deep you may penetrate into their psyches and still remain respectful of their boundaries. If they ask you to discuss their blockages in sexuality and you see indications of early sexual abuse, it may be permissible to bring that up. However, keep checking in with the client and know when to stop a particular line of discussion. Above all, remember that, while you are an astrologer and have the intention to be a healer, you are not a psychotherapist unless you have been formally trained as one. There are many situations where what is called for is a referral to another professional, and you should keep a list of these resources. It does not mean that you are an inadequate astrologer if you send a client to a specialist who has more expertise in the particular situations that face the client.

Again, many people will come to you because they have a blatant or gnawing problem, or a sense of malaise or confusion. Most often, this indicates some kind of major outer-planet transit that is triggering the chart and precipitating a crisis. Sometimes, one of the most reassuring things that you can tell them is:

> Given these transits, if you are having a meltdown, you are right on schedule with the unfoldment of your birth potential. If everything were fine in your life, then you would really have a problem.

What we are really addressing here is the need to establish rapport with your clients in the first few minutes of the session so they feel you have actually heard them, understand what is going on, and are sympathetic. For many people, opening their soul to a stranger and admitting their failings and shortcomings requires a huge leap of trust. As an astrologer, you also are up against the cultural bias that fortune-tellers take advantage of people's vulnerabilities. So, for your readings to be effective, your clients must feel they can trust you. You can reassure them of your trustworthiness by being completely present with them.

This involves listening carefully, asking probing questions, seeking greater clarification of their situation, and restating their concerns so that they know you understand what they conveyed. Then, you must mirror back to them that you are aware of the distress that they may be feeling, that there is something objective in the chart that indicates what is occurring, and that, however painful it may be, it is part of a larger process of timing that ultimately can bring them toward the next phase of their development as a realized being. If you are working within a one-hour session, all this must transpire within seven to ten minutes maximum from the moment the reading begins.

Based on what transpires in this initial interview, you will have a sense of what your clients' desires and expectations are for the reading, as well as their own relative degree of involvement in the process. There is a wide range of client styles and, as an astrologer, you need to adapt yourself to the various positions your clients will present. Here are some of the types of clients you may encounter:

- Some clients want the facts, the bottom line, whether it's good or bad news. That's what they are paying for. No psychological analysis, thank you.
- Some clients want you to reassure them that, no matter what is going on, everything will work out all right in the end.
- Some clients want you to see into their souls and validate them and tell them they are on the right path.
- Some clients are more interested in the "why" of what is occurring or in when to expect the event and when it will be over.
- Some clients want to be given options from which they can make up their own minds; some want precise directives as to what to do.
- Some clients want you to do all the talking; some want an interactive dialogue; some want to do all the talking and simply have you listen.
- Some clients are willing to disclose personal information; some are zipped-mouthed and want to see how much you can "get" on your own.
- Some clients come because it is a choice they themselves have made; some may have been pressured, forced, or gifted by a friend, partner, or family member, and thus may be skeptical and resistant.

WHO HAS THE ANSWERS?

One of the dangers of being an astrological counselor is an overweening pride that arises from the assumption that you know all the answers—that your clients are ignorant and should be the passive recipients of your wisdom. Both you and your clients can be complicit in fostering this situation, in which you can be terrified that your clients will discover that you may not know how to interpret some factor in their chart. This can cause you to assume a false bravado as to your competence. In other instances, your clients, in their confusion and fear, may project the archetype of savior onto you—and you may accept it.

The first thing you must admit is that you don't know everything, and that there may be parts of the chart that will evade your best attempts at interpretation. But even more than that, you must consider the possibility that your delineation of a client's chart may not be accurate. When clients cannot relate to what you are telling them about themselves, who is right? You or the client? Before you panic, double check to make sure you have used the correct birth data to calculate the chart. Ask your client to verify it. Then ask the client just where this information comes from—a birth certificate, or the parents' memory, or something they just always thought was true? If you think that the birth time is suspect, that error can affect the accuracy of the reading.

If the birth time is accurate and your client still cannot relate to your reading, don't jump to the conclusion that the client is in denial and ignore the possibility that your own powers of penetrating insight may be off the mark. Occasionally, denial is the case, but most often it is not. At this point, pause, come down a few notches, and try to work with the client to understand just what some factor signifies. We know that each symbol carries a range of significations and that there is an almost infinite variety of combinations that produce different results. You must respect your clients' feedback, because they know their own charts better than you do, since they reflect their own lives. In fact, your clients are your best source of education, because they provide immediate verification of a living chart in the moment. You do not lose stature when you are willing to interact with your clients to arrive at an interpretation that is meaningful to their lives.

Periodically, in the course of the reading, check in with your client to ensure that what is being said makes sense and is relevant to the life circumstances. To particularly reticent clients, I may say: I am speaking in general principles, hoping that they will trigger the specific circumstances in your mind. I do not need to know the details, as long as I know that I am on the right track. If they indicate that this is the case, then I proceed.

Another technique to diffuse the aura of "astrologer as God" is the art of skillful questioning, whereby you carefully lead clients to making the realization on their own. If, for example, you see the ruler of the third afflicted and in a harsh aspect to the ruler of the eighth, instead of telling your clients that a sibling is cheating them out of their inheritance, you can instead ask if there are problems in a sibling relationship that center around shared resources. In this way, you stimulate your clients to draw the conclusions themselves—conclusions that may be too intrusive or offensive to be made by you.

RECOGNIZING YOUR BIASES

No matter how much you try to put aside your own personal problems before a reading, everything you say to your clients cannot help but be filtered through your own personal orientation. The slant that you give to all your interpretations will be affected by your own values, conditioning, beliefs, and experiences. Therefore, it is incumbent on you to follow the maxim inscribed on the temple of the Delphic Oracle: Know thyself.

You must recognize your own biases and wounds, and how they affect what you say to your clients. If you were abused by your father, are you automatically suspect and unforgiving of your clients' relationships with their own fathers? If you had an abortion and later regretted it, does that predispose you to advise your clients against abortions, regardless of their own circumstances?

In this same vein, be vigilant about how your politics, your religion or lack thereof, your sexual orientation, or your morality may color how you discuss these issues with others or guide them in problem-solving. Can you be respectful of others' beliefs, even if they conflict with your own? If a woman client faced with a Pluto transit to a relationship point feels absolutely committed to a difficult marriage because of spiritual vows she took before God and you are an atheist, can you support her decision to stay and try to find some solution? Can you avoid being impatient or dismissive of her stance? If you are a staunch believer in marital fidelity, and especially if you have been betrayed by a partner, and your client has a varie-gated sexual life, can you be non-judgmental and hold the client with compassion?

This process of self-examination is very difficult. Astrologers who have psychological training often advise students to go through some kind of analysis or therapy so they can at least be conscious of the areas where their own blockages may affect the ways in which they guide others. How much personal work you have done, what kind of astrology you do, what kind of clients you attract, and how deep you go with them will determine how you should proceed fol-lowing another classical maxim: Physician, heal thyself.

Finally, what is your position on the fate/free-will issue? You must find a place on this continuum where you feel comfortable and be able give a good rationale for your stance. Sooner or later, a client will ask you: Do you think that the chart says that this situation is definitely going to happen in this particular way, or do you think that it is up to me how it will turn out? If the chart is an accurate depiction of a person's character and destiny, to what extent can choice and chance and therapy alter what has been ordained by the stars, and still have astrology work? How much freedom do individu-als actually have to fashion the course of their lives? Are there limits as to what is possible or probable, as determined by the planetary conditions?

The manner in which you answer these questions for yourself will affect the way in which you present the information to your clients. The more you pride yourself on accurate predictions, the less free will you afford your clients. Some astrologers who believe strongly in free will do not do predictive work at all, but rather use the chart as a springboard for discussing the client's issues without pronouncing any judgment. Other astrologers believe that astrology's capacity to predict is its greatest asset and benefit. This is a question that has yet to be resolved in 4000 years of astrological practice, and each and every practitioner of the art is forced to enter into the discussion. You can't avoid it. Furthermore, in your career as an astrologer, your views are likely to oscillate and change.

Setting Boundaries

There are a number of situations in which it is important to set boundaries with your clients. In some cases, you may even need to contain certain clients. You have to decide whether you will maintain firm boundaries or loose ones, and when you can be flexible and to what extent. Having no boundaries at all will encourage your clients to make your life crazy and unmanageable. Here are some of the situations you may face and on which you should take a position.

When you first discuss your services with a client, you indicate the length of the session. How do you respond if, when that time has elapsed, you have not covered what you wanted to or what the client requested? And what do you do if clients are so excited about what you are saying that they want more time? Do you continue, and do you charge for the additional time? How do you handle clients who won't hang up the phone or leave when the session is over, because they are trying to extract every last drop of essence from your brain? What do you do if they attempt to prolong their session by crying or having an emotional breakdown? What if they call back a few hours later with another slew of questions, or want you to clarify and repeat what you said earlier?

And speaking of payment, do you insist on receiving payment before the session? Or are you willing to trust that the client will send payment? And what if they want their money back or refuse to send payment because they are not satisfied with your reading?

Will you see clients only by pre-arranged appointment or will you make yourself available whenever they happen to call? If your best time for doing readings is in the mornings, will you allow clients to push you for an evening appointment because it is more convenient for them? If you reserve weekends for your own rejuvenation or family time, will you let pushy clients convince you to schedule a weekend session? If your client quota is filled for the day or the week, do you allow insistent clients to squeeze themselves in? How hungry are you for the money and does it affect your own well-being?

What do you do when a client does not allow you to direct the session and keep your focus, but instead constantly interrupts you,

asks irrelevant questions that take you off track, or disputes what you
say based on what another astrologer, psychic, or tarot reader said?
How do you respond when clients are more interested in hearing
themselves talk than in listening to you?

Suppose a client suddenly wants you to run the chart of a partner, child, boss, or parent, and compare it to his or her own or reveal
what is going on in that chart. Do you do it? Or do you say that you
agreed to read your client's chart, and that this entails another session? Do you say the client must ask permission of the other person
before you will work with that secondary chart?

Are you willing to do "blind readings," in which clients send
birth data and a check, and you prepare a cassette tape or written
interpretation, never having had any personal contact? If you have
discovered that this is not your forte, do you allow some clients to
talk you into doing it nevertheless?

How strict are you in maintaining client confidentiality? Do you
take clients who are in adversarial relationships with one another,
and if so, how do you use the information to which you are privy?
Do you discuss a difficult session with your best friend or partner,
because you need to process or vent or have a supply of amusing
conversation?

What happens when you run into one of your clients in some
kind of social situation or on the street? If the client is with someone
else, do you allude to your professional interaction? What if clients
see you and immediately launch into their charts, wanting to know
what is going on? What if they feel embarrassed, having bared their
souls to you, and now regret the exposure and want to avoid you?
How do you keep what happens in the consulting room in the consulting room, and not allow it to spill out and over into ordinary
life?

These are some of the many issues that arise in the life of an
astrological counselor. Each one of us deals with them differently,
depending on our own personalities and styles. You must examine
these situations carefully from your own personal perspective, and
think about the response that is best for you and why. If you encounter a difficult situation in which you are struggling to come up with
the right response, consult an experienced mental-health practitio-

ner or another practicing astrologer to help you deal with the issue. You do not have to solve these problems by yourself. Good therapists always have other therapists supervise them when needed.

Being clear on what is comfortable and acceptable for your own behavior affects how you interact with your clients. Individuals come into your consulting room seeking clarity, guidance, and healing. It is of the utmost importance that you see them as real living people and not just astrological symbols on a piece of paper. Make a genuine connection with your clients and, to the extent that they allow you, move past their physical appearance and engage with their person- alities; dip into their psyches and touch their souls if you are able. In order to illuminate the authentic self within each of your clients, you, as an astrologer, must be authentic in how you present yourself to them. And part of that authenticity entails being clear on your boundaries.

Bringing Closure to the Session

As you proceed through your consultation, stay aware of how much time has elapsed and how much remains. You have a general plan of what you want to cover, and, depending on the available time, you will condense or elaborate upon the material. Try to be about 95-percent complete by ten minutes before the session is over. At that point, pause and ask clients if they feel you have satisfactorily addressed their concerns and if they have any questions—either on what has been covered already or about anything else. Then, use the remaining time either to respond to their final queries or to men- tion some last details that are of secondary importance. Many clients appreciate a summary of the main points you have discussed. Try to end on a positive note so clients leave feeling inspired and hopeful, even if a difficult situation has emerged in the course of the consulta- tion.

Two minutes before the end of the session, tell clients you are coming to the end of their time. Finalize any issues about payment, confirm the correct address, and wish them the best. Have your schedule book available in the event that they want to make another appointment at this time.

What do you do if a client does not want to terminate the conversation or leave your office? Occasionally, you can go overtime ten to fifteen minutes if you feel that essential information or processing needs to occur. But generally, you should be firm. I often say I have another client waiting or that I have a medical appointment I have to keep.

Clients may ask if you feel you have covered all the important points in the chart or if there is more that you can say. This is how I respond:

> I could talk ten to twelve hours about your chart, but in my experience most people cannot take in anything more after one hour and fifteen minutes. However, I have covered what I think is most important for you at this time. If you are interested in discussing the finer points of your chart or going into more detail about anything, you are welcome to make another appointment after you have listened to the recording of this session and integrated what we have spoken about today. I do have some clients with whom I work in an ongoing manner, and many people schedule yearly updates.

At this point, clients can choose whether or not to schedule another session. This same general procedure applies to those who call back a few hours later with questions about their reading. However, you should be careful not to encourage unnecessary sessions so that you can build up your practice or foster in your clients a state of dependency in which they feel fearful and powerless to take any action without first consulting you.

After a client departs, blow out your candle and give silent thanks for the inspiration and guidance you have received. Wash your hands under cold running water to clear your psyche. Remember that you are a channel for divine inspiration and not a psychic sponge. You can be present in the moment with your clients' lives, but you should not take their situations into yourself and hold onto their difficulties. The ancient priestesses always bathed in the sacred springs in order to renew their virginity and be cleansed and purified for the next ritual encounter.

Study Guidelines

- Look over the various questions posed in this chapter concerning client styles, personal biases, and setting boundaries. Think about how you would answer them for yourself or handle such situations should they arise.
- If one of these challenging situations has already occurred in your practice and left you unnerved, describe what happened, what you did, and how you could handle it differently if you had the opportunity to do it over.
- Consult with another astrologer or counselor to share your concerns with someone who can understand the situation and give you reflection and feedback.

CHAPTER FIFTEEN

THE HEALING POWER OF MYTH
TO ADDRESS SUFFERING

In the process of giving readings for clients, you will inevitably see certain themes suggested in the birth chart that point to very sensitive issues that are difficult to discuss directly. They may refer to material that is sensitive, embarrassing, painful, shameful, hidden, or socially unacceptable—sexual violation, spousal abuse, or same-sex preference. Clients may not feel comfortable discussing these matters or may react with mortification at the implication that they had such an experience or have such an issue. They may feel as if their carefully guarded privacy has been violated and exposed. Yet, as an astrologer, you may suspect that this motif is central to their experience of who they essentially are, or to the suffering that permeates their lives. How do you address the elephant that is standing in the middle of the room?

The frank articulation of such issues is rarely appropriate, unless you have ascertained beforehand that the client is open and willing to discuss these topics. One effective way to speak to subjects that no one wants to acknowledge is to talk about them as universal stories as told in the myths that are common to many people. You can test the waters by recounting stories like Pluto's rape of Persephone, or Jupiter's spousal abuse of Juno, or Sappho's love for her female students. Then provide a space in which clients can offer information that reveals whether the story mirrors any of their personal experiences. In this way, you allow the client to lead the way or block the way into what some may consider taboo subjects beyond the scope of an astrological session. The telling of mythological stories can be a path by which to enter this hidden terrain of the psyche and initiate a process of understanding, acceptance, and healing.

The first portion of this book emphasizes a logical and analytical approach to chart delineation that can help you discern where problems may lie. In this chapter, we'll consider a more imaginal, psychological, and archetypal orientation to accessing the deeper meaning of the astrological symbols to facilitate healing.

Before we go more deeply into the use of myth as a healing modality in astrological counseling, let's digress briefly into a discussion of the theory behind the interpretation of myth and archetypal psychology. For those who question the validity of mythology associated with planetary bodies as a basis for astrological interpretation, and for those intrigued by the possibilities inherent in the union of mythology and astrology, I offer a rationale for a mythic approach to chart interpretation.

MYTH IN ARCHETYPAL PSYCHOLOGY AND ASTROLOGY

The corpus of mythology is comprised of the lives, deeds, and relationships of the various gods and goddesses of a culture. People in both ancient and modern times believed that either one or many deities were responsible for the generation and dominion of the world. The gods were worshipped in ritual ceremonies and invoked to avert troubles and to grant blessings.

Theoretical explanations of the nature of myths fall into two broad categories—external theories and internal theories. In the first, myths are interpreted as the recording and oral transmission of beliefs and history, an attempt to explain natural phenomena, or justifications for religious, social, or political institutions. In the second, myths are seen as the spontaneous expressions of the human psyche.[1] This is the understanding of myth that we will investigate in this chapter.

The psychological view that myths are projections of the structures of the human psyche is most useful for astrologers. Carl Jung called myths "the great dreams of humanity" and the "archetypes of the collective unconscious." He posited a human psyche that operates on two levels. The personal level derives from the experiences of our own biographical history. The collective level contains innate structures of the mind that, like the physical structures of the body, are common to all human beings and present from birth. This collective level is part of the unconscious and is composed of archetypes that are the universal primordial patterns representing the typical experiences of humankind. The contents of the archetypes are revealed in religion, the arts, creativity, dreams, visions, and myths.

In a cross-cultural comparison of mythologies, it becomes apparent that, while the gods and goddesses have different names and appearances, the pantheons of various cultures are generally comprised of the same archetypal figures. For example, Sumerian Inanna, Babylonian Ishtar, Phoenician Astarte, Greek Aphrodite, Egyptian Hathor, and Roman Venus are all identified as goddesses of love, beauty, and desire. This similarity suggests that mythic deities may be none other than the outer symbolic projections of the inner structures of the psyche that are common to most cultures. The myths, as projections of the unconscious psyche, contain the images and experiences through which we grasp the underlying reality of the human condition. Myths are not simply tales of happenings in the remote past, but eternal dramas that live themselves out repeatedly in our own personal lives and in what we see all around us.[2]

Jung gives an archetypal interpretation of psychology, suggesting that Olympian gods of old are now understood as various forms of neuroses.[3] Archetypes as living psychic forces demand to be taken seriously; when they are neglected, they become the unfailing causes of neurotic and psychotic disorders.[4] Murray Stein explains that the unconscious psychological contents that once created images of gods and mythic events have not disappeared with the waning of religious belief, but continue to affect human consciousness, revealing themselves in diseases and symptoms. Insight and therapy can be greatly enhanced by knowing the correspondences between mythic patterns and psychopathological symptoms.[5]

In fact, this perspective was also known to the Greeks. The earliest literature of Homer alludes to the divine causation of disease; illness and misfortune were sent by the gods as punishment for those who failed to honor them. Cure of the disease involved a pilgrim-

age to a cult site of the offended god, offerings at the temple, and
perhaps initiation into divine rites. Archetypal therapy recommends
a similar treatment, advising that the cure for psychological symptoms includes discovering which archetype (god) has been neglected
and then honoring it.[6] The symptoms are seen as messages from the
psyche indicating what the individual needs to do for greater psychological integration and healing. The modern word "therapy" is
derived from the Greek *therapeia*, which means "attendance upon
the gods."

In the astrological pantheon, the planets, asteroids, fixed stars,
constellations, and *nakshatras* all carry the names of deities. In the
cosmology of the Babylonians, and later the Greeks, the celestial
bodies were perceived as the visible manifestations of the divine
gods. This was the basis for the earliest proto-astrology in Mesopotamia over 4000 years ago, in which the appearance of a planet was an
omen heralding the presence of a god displaying its will to humanity. For example, a celestial omen from the first millennium B.C.E.
tells us: "When Ishtar stands on high, lovemaking on the land." The
planet we know as Venus was identified as the embodiment of Ishtar,
the goddess of love, and each of the other visible planets was likewise understood as a god. Thus, an intimate and explicit connection
between planets, gods, and human experience underwrites the very
foundation of astrology.

When the Greeks encountered the astronomy of the Babylonians
in the sixth century B.C.E., the Pythagoreans gave the names of the
Greek gods who most closely resembled their Babylonian counterparts to the planets—the planet called Ishtar was renamed the star
of Aphrodite; the planet Nebu, scribe of the gods, became the star
of Hermes for the Greeks and Mercurius for the Romans. The attributes associated with each deity became part of the significations
assigned by astrologers to the planet bearing its name.

Greek philosophers pondering cosmology put forth a number of
ideas that later provided a philosophical foundation for the validity
of astrology. The relationship between macrocosm and microcosm
and the notion of cosmic sympathy led to speculation that the planets might be the visible appearances of the gods, or that they might
signify the qualities of the soul or point to the concrete manifes-

tations of divine principles. Hermetic astrological texts are precise about the direct correlation between the planets and zodiacal signs to the parts of the human body, where the human being is a reflection of the structure of the cosmos.

In offering a rationale for the use of myth as a basis for astrological interpretation, we can say that myths are a culture's stories of the lives and deeds of its gods; archetypes are certain primordial structures in the psyche that are common to all human beings. Myths are one of the contents of the archetypes and, as such, they are the symbolic projections of the internal structures of the psyche. They describe the universal and timeless patterns of human experience that underlie and inform the expression of each individual's life. Astrology was based on the notion that the planets were one of the manifestations of the gods, and their appearances in the sky indicated the presence and influence of that god in earthly affairs. The attributes of the gods, as derived from their myths, became part of the significations of the planets, and the ancient gods are now understood to reveal themselves in the modern psyche as diseases and symptoms caused by the neglect of a particular archetype/god. Healing entails embracing and honoring a neglected part of the self.

Thus, if the nature of a celestial body has a chain of correspondences that manifest in the terrestrial and human realms, the mythological story associated with the planetary deity likewise shapes the life experiences of human beings. The birth chart, which depicts the placement of the celestial bodies in the sky at the moment of a person's birth, can be used as a map to identify which planetary bodies are most prominent. And the mythological motifs associated with those planets become the major themes that influence a person's life. Myths, as the archetypal expressions of the psyche, represent the basic dramas or scripts through which we live out the meaning of our lives and recognize our paths and purpose.

In ancient cultures, myths were not read, but recited aloud by story-tellers. Likewise, in the mythic approach to chart interpretation, it is the telling of the stories that initiates the process of internal recognition in the client. Through hearing the story, what may previously have been seen as unrelated incidents in the life are perceived as part of a larger story infused with an integrated theme. Furthermore, these stories, although experienced as personal, are also understood as archetypal, signifying universal patterns that others have experienced and endured. Once you begin to recite the mythic biography of a god or goddess whose planetary namesake occupies a prominent placement in a client's birth chart, you become a channel of expression for the power of the story and its timeless wisdom. You and your client discover that the ancient stories of the mythic deities are ever-present, and live on in the hearts and souls of us all.

In the analytical approach to chart interpretation, you relied on astrological techniques. In the mythic approach, it is the story itself that constellates a healing in the client. The sign, house, and aspects of the planetary bodies give specific details of how the story plays out, in much the same way that each theatre group that enacts a play has different costumes, sets, and props, but still delivers the same core features of the drama. In my experience, the details of sign, house, and aspect are almost insignificant compared to the power of the story itself, which, stripped bare of astrological considerations, can convey the essential meaning and trials of the human condition.

The mythic approach to chart interpretation entails knowing the myths and knowing which deities have natural relationships with one another from their mythic biographies. The inclusion of the asteroids, thousands of which are named after deities from various cultures, expands the mythic pantheon on which you can draw for meaning. You can also use this approach to discuss the fixed-star constellations that carry the names of gods and heroes—like Perseus and Hercules, or the *nakshatras* in Vedic astrology that are named after Hindu deities. The reading can become primarily a telling of stories—stories that you choose based on the prominence of that celestial body at the birth moment. When clients hear their own personal stories, they experience a sense of internal integration and self-acceptance.

USING MYTH IN COUNSELING

Now let's look at a few examples of this approach. If a client has Juno prominent in the chart, perhaps configured with Pluto or Mars, suggesting a theme of power struggles, obsession, or potentially violent conflict within relationships, be sure to mention how Juno was continually betrayed and humiliated by her husband Jupiter's many infidelities. When telling the story of Juno, include the fact that, when she protested her subjugation and domination, her husband hung her upside down from the heavens with her wrists weighted with heavy golden bracelets. You can also recount how Juno valued the honoring of her marriage vows and repeatedly tried to reconcile with Jupiter in hope that the marriage would work. To the extent that your client sees a parallel between this story and his or her own life and offers that information, you can begin to explore that issue in more detail. This is a more subtle and compassionate way to address the potential of these themes in a client's chart, rather than asking point blank: Your mate is unfaithful and abusive so why do you remain in this marriage? Or perhaps, even worse, ignoring altogether a core issue in a client's life that he or she may be too ashamed to mention.

Same-sex preference is another taboo subject. This is slowly becoming more openly acknowledged, but, for many, continues to be a difficult thing to admit for fear of being ostracized by society. The asteroid Sappho, when prominent in the chart or conjoined to Venus, the ruler of the seventh house, or to Juno may be a story that can open up the gay/lesbian conversation. Sappho was a historical personage, born on the island of Lesbos in the sixth century B.C.E. Famed as a poet, she was called the tenth muse by Plato. Sappho composed lyric love poetry detailing the emotional terrain of intimacy. Many of her poems were dedicated to Aphrodite and addressed to her female students. After giving the biographical details of her life, you can say that Sappho in the birth chart indicates an aptitude for poetry, the education of women, especially in the fine arts, extreme sensitivity regarding affairs of the heart and sexuality, or a strong emotional or physical connection with members of the same sex. Sappho does not always indicate a client is gay or lesbian. By giving choices as to her signification in a particular chart, you leave it open to your clients to locate and discuss how they may or may not experience this archetype in their lives.

Because Ceres was such an important goddess in the Greek pantheon and religious life, her story embraces many different themes that are actually connected by means of the story. Ceres, as we saw in chapter 9, can have powerful implications for a chart. One of my clients has Ceres conjunct her Capricorn Ascendant. As a young woman, divorced with a child, she and her current partner set out across the country to search for a new home. En route, the child suddenly died in a freak accident. As her partner was unable to father children, she was faced with remaining childless. After years of grief and depression, they arranged for the private adoption of a child rejected by his alcoholic mother. The client was intensely devoted to gardening and preparing nutritious meals. This led to the creation of a home-based organic bakery business. She went to school for nutritional counseling and discovered that most of her clients had eating disorders from an inability to take or keep nourishment, and that most of them had developed these illnesses after having been sexually abused as children. She continued her education in therapy, and now works with sexually abused children trying to heal these wounds and prevent the wounds from destroying their adult lives. I am waiting to see if, near the end of her life, she becomes involved in hospice work and facilitates conscious dying.

This case history illustrates how the major themes in the client's life correspond to the mythic biography of Ceres, which included growing food, the loss of a child, the fostering of another child, working with clients for whom withholding of food is an act of power, and counseling the trauma of children abducted into underworld experiences. Without a mythic perspective, however, the client may not be able to identify the connection that unifies all of these life circumstances and events into a larger picture. Once clients recognize them as related, they can acknowledge that their individual lives are unfolding in conformity with a universal motif, and this can lead to a transpersonal understanding of their place in the larger whole.

Myth provides the integrated image that connects all individual thematic threads. There is some comfort to clients in the realization that many other people have also experienced the particular pathos that they thought was their own personal cross to bear. This allows them to accept the circumstances of their life predicament more fully, in the realization that the broad outline of their lives is one of the templates that arise from within the collective psyche. These archetypal templates, envisioned through myths, are the very means by which we can follow the paths that guide us to live life with a sense of meaning and purpose. It is at this instant that astrology becomes a therapeutic modality.

An archetypal approach to the healing of the psyche enables you to help clients identify malaise as a psychosomatic response to a part of themselves, as symbolized by the planetary deity that has been neglected. Chronic depression may be the symptom of an individual who has a prominent Ceres and who has suffered the loss of parents or children. Finding a way to express the fundamental need to nurture another being—fostering an abandoned child, caring for a pet, or growing a garden to feed others—may be various means by which the neglected Ceres archetypal energy is actively integrated back into the life. The motif of nurturing is expressed in the archetype of Ceres' daughter as well. Eating disorders are often the symptoms of women who have been molested as children. As for Persephone herself, who refused to eat during her time of captivity when she felt powerless and victimized, the withholding of food with which to nourish the self appears to be an avenue of maintaining some kind of control in the life. Eating disorders thus tend to be the bodily expression of the ongoing terror of the Persephone child, who needs the reassurance of feeling safe and protected.

When you encounter Persephone as the prominent archetype, tell the story of the abduction from the child's point of view. Focus on the scene in the story where Persephone is left behind briefly by her mother, told to play with the other maiden nymphs picking flowers in the fields, but to stay away from the narcissus flower, known to symbolize sexual awakening. Irresistibly drawn to the intoxicating fragrance of the flower, Persephone precipitates the rest of her archetypal story. Her appearance as a prominent archetype thus often indicates some kind of early childhood trauma. The child has an expectation of being watched over by the mother, but for some unexpected reason is plunged into an underworld experience where it encounters loss, terror, confusion, and feelings of abandonment. This can be due to factors such as the death of the parents, divorce or illness in the family, a physical accident, or abuse. The child often survives by disassociating and retreating into some kind of fantasy world. As an adult, he or she remains frozen at the age of the emotional trauma and spends much time living in some kind of internal alternate reality. This is also the Persephone child's earliest initiation into the spirit world. A sense of victimization overshadows the life, with feelings of being powerless to control the outer circumstances of a harsh world.

Let's take another example. A woman has a configuration in her chart consisting of the Sun, Moon, and Ceres conjoined to the asteroids Persephone and Nyctimene, all within a 5-degree range located in the fifth house. Persephone is located within 1 degree of the Sun. In mythology, Nyctimene, a daughter of the King of Lesbos, is seduced by her father. Out of shame, she hides herself in the forest, and is later changed into an owl (a bird that comes out only at night) by Athena. Putting these two myths together, you can surmise that this woman was sexually abused by her father and is still reeling from the trauma. In fact, this was exactly the case. The first time I saw this client, I simply related the stories, without stating the conclusion. The client remained silent and did not offer any commentary, and so I went on to other factors in the chart. The following week, she called and told me that she was not ready at the time of the first reading to acknowledge that pivotal episode in her life, but that now she wanted to do a follow-up and explore the symbolism in greater depth. In ensuing years of psychological counseling, she has seen how the turbulent emotions generated by this act of violence have fueled the creative output of her artistic and musical compositions. This corresponds to the planets' presence in the fifth house of artistic creativity.

A male client has the asteroid Persephone conjoined to his Sun. As a seven-year-old child, he discovered his mother's suicide by hanging and was told by a distraught relative that his mother had killed herself because he was such a naughty boy. From the age of eleven, he anesthetized his pain and shame by drinking alcohol every day. For him, just being able to get up every day and go to work was a victory. Some Persephone children remain trapped in the underworld due to the severity of the wounding.

In some cases, the telling of the myth gives clients another broader and more inclusive perspective with which to better understand their lives. In other cases, this is not enough. The myth, combined with the astrology, can point the way toward the healing of the psyche, and offer clues for the alchemical transformation of lead into gold. In other words, the next step in the healing process can involve a discussion of how the experience of the pain and suffering can lead a person to a state of greater wisdom and positive purposeful action. It is often in the process of helping others that we can alleviate our own suffering. This leads us into a deeper exploration of the wounded-healer archetype, and the astrological indications as to whether this is a central motif in the life. It is important for clients to acknowledge difficult life experiences, and to attempt to put them into a perspective that gives some kind of redeeming meaning.

THE ARCHETYPE OF THE WOUNDED HEALER

An analytical approach to astrology acknowledges the likelihood that certain events in clients' lives will be problematic, bringing illness, poverty, misfortune, failure, loss, or pain. Unfortunately, the chart does not tell you why these bad things happen to seemingly good people. You will have clients, however, who will ask you what they have done to deserve such suffering, or why God has punished them so. The pat response, and not an incorrect one, is that astrology itself cannot provide this kind of answer. And yet, as a counseling astrologer, you must learn to deal with and acknowledge the pervasive condition of human suffering.

If you subscribe to the Eastern doctrine of karma and reincarnation, you may think that current misfortunes are the result of harmful actions from past lives, but that train of thought is generally not helpful in the immediacy of a client's predicament. Or if you approach the situation from a Christian perspective, you can fall back on the saying that God works in mysterious ways and who are we to know God's will for us. While both of these statements may be true in their own context, your client is still left with abstract explanations and the distant possibility that things may be better in the next life or in eternal life after death if he or she does good deeds now or has more faith. How can the insights of both of these spiritual approaches be made more concrete within an astrological context that has severed itself from its religious origins?

The archetype of the wounded healer offers a way to discuss how painful experiences can sometimes be a training ground for the knowledge and compassion required to assist others in similar situations. It may also be the case that this activity leads us toward our destiny. Two mythic figures that speak to this situation are Persephone and the centaur Chiron. The wounded-healer motif can also be suggested by the location of planets in the twelfth house.

Chiron is a celestial body—most likely a comet that arrived from outside our solar system—that revolves around the Sun. It does not travel in the asteroid belt, but rather between the orbits of Saturn and Uranus. It was photographed on October 31, 1977, on All Hallows Eve, and recognized as a new body the following morning on All Souls Day, November 1. According to folklore, on that eve the veil between the worlds is most transparent, allowing the easy passage of spirits from the realm of the dead into that of the living. Chiron was named after the mythological centaur from the Mount Pelion area who was half man and half horse. He was conceived through an illicit union between his father, Saturn, disguising himself as a stallion, and an unsuspecting nymph, Philyra. When his mother saw the monstrosity she had borne, she immediately cast him aside. Chiron's first wound was abandonment by the mother and denial by the father. He was found and fostered by Apollo and Artemis.

Unlike the other centaurs, who were boisterous and rowdy drunkards, half-immortal Chiron was famed for his wisdom and kindness. In a cave beneath the summit of Mount Pelion, the parentless child in his adulthood became a foster parent to many Greek youths, raising them and educating them in whatever they needed to fulfill their heroic destinies. Among his students were Jason, Achilles, and Actaeon. Chiron was noted for his knowledge of medicine, which he taught to the divine physician Asclepius, including instruction in the use of many medicinal herbs that grew profusely in the Pelion area.

Some say that Chiron was king of the centaurs, who, in a prolonged battle with their hereditary enemies the Lapiths, were driven to take refuge on Mount Malea in the southern Peloponnese. On their way, they encountered Heracles in a skirmish, and Chiron was wounded in the thigh, knee, or ankle by a poisoned arrow dipped in the blood of the Hydra. Chiron's wound was fatal, but because he was partly immortal, he could not die and so was doomed to a life of eternal suffering. Chiron eventually became aware of the plight of the Titan Prometheus, who was punished for giving the fire of the gods to humankind by being bound to the highest crag in the Caucasus Mountains, where an eagle devoured his liver daily. Prometheus could be released only if some other immortal took his place in the underworld. So Chiron, founder of the art of healing who himself had a wound he could not heal, went into the underworld, taking upon himself the suffering and death of Prometheus so that a benefactor of mankind could be liberated. Zeus later transformed Chiron into the Centaur constellation in honor of his service.

Chiron symbolizes the quintessential shamanic healer. What distinguishes a shaman from any other kind of healer is that the shaman is always wounded first. It is the descent into the pain and suffering of the wound that leads the shaman to an encounter with the spirit realm where wisdom and insight are received. The destiny of the shaman is to be of service to his or her community, bringing back messages from the spirit world about the healing of the body and soul. The credentials of the chironic healer are those of direct real-life experience, as opposed to the theoretical knowledge gained in books and classrooms. Concurrent with Chiron's discovery in 1977 was the emergence of many twelve-step recovery programs, in which those who have suffered trauma or addiction facilitate the healing of others in similar predicaments. In Chiron's world, the wound is never completely healed and, to varying degrees, the individual is in a continual process of both suffering and recovery.

Wherever Chiron is placed in the natal chart, it signifies some kind of core wounding in the life that becomes a central challenge. However, dealing with the challenge can lead a person to his or her destiny. When Chiron is a prominent archetype, located with either of the two lights or with the Ascendant ruler or on the angles, the motif of wounded healer becomes part of the essential meaning of the life path. As a counseling astrologer, when you see this pattern, give guidance to the client that one reason for the suffering may be to gain personal knowledge of a condition that will enable him or her to help others. Often, a sympathetic ear and expression that conveys, "I know just what you are going through, because that happened to me too" can be a tremendous source of emotional support to another. In other cases, what you do will have a much larger impact than the simple expression of compassion.

A client had natal Chiron in the first house, and I suspected that wound might occur in the physical body. When the client was twenty years old, the transit of Pluto passed over the natal Chiron, and she was diagnosed with cervical cancer. Traditional treatment recommended surgery that would most likely prevent her from bearing children in the future. She researched alternative treatments, and found an herbal protocol that was successful. In the ensuing years, she pursued training and certification in herbal studies, and is now an established body worker. It was the confrontation with the near-fatal wound that catalyzed her future path as a healer.

So when a client looks at you and says, "Why has this terrible thing happened to me," look at the chart and see if the person has some afflicted and debilitated planet signifying the matter. Simply telling the client that the condition of the Moon is wretched is not helpful in and of itself, however. You must help the client find some kind of redeeming value in the suffering. Most basic and true guidance will lead clients to see how they can use the suffering to help another. It is in the process of helping others that they can ultimately bring healing to themselves.

Let's return to Persephone. Like Chiron, she also made a descent into the underworld. According to the compromise reached between her mother, Ceres, and her husband, Pluto, to share her presence for part of each year, she returns to the realm of the dead after the annual harvest has been safely stored in the world above. She is a fluid traveler, passing back and forth between the world of the living and the world of the dead. During her annual sojourns in Hades, she watches over the souls of the dead and initiates them into the rites of rebirth. As we mentioned before, the Persephone child's early tragedy brings him or her into an encounter with the spirit world.

This may speak to the Persephone person's destiny as a psychic who brings messages from the astral plane, or as a psychotherapist, guiding others through the terrain of the unconscious and facilitating psychological rebirth. In recent years, a healing modality called soul retrieval has emerged. In this healing, the Persephone healer may engage in methods to help people reintegrate parts of their psyche that have split off and become dissociated in order to survive the trauma. Work in hospice and care for the dying, befriending young children who have been abused or are at risk, or counseling substance addicts whose addictions are frequently a response to the need to numb the memory of trauma are all vocations that can bring a redemptive value to the suffering of those who carry the archetype of Persephone. It is the telling of the myth that evokes the archetype and thereby stirs the unconscious into a chain of images and associations that makes the client more receptive to the information that follows.

THE TWELFTH HOUSE

The final wounded-healer motif we will discuss is the twelfth house. While this house does not directly correspond to a mythic archetype like those symbolized by the celestial bodies, we can continue to utilize the archetypal approach to this area of the chart through a discussion of the concept of *bodhicitta* found in Eastern philosophical and religious doctrines.

Traditionally, the twelfth house signifies suffering, loss, affliction, enemies, and confinement. Modern astrology has added the meanings of karma, the collective unconscious, solitude, retreat, and hidden motivations. Influenced by Vedic astrology, which assigns the concept of *moksha,* or spiritual liberation, to the twelfth house, it now also carries the connotations of spiritual transcendence and selfless service. Generally, when an individual has placements of planets in the twelfth house, he or she experiences some kind of loss, suffering, or difficulty with regard to the significations of that planet and to the topics of the houses it rules—more so if the planet is in poor condition.

Depending on the belief system of the astrologer and the client, these themes can be framed in terms of karma and reincarnation, making the difficult experiences the results of past actions, trauma, and unresolved issues from previous lives that seek healing and resolution in this lifetime. Or it may be that commitments in the form of an "I owe you" have been made in previous lives whose chips, so to speak, are now being called in. Or these disturbing events may be eruptions from the unconscious of negative and toxic mental and emotional patterns that are either carried over from the past or residues of events that occurred before the client's own biographical memory. The living out of shadow motifs in the personal life that have collective significance or are the hereditary issues of one's family, religious, or cultural trials may also be a factor.

While all of these approaches may offer somewhat satisfying explanations for the pathos of twelfth-house planets, they do not necessarily help a client move through the suffering or utilize the suffering for some kind of beneficial action, thereby transforming it. The crises that are experienced in the twelfth house often do illuminate the wounded-healer archetype, in that early difficulties can become the formative experiences that enable a person to recognize that particular pain in others and feel moved with compassion to help them. This takes us to a discussion of the archetype of the *bodhisattva*, which can be one of the highest expressions of the twelfth house.

In Eastern doctrines, a *bodhisattva* is an enlightened being who consciously chooses to incarnate in order to alleviate suffering and to assist others in the search for liberation. Bodhicitta is the enlightened motivation or attitude that inspires a person to become a bodhisattva in order to benefit all beings. You don't need to subscribe to an Eastern religion to emulate the altruistic behavior that ensues from the cultivation of bodhicitta.

Depending upon the belief system, you can suggest that, if there is some kind of consciousness prior to incarnation, the evolving soul may make decisions to take on the burdens of others willingly and out of compassion for their plight, or for personal redemption, or because it sees the necessity for self-sacrifice for the benefit of the greater good. This can be indicated by the location of planets in the twelfth house, where the individual carries a heavier burden than others do—not due to punishment for wrongdoing or past trauma held in the unconscious, but through a voluntary undertaking arising from an enlightened awareness.

I want to close this chapter with a teaching from one my own teachers, Lama Tsering Everest. I asked her what a birth chart actually represents. Her response was that, from a Buddhist perspective, the chart is a picture of our basic karmic situation in life, as the fruition and result of our actions from previous lives. As such, it represents our limitations and negative emotional patterns, which are the source of our suffering. However, simultaneously, the birth chart is a picture of what we would look like as enlightened beings if we were able to transform the negative karmic mental patterns into their corresponding wisdom qualities through meditative practice and right action.

The archetypal approach to therapy postulates that suffering is a message from the psyche—from some neglected part of the self crying out in pain to be noticed. In Buddhist philosophy, suffering is the result of wrong thinking that leads us to wrong actions and reinforces the predisposition to future suffering. Astrology is one means by which we can recognize the indicators of suffering as depicted in the birth chart. As astrological counselors, we can acknowledge the reality of the difficulties our clients have, in fact, experienced, and discuss various ways that the suffering can hold the key to self-healing, to realization of potential, and to spiritual progress through altruistic action to benefit others. Archetypal mythology and the telling of these timeless universal stories offers us an entry point into this path of healing.

Study Guidelines

- Look at your practice chart and determine if you see any sensitive issues that can be approached by mythic storytelling. Practice by telling this story to your "client"; ask if the story mirrors any events from his or her own life experiences.
- Carefully explore the factors associated with the twelfth house—the sign occupying it, any planets located there, and the planet that rules it. Ask your "client" if he or she has experienced any difficulties, losses, or suffering with regard to the significations of these planets or to the psychological qualities of the sign. Does a discussion of the wounded-healer archetype offer any solace or guidance to the healing of these issues?

Epilogue:

The Astrologer as Counselor

The quandary for astrological counselors is that they must straddle the gap between science and art—between logical analysis and compassionate healing. For astrologers dedicated to mastering the discipline of accurately discerning the celestial signatures for a nativity, it is a point of honor to be competent and to recognize the truth of what the chart reveals. But counselors understand that a dispassionate recitation of the stark unadorned facts may not always serve the best interests of the client. How can you be true to what the astrological symbols in the chart indicate, yet convey hope rather than despair if they point to problematic outcomes? How can you acknowledge the operation of karma or fate as an explanation for what may otherwise be untenable circumstances, yet give a redemptive meaning to a person's suffering? The ultimate challenge for astrological counselors is to be truthful to the objective reality of the birth chart and, at the same time, give the client a positive and spiritually uplifting vision for living a life that has purpose and meaning for themselves and also benefits others.

Occasionally, this is a relatively easy task, since some charts show mostly good fortune. It is a joy to communicate glowing information to those who have had the fortune to be born under a chart that, according to classical guidelines, is easy, positive, and designed for success and happiness. Here, you can feel confident and secure in waxing eloquent about your client's life and future, knowing that you stand on firm ground. You have a blissful client who will love you as the bearer of good news. But often, those with easy lives are less likely to seek counseling and guidance; it is generally when things are going badly that people reach out for help. Most people who come to astrologers for insight and advice are driven by some kind of malaise, either temporary or chronic, about which they may be more or less aware. Few of us are without our own particular kind of suffering in the deep places of our hearts.

As Homer tells us in the *Iliad*, only gods have been given all good lots in life; most mortals receive a mixture of good and bad, and some end up with only bad as their allotted portion. The real test of an astrological counselor is to know what to say when the chart indicators point to problematic outcomes that describe difficulties the client has already experienced or is concerned about for the future. What is your responsibility when you see a pattern in the birth chart that does not bode well for individuals and for their hopes for their lives? What do you say when the chart indicates that it is unlikely that they will get what they want, or the things that many others take for granted—and if they do, that it may not turn out to be in their best interests? How can you be truthful and not negate or dismiss the reality of the problems in their lives, but at the same time reframe the situation so you do not leave clients in a state of despair?

We can speculate about the extent to which people are capable of transforming the bad into the good, and, indeed, most religions, spiritual practices and psychological therapies are predicated on the premise that this is within the realm of human potential. We may never really know the absolute truth of this matter. But it is apparent that we must live our lives as if it were true; the alternative leads us into resignation and hopelessness. As astrologers, we must confront our own beliefs about what the natal chart actually represents and to what extent the patterns depicting character and destiny are fixed or flexible. If we consider the possibility that individuals can take conscious action to alter the indications of the chart significators or express the energies at the more skillful range of their manifestations, we give guidance as to the strength of human will to overcome obstacles. Reliance on higher powers, belief in the capacity of focused thought to create reality, positive thinking, psychological therapy to release blocked energies, spiritual practice and intercession, the implementation of right action, and remedial measures to counteract otherwise destructive forces are all ways to bring this about.

However, if we suspect that the arrangement of the stars at the birth moment is an accurate depiction of the seed imprint that determines the shape and timing of who we are over the entire span of our lives, then it may become a matter of changing our perspective on how we view the reality of the objective condition of our lives. The Western astrological tradition developed under the umbrella of Stoic philosophy, which held that everything in nature proceeds according to a natural law that connects, orders, and determines all things. Happiness and freedom arise out of a willingness to accept the wisdom of this natural law and live in conformity with it. Suffering is the result of a futile struggle to obtain something that was not meant to be.

While some may take this to imply a strict determinism that denies our free will to make choices and consciously direct our lives, that begs the following questions: Given that these are the circumstances of my life, what is the best expression for the greatest good that I can give to them? How can I make the best use of this situation for the realization of what my chart supports rather than what I desire or imagine will make me happy? This is a very different approach than one that attempts to change what is or create what we may want. It does not mean resignation to the adversity of fate, but rather raises the question: If the chart is denying the realization of some topic, why? And what is being asked of the person instead?

When it seems impossible to change, transform, and re-create a client's reality, there are several alternatives you can suggest. One involves spinning and reframing the situation to gain a different perspective that makes sense and that the client can accept. A second is to make peace with what is unlikely to occur and focus instead on what else the chart supports for the realization of success and good fortune, and develop the life energies there. A third is to allow the pain to open the heart to compassion and, from that place, take action to alleviate the suffering of others. None of these possibilities is mutually exclusive.

Throughout this book, I have emphasized the importance of knowing what a chart indicates before deciding on how and when to "spin" the reading. Metaphorically, the work of the *Moirai*, the Three Fates, was to spin and weave the fabric of a person's life. In this context, "spinning" does not mean saying something other than

or opposite to what actually is, but rather giving an alternate perspective that reframes the situation in a manner that both is reasonable and offers a path of positive action.

Say a man arrives in your office concerned about an ongoing
crisis in his marriage. He has a Libra Ascendant, with Venus the
ruler of the Ascendant as steersman in Aries in the seventh house
of marriage guiding his life. The seventh house is thus occupied by
the sign Aries, and its ruler, Mars, is located in Virgo in the twelfth
house of afflictions conjoined to Saturn; Mars rules the Scorpio second house of money earned from livelihood as well. The man has
had three long-term relationships with angry, domineering women
who constantly criticized and berated him, focusing on his meager
earnings despite the fact that he is a hard worker and skillful crafts-
man. And yet he remained committed to the marriages until forced
to leave by his partners.

You may think it unlikely that this person will find happiness
and peace with a partner who is gentle, kind, and appreciative. Yet
it is the topic of relationship that guides his life, and the thought
of not being in a relationship is untenable to him. How can you
reframe these chart indicators to make sense of his predicament?
The counselor in you might speculate that he may have taken on
a karmic commitment (ruler of seventh in the twelfth) to women
who are filled with inner rage toward men due to their own previous circumstances (his Venus in Aries in the seventh). Because he
is secure enough in his own inner strength, he is able to withstand
their tirades and give them unconditional love, commitment, continual help, and emotional support to bring some healing into their
lives. Everyone can benefit from and heal by being loved, and it may
be that he is able and willing to extend this compassion to a type of
woman who needs it very much. The question here is how to find
peace with a situation a person is unable or unwilling to change by
viewing it in a way that affirms the higher impulses of the individual.
Had the client been open to the possibility of leaving the relationship, the discussion might have taken a different turn.

Or say a chart denies you what you want. What may it be asking you to do instead? A man has had a lifelong unfulfilled yearning
for his own children, but his wife did not want to give birth or raise

a family. He has Mars, the ruler of his Ascendant, placed in the fifth house of children; the Sun, ruler of the tenth house of profession or what we do, is also located there. Mars closely conjoins the Sun, and both are opposed by Saturn, indicating some of the problems. In addition, the planet Pluto and the asteroid Ceres are partile (exact to the degree) conjunct one another at the degree of his MC. His only child died before birth. However, the partners of two of his close friends died, leaving teenage children behind. He has joyfully taken on the responsibilities of befriending, mentoring, and helping to raise them. In addition, he has written several books relating to the emotional healing of children (the Sun, ruler of the tenth of profession in the fifth of children and the ruler of the fifth in the third house of writing). The books have been his creative children.

You can point out that, had he had children of his own, his energies might not have been available to help these other children as he has done. In addition, the natural impulse toward children as indicated in his chart is being asked to reach a larger audience through his writings. Through helping the children of others, he not only redeems his own suffering, but actualizes the essential meaning and purpose of his own life.

Let's look at the chart of artist Frida Kahlo, who demonstrates the channeling of suffering into other endeavors, and thereby finds redemptive meaning. Her Sun, ruler of the Ascendant, is located in Cancer in the twelfth house opposed by an exalted Mars in Capricorn in its joy in the sixth house. Mars signified a great illness, accidents, and countless surgeries that brought her life-long physical pain and subsequent emotional suffering from an inability to bear children. You clearly see that poor health is one of the outstanding circumstances of her life. You also see that both of these planets are configured by sextile and trine to a tenth-house exalted Taurus Moon that rules the twelfth. You can affirm that her basic life purpose is expressed through the transfiguration of her own emotional and physical suffering, which she actualizes through a successful profession in the creative arts; her pain was the content of her artistic expression and gift to the world, from which she received much recognition and honor.

In the above examples, I am not trying to whitewash the reality of painful situations or to deny and ignore the difficulties of these people's lives. Nor am I telling them to employ a variety of methods to change and transform their lives according to their wishes. I am acknowledging the truth of the chart, but offering another point of view that makes sense of the facts in a way that allows them to live life with a positive sense of meaning. When you stop struggling to be other than who you are, or to obtain a life other than your own, you enter a peaceful state of mind, as described in the Serenity Prayer of Alcoholics Anonymous: God grant me the serenity to accept the things I cannot change, the courage to change the things I can, and the wisdom to know the difference. Focusing on what you *can* control liberates great energy to actualize fully the best possible expression of the potentialities inherent in your chart. Ultimately, the quest is to discover your authentic self so that you can willingly embrace your destiny.

Your job as an astrological counselor is to benefit your clients with an honest and compassionate appraisal of the circumstances of their lives. The celestial arrangement of the astrological symbols in the birth chart reflects the intersection of a person's karma from the past, their fate in the present, and their destiny that yearns to be fulfilled in the future. Your technical proficiency as an astrologer allows you to assemble and read the symbols in a way that illuminates the celestial configuration that expresses your clients' authentic self. Your wisdom as a counselor enables you to convey this vision in a manner that makes sense of your clients' suffering and inspires them to live out that purpose for the greater good. When you integrate your skill as an astrologer with your wisdom as a counselor—when you hold your clients with compassion—you place the analytical power of astrology in the service of your clients' personal healing in a way that radiates it outward to benefit the larger whole.

How to Determine Your Natal and
Progressed Lunation Phases

The following set of instructions will guide you through the process of determining your natal lunation phase and the dates of your
progressed lunation phases. You will need a copy of your natal birth
chart and a computer report giving your progressed lunation phases
for a 100-year period. These documents can be ordered through
ASTROLABE at 1-800-THE NOVA. Tell them you want to use
them in connection with this book. Alternately, many computer
software programs can generate the dates for the progressed lunation
phases; the report illustrated here is from the Solar Fire Program.

Natal Lunation Phase

To determine your natal lunation phase, calculate the number of
degrees between the Sun and the Moon in your birth chart. Using
the Sun as a reference point, count the degrees from the Sun to the
Moon in the order of the signs (in a counterclockwise direction).
Each sign contains 30 degrees and each degree contains 60 minutes.
Add the total number of degrees and minutes between the Sun and
the Moon and use Table 7 on page 292 to find your lunation phase.

Bill's Sun is at 24 degrees Scorpio 23 minutes. His Moon is at 9
degrees Aquarius 51 minutes. So the distance from the Sun to the
Moon in Bill's chart is calculated by adding:

5°. 37" remaining in Scorpio
30°. 00" Sagittarius
30°. 00" Capricorn
9°. 51" Aquarius
75°. 98" = 76°. 38" between the Sun and Moon

Table 7. Lunation Phases by Degrees and Minutes
between the Sun and Moon

Degrees between Sun and Moon	Lunation Phase
0.00 - 45.00	New Moon
45.01 – 90.00	Crescent Moon
90.01- 135.00	First Quarter Moon
135.01- 180.00	Gibbous Moon
180.01 – 225.00	Full Moon
225.01 – 270.00	Disseminating Moon
271.01 – 315.00	Last-Quarter Moon
315.01 – 360.00	Balsamic Moon

Remember, there are 30 degrees in each sign and 60 minutes in each degree. Do not carry over the sums between the degree and minute columns, but tally each one separately. In the above example, 98 minutes is equal to 1 degree (60 minutes) and 38 minutes. Thus we add one degree (equal to 60 minutes) to 75 degrees for a result of 76 degrees and 38 minutes.

According to this calculation, Bill's natal lunation phase is Crescent Moon.

PROGRESSED LUNATION PHASE

I will illustrate how to determine the dates of your progressed lunation phases using a computer report generated by the *Solar Fire* software program in the Dynamic Menu (see figure 16). If you do not have access to this astrological software, you can order a report from Astrolabe at 1-800-THE NOVA. Tell them that you want to use it in connection with this book.

In the second column from the left are glyphs for various aspects between the position of the progressed Moon (first column) and the progressed Sun (third column).

• Run your finger down this column until you come to the first entry for the glyph that represents the conjunction aspect ♂. In the space to the left, write the words "New Moon."

• Immediately beneath the glyph for the conjunction aspect is the glyph that represents the semi-square aspect ∠. Opposite this glyph, write the words "Crescent Moon."

- Beneath the glyph for the semi-square aspect is the glyph that represents the square aspect □. Opposite this glyph, write the words "First Quarter Moon."
- Beneath the glyph for the square aspect is the glyph that represents the sesi-quadrate aspect ⬛. Opposite this glyph, write the words "Gibbous Moon."
- Beneath the glyph for the sesi-quadrate aspect is the glyph that represents the opposition aspect ☍. Opposite this glyph, write the words "Full Moon."
- Beneath the glyph for the opposition aspect is the glyph that represents the sesi-quadrate aspect ⬛. (This is the same glyph as that for the Gibbous Moon). Opposite this glyph, write the words "Disseminating Moon."
- Beneath the glyph for the sesi-quadrate aspect is the glyph that represents the square aspect □. (This is the same glyph as that for the First Quarter Moon.) Opposite this glyph, write the words "Last Quarter Moon."
- Beneath the glyph for the square aspect is the glyph that represents the semi-square aspect ∠. (This is the same glyph as that for the Crescent Moon.) Opposite this glyph, write the words "Balsamic Moon."
- The next glyph is that of the conjunction ☌. Repeat this sequence until you reach the end of the column at the bottom of the page.
- Now return to your starting point, but this time move up the column toward the top of the page and enter the words for the lunation phases in reverse order next to each glyph: Balsamic, Last Quarter, Disseminating, Full, Gibbous, First Quarter, and Crescent.
- When you reach the top of the column, enter the next lunation phase in the sequence, even though there is no glyph next to it. This is your natal lunation phase.

The dates to the right of the progressed Sun are the dates on which each of these lunation phases began.

Progressed Lunation Phases

☽ Phase	Aspect	☉	Date	Position	Position
(3) First Quarter	□	(12)	Mar 16, 1941	25°≈43' D	25°♏43' D
(5) Gibbous	⚼	(12)	Apr 26, 1945	14°♈52' D	29°♏52' D
(7) Full	☍	(1)	Feb 22, 1949	03°♊44' D	03°♐44' D
(8) Disseminating	⚼	(1)	Sep 1, 1952	22°♋18' D	07°♐18' D
(10) Last Quarter	□	(1)	Feb 3, 1956	10°♍47' D	10°♐47' D
(11) Balsamic	∠	(1)	Jul 22, 1959	29°♎17' D	14°♐17' D
(1) New	☌	(1)	Feb 20, 1963	17°♍56' D	17°♐56' D
(3) Crescent	∠	(1)	Dec 26, 1966	06°≈51' D	21°♐51' D
(4) First Quarter	□	(1)	Feb 9, 1971	26°♓03' D	26°♐03' D
(6) Gibbous	⚼	(2)	Feb 13, 1975	15°♉08' D	00°♑08' D
(8) Full	☍	(2)	Sep 16, 1978	03°♋47' D	03°♑47' D
(9) Disseminating	⚼	(2)	Jan 17, 1982	22°♌11' D	07°♑11' D
(11) Last Quarter	□	(2)	Jun 8, 1985	10°♎38' D	10°♑38' D
(12) Balsamic	∠	(2)	Jan 7, 1989	29°♏18' D	14°♑18' D
(2) New	☌	(2)	Oct 22, 1992	18°♑09' D	18°♑09' D
(4) Crescent	∠	(2)	Nov 4, 1996	07°♓16' D	22°♑16' D
(5) First Quarter	□	(2)	Dec 29, 2000	26°♈30' D	26°♑30' D
(7) Gibbous	⚼	(3)	Oct 28, 2004	15°♊24' D	00°≈24' D
(9) Full	☍	(3)	Mar 15, 2008	03°♌50' D	03°≈50' D
(10) Disseminating	⚼	(3)	Jun 7, 2011	22°♍07' D	07°≈07' D
(12) Last Quarter	□	(3)	Nov 5, 2014	10°♏35' D	10°≈35' D
(1) Balsamic	∠	(3)	Jul 29, 2018	29°♐22' D	14°≈22' D
(3) New	☌	(3)	Jul 21, 2022	18°≈24' D	18°≈24' D
(5) Crescent	∠	(3)	Sep 13, 2026	07°♈36' D	22°≈36' D
(6) First Quarter	□	(3)	Oct 8, 2030	26°♉42' D	26°≈42' D
(8) Gibbous	⚼	(4)	May 27, 2034	15°♋22' D	00°♓22' D
(10) Full	☍	(4)	Aug 23, 2037	03°♍38' D	03°♓38' D

Legend

☌	New	(0°)	⚼	Disseminating	(225°)
∠	Crescent	(45°)	□	Last Quarter	(270°)
□	First Quarter	(90°)	∠	Balsamic	(315°)
⚼	Gibbous	(135°)	☌	New	(0°)
☍	Opposition	(180°)			

FIGURE 16. *Bill's progressed lunation phase report.*
Calculations courtesy of Solar Fire.

Appendix B:

Resources for the Study of Asteroids

A Selection of Mythic and Concept Asteroids

(See pages 296–97 for a list of Bill's Asteroids)

Books

George, Demetra and Douglas Bloch. *Asteroid Goddesses.* Berwick, ME: Ibis, 2003.

George, Demetra. *Finding Our Way through the Dark.* Tempe, AZ: AFA, 2008.

Guttman, Ariel and Kenneth Johnson. *Mythic Astrology Applied, Part III.* St. Paul, MN: Llewellyn, 2004.

Larousse Encyclopedia of Mythology. London & New York: Hamlyn, 1978.

Schmadel, Lutz D. *Dictionary of Minor Planet Names.* Berlin & New York: Springer-Verlag, 2006.

Tripp, Edward. *The Meridian Handbook of Classical Mythology.* New York: Meridian, 1974.

Web Sites

www.theoi.com for Greek mythology.

www.entheos1.com/Asteroid.htm for THE MUSE—personal asteroid positions and ephemerides order forms for 12,000 asteroids.

www.astro.com/swisseph/astlist.htm for the name and numbers of all the asteroids and the positions for individual asteroids on a given date.

Software

Mark Pottenger, *CCRS Asteroid Program,* an ephemerides of all named asteroids with a Windows program to display positions for a date and time. (markpott@pacbell.net).

Fei Cochrane, Kepler Astrology Software, *Cosmic Patterns Software,* for an asteroid add-on module that calculates all named asteroids (kepler@ AstroSoftware.com) .

Asteroid Report

```
Bill
NOV 17,   1939   15:30: 0 UT  (delta T is   24   seconds)
Geocentric Asteroids in sorted order
```

1282	Utopia	2♈13R	2	Pallas	2♌ 9
271	Penthesilea	2♈45R	-10	Pluto	2♌53R
20000	Varuna	15♈32R	212	Medea	4♌22
90377	Sedna	19♈30R	1958	Chandra	4♌57
313	Chaldaea	19♈37R	1221	Amor	8♌55
238	Hypatia	23♈45R	1181	Lilith	9♌16
4	Vesta	25♈36R	5708	Melancholia	10♌19
-7	Saturn	25♈49R	244	Sita	12♌31
227	Philosophia	27♈45R	14367	Hippokrates	14♌ 0
-12	South Node	27♈54	318	Magdalena	15♌35
90	Antiope	29♈20R	2440	Educatio	16♌24
7066	Nessus	29♈52R	2340	Hathor	18♌37
1589	Fanatica	0♉ 1R	6	Hebe	21♌18
2415	Ganesa	1♉39R	1896	Beer	1♍25
580	Selene	1♉51R	258	Tyche	2♍50
3200	Phaethon	11♉15R	216	Kleopatra	3♍13
-8	Uranus	19♉46R	2791	Paradise	3♍51
3063	Makhaon	20♉21R	105	Artemis	6♍41
101	Helena	22♉ 4R	2847	Parvati	6♍47
423	Diotima	22♉ 7R	57	Mnemosyne	6♍48
2365	Interkosmos	22♉24R	1	Ceres	8♍11
588	Achilles	28♉33R	140	Siwa	8♍45
870	Manto	28♉44R	8	Flora	9♍ 2
621	Werdandi	29♉57R	30	Urania	11♍41
4086	Podalirius	1♊19R	84	Klio	12♍ 3
8990	Compassion	1♊27R	273	Atropos	15♍50
10295	Hippolyta	5♊54R	6805	Abstracta	17♍ 4
1042	Amazone	6♊26R	1154	Astronomia	17♍11
4450	Pan	9♊10R	1198	Atlantis	17♍43
2597	Arthur	9♊20R	3402	Wisdom	18♍ 8
4138	Kalchas	13♊35R	46	Hestia	18♍44
1924	Horus	13♊38R	2041	Lancelot	20♍27
3671	Dionysus	14♊52R	76	Freia	21♍49
49036	Pelion	15♊ 1R	-9	Neptune	25♍ 3
1143	Odysseus	17♊54R	158	Koronis	26♍18
975	Perseverantia	21♊17R	433	Eros	28♍19
5143	Heracles	21♊24	80	Sappho	29♍24
168	Sibylla	21♊36R	3554	Amun	29♍28
2815	Soma	25♊ 6R	5863	Tara	1♎18
881	Athene	26♊21R	8958	Stargazer	3♎14
577	Rhea	0♋27R	1866	Sisyphus	3♎39
12524	Conscience	1♋17R	37452	Spirit	6♎ 9
5239	Reiki	2♋32R	9	Metis	6♎55
1813	Imhotep	6♋25R	1108	Demeter	8♎37
4386	Lust	7♋41R	114	Kassandra	9♎55
875	Nymphe	10♋15R	33	Polyhymnia	11♎22
2212	Hephaistos	12♋28R	2483	Guinevere	11♎39
3497	Innanen	12♋34R	905	Universitas	12♎32
2174	Asmodeus	14♋46R	4342	Freud	17♎46
3688	Navajo	17♋11	29	Amphitrite	18♎20
1862	Apollo	18♋ 9R	4679	Sybil	18♎50
3989	Odin	19♋17	490	Veritas	26♎ 0
2060	Chiron	19♋51R	672	Astarte	26♎34
6630	Skepticus	21♋ 1R	6123	Aristoteles	27♎44
112	Iphigenia	22♋ 0	-11	North Node	28♎59
2598	Merlin	22♋ 8	3258	Somnium	29♎25
643	Scheherezade	24♋38	42	Isis	0♏33
179	Klytaemnestra	26♋ 0	75	Eurydike	1♏11
259	Aletheia	29♋33	829	Academia	2♏36
24626	Astrowizard	29♋47	2202	Pele	3♏ 4
2878	Panacea	0♌47			

```
Bill
NOV 17,   1939   15:30: 0 UT  (delta T is  24  seconds)
Geocentric Asteroids in sorted order
```

#	Name	Position		#	Name	Position
1923	Osiris	3♏39		12472	Samadhi	6♑33
86	Semele	4♏58		1629	Pecker	7♑25
78	Diana	5♏13		1566	Icarus	9♑ 2
11518	Jung	6♏18		1809	Prometheus	11♑18
916	America	7♏14		287	Nephthys	12♑18
2101	Adonis	8♏28		4227	Kaali	13♑12
2938	Hopi	8♏41		2063	Bacchus	14♑11
26	Proserpina	9♏19		4581	Asclepius	14♑11
1685	Toro	9♏34		209	Dido	15♑21
6143	Pythagoras	10♏20		120	Lachesis	15♑44
953	Painleva	10♏35		2082	Galahad	15♑59
201	Penelope	12♏22		1172	Aneas	18♑32
214	Aschera	14♏37		10	Hygiea	19♑24
4341	Poseidon	15♏58R		399	Persephone	22♑ 8
81	Terpsichore	20♏ 3		1173	Anchises	22♑12
908	Buda	21♏22		430	Hybris	25♑ 6
65803	Didymos	21♏49		7	Iris	26♑46
1122	Neith	23♏ 7		638	Moira	29♑23
679	Pax	23♏23		43	Ariadne	29♑49
944	Hidalgo	23♏37		3317	Paris	1≈57
1170	Siva	24♏ 1		5731	Zeus	7≈21
-1	Sun	24♏23		-2	Moon	9≈52
451	Patientia	25♏17		14	Irene	10≈18
7088	Ishtar	28♏49		16	Psyche	10≈37
14827	Hypnos	29♏14		9500	Camelot	11≈35
3908	Nyx	0♐21		4401	Aditi	14≈52
2155	Wodan	0♐26		6063	Jason	16≈ 3
5450	Sokrates	0♐37		499	Venusia	17≈19
55	Pandora	2♐34		8992	Magnanimity	19≈30
3811	Karma	6♐56		251	Sophia	20≈54
432	Pythia	7♐38		8275	Inca	21≈42
8732	Champion	7♐55		69230	Hermes	25≈15R
5381	Sekhmet	8♐46		3	Juno	25≈36
93	Minerva	10♐11		149	Medusa	26≈29
-4	Venus	13♐ 6		-5	Mars	28≈44
367	Amicitia	13♐17		65	Cybele	1♓ 9
309	Fraternitas	13♐19		1915	Quetzalcoatl	1♓35
-3	Mercury	13♐55		100	Hekate	4♓16
53	Kalypso	14♐ 7		886	Washingtonia	6♓48
77	Frigga	14♐39		270	Anahita	13♓21
2102	Tantalus	19♐52		19521	Chaos	14♓44R
275	Sapientia	21♐ 7		1812	Gilgamesh	15♓59
2150	Nyctimene	21♐ 9		103	Hera	16♓ 3
1810	Epimetheus	22♐ 1		1930	Lucifer	16♓48
763	Cupido	23♐14		1184	Gaea	17♓ 2
1009	Sirene	25♐35		1027	Aesculapia	18♓58
1912	Anubis	26♐11		9602	Oya	20♓46
19	Fortuna	26♐47		896	Sphinx	21♓31
3361	Orpheus	26♐55		40	Harmonia	21♓49
34	Circe	28♐ 2		167	Urda	25♓ 7
7853	Confucius	28♐53		1130	Skuld	27♓33
1864	Daedalus	29♐23		24	Themis	28♓34R
443	Photographica	29♐49		-6	Jupiter	28♓58R
382	Dodona	0♑ 4				
97	Klotho	0♑38				
5451	Plato	1♑37				
128	Nemesis	3♑35				
174	Phaedra	4♑ 1				
3218	Delphine	4♑14				
1388	Aphrodite	6♑24				

Asteroid calculations compiled in CCRS software by Mark Pottenger

George, Demetra and Douglas Bloch. *The Asteroid Goddess Report Writer.* Brewster, MA: Astrolabe, Inc., 1995 (astrolabe@alabe.com).

Jacob Schwartz, *Asteroid Signatures*, indexes and annotates all asteroid citations, www.AstroSoftware.com/Asteroid Signatures.htm.

Publications

Dobyns, Zipporah. *Mutable Dilemna/Asteroid World*, www.ccrsdodona.org.

Gaia (Gathering Information by Astrologers), contact National Council of Geocosmic Research Asteroid Special Interest Group, www.geocosmic. org.

ENDOTES

Introduction

[1] James Hillman, *The Soul's Code* (New York: Warner Books, 1996), p. 6.

[2] Plato, *Timeaus*, 30 c.

Chapter One

[1] In the Whole Sign house system, the MC degree can appear in either the ninth, tenth, or eleventh houses; it is not the cusp of the tenth house as in quadrant-house systems like Placidus or Koch. Likewise the Ascendant degree falls somewhere in the first house; it is not the cusp between the twelfth and first houses although it does mark the horizon.

[2] See Douglas Bloch and Demetra George, *Astrology For Yourself* (Berwick, ME: Ibis Press, 2006), pp. 153–174 for a template for beginning-level interpretation of planetary aspects.

Chapter 2

[1] In *Elements of Hellenistic Astrology* (forthcoming), I give an exhaustive treatment of this inquiry from the Hellenistic perspective.

[2] Each planet is a general significator of certain topics in everyone's chart (e.g., the Moon for the mother. In addition, each planet is a particular significator for a certain topic based upon the house or houses it rules in any particular chart, and this varies from one chart to another. For example, the Moon also governs the particular topic of marriage if Cancer, the sign it rules, happens to occupy the seventh house of marriage.

[3] *Tetrabiblos*, I, 4.

[4] You can easily tell a morning-star Mercury because it has a lesser zodiacal degree than the Sun, while an evening-star Mercury has one greater than the Sun.

[5] In Hellenistic astrology, the rulership categories trigon, bound, and decan are equivalent to the medieval usage of dignities as triplicity, term, and face, respectively.

[6] *Mathesis*, 3; 1, 10.

[7] Antiochus, *Introduction*, I, 19.

[8] Robert Schmidt, *PHASE Conclave 2006 Lecture*, Cumberland, MD.

[9] Valens, *Anthology*, IV, 11.

[10] Paulus Alexandrinus, *Introductory Matters*, 10.

[11] Porphyry, *Introduction to Ptolemy*, 28.

[12] A planet is enclosed when it is located between two other planets. When two malefics enclose a planet, the medieval tradition said the enclosed planet was besieged; the Vedic astrologers said it was "scissored." Traditions vary in far away in terms of zodiacal degrees the malefic or benefic planets had to be from the enclosed planet.

[13] Paulus Alexandrinus, *Introductory Matters*, 14; Porphyry, *Introduction to Ptolemy*, 2.

[14] Antiochus, *Thesaurus*, I, 1.

[15] Ptolemy, *Tetrabiblos*, I, 24.

[16] Antiochus, *Thesaurus*, 1.1; Paulus Alexandrinus, *Introductory Matters*, 14).

[17] An applying aspect occurs when a faster-moving planet approaches a slower-moving planet (Venus at 5° Aries applying to a sextile of Saturn at 8° Gemini). A separating aspect occurs when a faster-moving planet moves away from a slower-moving planet (Venus at 10° Leo separating from a sextile to Saturn at 8° Gemini).

Chapter 3

[1] For information on chart patterns, see Marc Edmund Jones, *Guide to Horoscope Interpretation*; Dane Rudhyar, *Person-Centered Astrology*.

Chapter 5

[1] Paulus Alexandrinus, *Introductory Matters*, 3.

[2] Vettius Valens, *Anthology*, I. 1.

[3] Vettius Valens, *Anthology*, I.1.

Chapter 6

[1] See Demetra George, *Finding Our Way through the Dark*, Tempe, AZ:AFA, 2008 for a complete exposition of the lunation cycle, natal and progressed.

[2] If you do not know what a transit is, how to read an ephemeris to determine the positions of the transiting planets, or how to identify the aspects that transiting planets make to natal planets, see "Astrological Timing" in Bloch and George, *Astrology For Yourself*.

[3] Adapted from Bloch and George, *Astrology For Yourself* .

[4] Brian Clark, *Secondary Progressions* (Australia: AstroSynthesis, 1994).

Chapter 7

[1] Vettius Valens, *Anthology*, II.36.

[2] Paulus Alexandrinus, *Introductory Matters*, 16.

[3] Dane Rudhyar, *The Lunation Cycle* (Santa Fe, NM: Aurora Press, 1967).

[4] Adapted from Demetra George, *Finding Our Way Through the Dark*, AFA 2008. This source gives a more comprehensive discussion of the natal lunation phases and the progressed lunation cycle, and contains a workbook to help you chart out your lifetime lunar progressions.

Chapter 8

[1] The calculation of the Lot of Spirit belonging to the Sun is the reverse of this formula—in a day chart from the Moon to the Sun and in a night chart from the Sun to the Moon.

[2] Vettius Valens, *Anthology*, I, 15; V, 2.

[3] Ariel Guttman and Kenneth Johnson, *Mythic Astrology* (St. Paul, MN: Llewellyn Publications, 1993), p. 74.

[4] Dane Rudhyar, *The Astrology of Personality* (New York: Doubleday, 1970), p. 296.

Chapter 9

[1] For a full treatment of major asteroids and a selection of minor ones, see Demetra George and Douglas Bloch, *Asteroid Goddesses* (Berwick, ME: Ibis, 2003).

Chapter 11

[1] Vettius Valens, *Anthology*, II, 38.

[2] Ptolemy, *Tetrabiblos*, IV, 4.

[3] Paulus Alexandrinus, *Introductory Matters*, 26.

[4] In the *Olympidorus Commentary* to Paulus Alexandrinus, several formulas are given for the Lot of Action (Praxis): 1. From Mercury to the Moon, projected from the Ascendant (reverse for nocturnal births); 2. From Mercury to Mars, projected from the Ascendant (reverse for a nocturnal birth).

Chapter 12

[1] Hephaisto, *Apotelesmatics*, II, 27.

Chapter 15

[1] Robert A. Segal, *Myth: A Very Short Introduction* (New York: Oxford University Press, 2004).

[2] Edward Edinger, *The Eternal Drama* (Boston & London: Shambhala, 1994), p. 3.

[3] Carl Jung, "Commentary on 'The Secret of the Golden Flower,'" in *Collected Works*, vol. 13. (Princeton: Princeton University Press, 1967), paragraph 54.

[4] Carl Jung, "The Psychology of the Child Archetype," in *Collected Works*, vol. 9, part 1. (Princeton: Princeton University Press, 1990, paragraph 266.

[5] Murray Stein, *In Midlife* (Dallas, TX: Spring Publications, 1983), pp. 64-65.

[6] Stein, *In Midlife*, p. 65.

Bibliography

General Bibliography

Bloch, Douglas and Demetra George. *Astrology for Yourself*. Lake Worth, FL: Ibis Press, 2006.

Clark, Brian. *Secondary Progressions*. Australia: AstroSynthesis, 1994.

Costello, Priscilla and James Wasserman. *The Weiser Concise Guide to Practical Astrology*. San Francisco, CA: Red Wheel/Weiser, 2008.

Edinger, Edward. *The Eternal Drama*. Boston & London: Shambhala, 1994.

George, Demetra and Douglas Bloch. *Asteroid Goddesses*. Lake Worth, FL: Ibis Press, 2003.

George, Demetra. *Finding Our Way through the Dark*. Tempe, AZ: American Federation of Astrologers, 2008.

——————. *Mysteries of the Dark Moon*. San Francisco: Harper Collins, 1992.

——————. *Elements of Hellenistic Astrology*. Forthcoming.

Guttman, Ariel and Kenneth Johnson. *Mythic Astrology Applied*, Part III. St. Paul, MN: Llewellyn, 2004.

Hillman, James. *The Soul's Code*. New York: Warner Books, 1996.

Jung, Carl. *Collected Works*. Princeton: Princeton University Press, 1967 - 1990.

Rudhyar, Dane. *The Lunation Cycle*. Santa Fe, NM: Aurora Press, 1967.

——————. *The Astrology of Personality*. Santa Fe, NM: Aurora Press, 1987.

——————. *Person Centered Astrology*. Santa Fe, NM: Aurora Press, 1990.

Schmidt, Robert. *PHASE Conclave 2006 Lectures CD set*, Cumberland, MD: Project Hindsight, 2006.

Segal, Robert A. *Myth: A Very Short Introduction*. New York: Oxford University Press, 2004.

Stein, Murray. *In Midlife*. Dallas, TX: Spring Publications, 1983.

Primary Sources for a Study of Hellenistic Astrology

Cumont, Franz, Alexander Oliveri, et. al., eds. *Catalogus Codicum Astrologorum Graecorum (CCAG)*, 12 vols. Brussels: 1898-1953.

Goold, G. P., trans. Marcus Manilius, *Astronomica*. Cambridge, MA: Harvard University Press, 1977.

Greenbaum. Dorian, trans. *Late Classical Astrology: Paulus Alexandrinus and Olympidorus*. Reston, VA: ARHAT, 2001.

Lopilato, Robert, trans. Manetho, *Apotelesmatika*. Providence, RI, 1998. Ph.D. dissertation.

Maternus, Julius Firmicus. *Mathesis*, translated as *Ancient Astrology: Theory and Practice, Jean Rhys Bram*. Park Ridge, NJ: Noyes Press, 1975.

Pingree, David, ed. and trans. Dorotheus of Sidon, *Carmen Astrologicum*. Leipzig: BSG B.G. Teubner Verlagsgesellschaft, 1976.

————————, trans. and commentary. *The Yavanajataka of Sphujidhvaja*. Cambridge: Harvard University Press, vols. 1 &2, 1978.

Robbins, F. E., trans. Claudius Ptolemy, *Tetrabiblos*. Cambridge, MA: Harvard University Press, 1930.

Schmidt, Robert, trans. Antiochus of Athens. *The Thesaurus*. Berkeley Springs, WV: Golden Hind Press, 1993.

————————, trans. Claudius Ptolemy, *Tetrabiblos*. Berkeley Springs, WV: Golden Hind Press, Books 1, 3, & 4, 1994, 1996, 1998.

————————, trans. Claudius Ptolemy, *The Phases of the Fixed Stars*. Berkeley Springs, WV: Golden Hind Press, 1993.

————————, trans. and commentary. *Definitions and Foundations: Antiochus, with Porphyry, Rhetorius, Serapio, and Antigonus*. Cumberland, MD: Golden Hind Press, 2008.

————————, trans. Dorotheus, Orpheus, Anubio, & Pseudo-Valens, *Teachings on Transits*. Berkeley Springs, WV: Golden Hind Press, 1995.

————————, trans. Hephaistio of Thebes, *Apotelesmatics*. Berkeley Springs, WV: Golden Hind Press, Books 1 & 2, 1994, 1998.

————————, trans. Paulus Alexandrinus, *Introductory Matters*. Berkeley Springs, WV: Golden Hind Press, 1993.

————————, trans. Vettius Valens, *The Anthology*. Berkeley Springs, WV: Golden Hind Press, Books 1-7, 1993-2001

————————, trans. *Companion to the Greek Track*. Berkeley Springs, WV: Golden Hind Press, 1994.

————————, trans. *The Treatise of the Fixed Stars*. Berkeley Springs, WV: Golden Hind Press, 1993.

Schmidt, Robert. *Sourcebook of Hellenistic Astrological Texts: Translations and Commentary*. Cumberland, MD: Phaser Foundation, 2005.

Schmidt, Robert and Robert Hand, eds. and trans. *Astrological Record of Early Greek Sages*. Berkeley Springs, WV: Golden Hind Press, 1995.

Zoller, Robert, trans. Hermes, *Liber Hermetis*. Berkeley Springs, WV: Golden Hind Press, Books 1 & 2, 1993.

Glossary

angle

Term used to refer to any one of the four cardinal points in a horoscope relative to the Sun's motion, as observed in the Northern Hemisphere facing south. They are the Ascendant (sunrise point on the eastern horizon), the Midheaven, also called *Medium Coeli* and abbreviated MC (the Sun's highest elevation overhead in the southern sky), the Descendant (sunset point on the western horizon), and the *Imum Coeli*, abbreviated IC (Sun's lowest passage under the Earth). In Greek, the angles are called *horoskopos*, *mesouranema*, *dusis*, and *hupogeion* respectively.

angular house

The first, fourth, seventh, and tenth houses. Traditional astrology holds that planets are the strongest when located in the angular houses. In Greek, an angular house is called a *kentron*.

annual profections

Symbolic timing procedure where each sign moves around the chart at a fixed rate. Annual profections move one sign per year; monthly profections move one sign per month; daily profections move one sign every 2 ½ days. The matters of the house occupied by the profected sign are emphasized for that period of time and the planet that rules that sign plays a role in the determination of the outcome of the matters of the house. The annual profected time lord is the planet that rules the annual profected sign, and this planet governs the life for the duration of one year. During that year, it has the opportunity to bring about its significations as indicated in the natal chart.

annual lord of the year

A planet that assumes governance of the chart for the duration of one year based upon a time-lord procedure.

applying aspect

A term used to describe a faster-moving planet approaching, or applying to, the forming of an aspect to a slower-moving planet. Aspects are considered more powerful when forming/applying rather than when separating.

Arabic part

A mathematical analog calculated by taking the distance between two planets or between a planet and a house degree, and then projecting this distance as an arc from the Ascendant. Originally known as a Greek lot, the best-known Arabic part is the Lot of Fortune. Hellenistic and Medieval astrology utilized hundreds of various lots such as the Lot of Spirit, the Lot of Marriage, the Lot of the Father, and the Lot of Death. The Latin terms for part is *pars*.

Ascendant

The exact degree of the zodiacal sign that is rising above the eastern horizon at the moment of the birth. The sign in which the Ascendant degree is located is known as the rising sign and is generally used as a descriptor of appearance and character. The Greek term is *horoskopos*, from which the word horoscope is derived.

ascending node

The point where the plane of the Moon or a planet in its orbital motion crosses the ecliptic from a southerly to northerly direction. The Greek term is *anabibazo*, which means "to go up." Also known as the north node, it is called the north lunar node when referring to the orbit of the Moon.

ascensional time

The amount of time it takes for a sign to ascend fully over the eastern horizon. It is also known as oblique ascension. The ascensional time of a sign varies according to geographical latitude.

aspect

The angular relationship between two planets or other celestial bodies. Ancient astrologers understood this relationship as the configuration made by two planets occupying signs in conformity to the sides of regular polygons, such as a sextile from the sides of a hexagon, a square from the sides of a square, and a trine from the sides of a triangle. Modern astrologers define this relationship as planets separated by an arc of a certain number of degrees that are derived from the division of the circle by whole numbers, regardless of the signs these planets occupy. Both approaches agree that planets linked in this manner influence each others' significations in harmonious or unharmonious ways. The closer the planets are to the exact arcs of separation specified by 0 (conjunction), 60 (sextile), 90 (square), 120 (trine), or 180 (opposition) degrees, the more active the influence. Traditional astrologers use only these five aspect configurations; modern astrologers employ a host of additional aspects.

aspect pattern

Geometrical configuration made by three or more planets in aspect to one another, such as a grand trine, where three planets that are trine one another form an equilateral triangle, or a Grand Cross, where four planets square each other form a square.

aversion

A term used by ancient astrologers to refer to planets occupying signs that are unconnected to one another, specifically the semi-sextile (30 degrees) and the inconjunct (150 degrees). The Greek term is *apostrophe*, which means "to turn away" or "avert."

benefic

A planet that is literally a "doer of good," usually ascribed to Venus and Jupiter. The Greek term is *agathopoios*.

bi-wheel chart

Arranges one set of planetary positions (for instance progressions, transits, or Solar Returns) in an outer wheel relative to another chart (for instance a natal chart) in the inner wheel.

bonification

Enhanced favorable significations or lessened unfavorable significations resulting from certain relationships with the benefic planets Venus and Jupiter, such as conjunction, sextile, and trine configurations, as well as other conditions.

bound/term

The five unequal divisions of each sign where each segment is under the rulership of a different planet—Mercury, Venus, Mars, Jupiter, or Saturn, but not the Sun and Moon. Called "terms" in Medieval astrology. When a planet occupies the bound degrees of another planet, the bound ruler planet sets the rules of operation for whichever planets occupy its territory; when a planet occupies its own bounds it is autonomous, subject only to its own rules. There are several different systems of bounds recorded in the ancient astrological literature. The Greek word is *horion*.

cadent house

The third, sixth, ninth, and twelfth houses. Traditional astrology considers that planets are weak when located in the cadent houses. In Greek, a cadent house is called *apoklima*.

celestial latitude
Measures the distance of a planet north or south of the ecliptic.

celestial longitude
Measures the distance of a planet along the ecliptic.

circumambulation
A term used in traditional timing techniques for advancing a planet around the chart at some fixed rate. Literally meaning "to walk around," this term is used to establish a series of time lords that govern the life for various periods of time, as well as in length-of-life determinations. Circumambulations are similar conceptually to primary directions; the Greek term is *peripatesis*.

combust
When the Sun conjuncts a planet, usually within 5-8 degrees. This is a term used in Medieval astrology to describe a condition that is thought to burn up and weaken the planet's significations.

configuration
A term in traditional astrology that refers to sextile, square, trine and opposition aspects envisioned as planets standing in conformity to the sides of regular polygons. Planets can be configured either by whole sign or by degree.

corruption
The condition of a planet that is corrupted, harmed, or damaged in its capacity to bring forth its positive significations as a result of certain configurations with the malefic planets Mars and Saturn, such as conjunction, square, and opposition, as well as other conditions. Corruption may also be referred to as maltreatment.

decan/face
Sub-division of a sign into three equal portions where each 10-degree *decanate* is ruled by a different planet and influences how a planet that occupies that decan functions. Decans, originally thirty-six star sets associated with a divinity, are the indigenous Egyptian contribution to Hellenistic astrology; they are called faces in Medieval astrology. The Greek word is *dekanos*.

decennial
Timing system used in Hellenistic and Medieval astrology where the life is divided into equal 10-year-9-month intervals, each under the rulership of a certain planet that has governance over the life during that period.

descending node
The point where the plane of the Moon or a planet in its orbital motion crosses the ecliptic from a northerly to southerly direction. Also known as the south node; the Greek term is *katabibazo*, which means "to go down." When referring to the orbit of the Moon, this is also called the south lunar node.

detriment
The condition of a planet that occupies the sign opposite that of its domicile rulership. Generally speaking, a planet in detriment has difficulty bringing forth or sustaining the matters it represents. Aquarius is the detriment of the Sun, Capricorn of the Moon, Sagittarius and Pisces of Mercury, Aries and Scorpio of Venus, Taurus and Libra of Mars, Gemini and Virgo of Jupiter, and Cancer and Leo of Saturn.

direct motion
A planet that is moving in a forward motion, as opposed to retrograde, when a planet is moving in apparent backward motion.

disjunct
See aversion.

dispositor
The planet that rules the sign in which a planet is located and adds its influence to how the planet operates. For example, when Venus is in Cancer, the Moon is the dispositor of Venus since the Moon rules the sign Cancer. In Hellenistic astrology, the dispositor is referred to as the domicile lord.

diurnal chart
A chart in which the Sun is above the horizon, as defined by the Ascendant/Descendant axis. The diurnal sect is composed of the Sun (as sect leader), Jupiter, Saturn, and morning-star Mercury (rises before the Sun).

domicile
The sign in which a planet resides or, in modern terminology, the sign a planet rules. Translation of the Greek word *oikos*. The domicile of the Sun is Leo; the domicile of the Moon is Cancer; the domiciles of Mercury are Gemini and Virgo; the domiciles of Venus are Taurus and Libra; the domiciles of Mars are Aries and Scorpio; the domiciles of Jupiter are Sagittarius and Pisces; the domiciles of Saturn are Capricorn and Aquarius. In traditional astrology, planets are thought to have the greatest power in terms of self-sufficiency when located in their own domiciles.

ecliptic
The apparent path of the Sun as seen from Earth. Sometimes called the zodiacal circle, as this path can be seen against the backdrop of the zodiacal constellations.

electional chart
A chart that is "elected" or deliberately chosen for an auspicious outcome for the initiation of a certain event, such as a surgery, marriage, or business opening.

enclosure
A planet that is hemmed in by other planets on both sides. In Medieval astrology, when a planet was enclosed by two malefics, it was said to be besieged and this was considered an unfortunate condition. A planet can also be enclosed by two benefics, in which case it is thought to be protected.

exaltation
The condition of a planet whose matters of life are raised high, honored, and respected. The Sun is exalted in Aries, the Moon in Taurus, Mercury in Virgo, Venus in Pisces, Mars in Capricorn, Jupiter in Cancer, and Saturn in Libra. The Greek term is *hupsoma*.

fall
The condition of a planet in the sign opposite its exaltation sign. Traditional astrology posits that the matters the planet represents are brought down low, dishonored, and not respected. The Sun is in its fall in Libra, the Moon in Scorpio, Mercury in Pisces, Venus in Virgo, Mars in Cancer, Jupiter in Capricorn, and Saturn in Aries. The Greek term is *tapeinoma*.

gender
A classification of planets and signs in accordance with masculine or feminine energies as active or receptive. Events signified by planets occupying masculine signs are more active and thus come about at an earlier age; events signified by planets in feminine signs move more slowly and thus occur at a later age. Masculine gender signs are Aries, Gemini, Leo, Libra, Sagittarius, and Aquarius; feminine gender signs are Taurus, Cancer, Virgo, Scorpio, Capricorn, and Pisces. Masculine gender planets are the Sun, Mercury, Mars, Jupiter, and Saturn; feminine gender planets are the Moon and Venus.

heliacal rising
When a star or planet first appears in the predawn hours, rising before the Sun in the eastern sky, after its period of invisibility due to its prior conjunction with the Sun.

heliacal setting
When a star or planet can be seen setting on the western horizon just after sunset, right before its period of invisibility due to its forthcoming conjunction with the Sun.

imum coeli
See angle.

inconjunct
See aversion.

joy
A condition in which a planet rejoices and finds delight when located in a particular house. Mercury has its joy in the first house, the Moon in the third, Venus in the fifth, Mars in the sixth, the Sun in the ninth, Jupiter in the eleventh, and Saturn in the twelfth. When a planet is happy, it tends to bring about more favorable outcomes.

line of the horizon
The axis formed by the Ascendant and Descendant depicting the sunrise and sunset points on the horizon.

Lot of Fortune
The kind and amount of accidental good fortune that a person may expect in life. Also known as the Part of Fortune in Medieval and modern astrology. Many traditional astrologers calculate this and other lots differently in diurnal and nocturnal charts by taking the arc from the Sun to the Moon in a diurnal chart or the arc from the Moon to the Sun in a nocturnal chart, in the order of the signs and projecting this arc from the degree of the Ascendant. The Greek term is *kleros tuche*.

lot
The Greek term equivalent to Arabic part.

lunar node
See ascending and descending node.

Lunar Return
A chart that can be set up each month when the Moon returns to the same degree it was at at birth. The chart can be interpreted as a snapshot of the current month's opportunities and challenges.

lunation phase
The phase, or arc of separation, between the Sun and the Moon.

malefic
A planet that is literally a "doer of bad," usually ascribed to Mars and Saturn. The Greek term is *kakopoios*.

modality
Categories that describe signs as cardinal, fixed, and mutable in modern astrology. In traditional astrology, this term is "quadruplicity" and the three categories are called tropical, fixed, and bi-corporeal.

mutual reception
Occurs when two planets receive one another when they occupy each others' domiciles, or signs of rulership, such as the Sun in Scorpio and Mars in Leo. It is thought to give more power to each planet than it would otherwise have.

nadir
The point directly underneath the zenith. The zenith is the point immediately overhead in the sky; the nadir is the lowest point underneath the Earth. Technically, these two points together are referred to as the Pole of the Horizon and should not be confused with the MC and IC degrees, or with the tenth and fourth houses.

nativity
A term used in traditional astrology to refer to a birth chart. From the Latin *natus*, meaning "birth."

nocturnal chart
A chart in which the Sun is below the horizon, defined by the Ascendant/Descendant axis. The nocturnal sect is composed of the Moon as sect leader, Venus, Mars, and evening-star Mercury (Mercury rises after the Sun).

node
See ascending and descending node.

non-precessed Solar Return
A chart calculated each year around the birthday, when the Sun returns to the exact degree and minute that it was at in the birth chart.

north node
See ascending node.

orb
The range of degrees on either side of exactitude. This term is commonly found in discussions of aspects. For instance, a 90-degree square aspect may have an orb of 0 to 8 degrees on either side of 90.

partile apect
An aspect that is exact to the same degree of longitude in each of the planet's respective signs, such as a partile sextile aspect between the Moon at 8 Leo and Venus at 8 Gemini.

phasis
A condition in which a planet makes a helical rising or setting (with an exact 15-degree separation from the Sun) or is making a station, either direct or retrograde. From the word meaning "phase," Hellenistic astrology considers this condition an intensification of the planet's energy.

planetary condition
The evaluation of a planet according to sect, sign, house, aspect, and solar and lunar considerations to determine how effective it is in bringing about its significations and to what extent the outcome of its matters will be favorable or unfavorable.

planetary node
See ascending and descending node.

precessed Solar Return
A chart calculated each year around the time of the birthday, when the Sun passes over the degree of the precessed Sun in the current year, as determined by its position relative to the sidereal rather than tropical zodiac. Because of the Earth's precessional motion, this will be different from the natal degree of the Sun by about 50 seconds of arc for each year of life, and thus will yield a different Ascendant than the non-precessed Solar Return.

precession

A gyrating motion resulting from the ellipsoid shape of the Earth. The effect of this is that the intersection of the vernal equinox point with that of the celestial equator drifts backward through the zodiacal signs at the rate of approximately 50 seconds per year, one degree every 72 years, and a complete cycle in 25,695 years. In recent literature, this phenomenon has been discussed in terms of the precession of the equinoxes and historical ages, such as the Age of Aquarius put forth in a popular song.

pre-natal lunation

The New Moon or Full Moon seen previous to birth. The degree of this lunation remains as a sensitive point throughout the life.

primary directions

A symbolic timing system used to investigate future events where planets are moved ahead to the exact aspects made to other planets or angles based on the measure of right Ascension as the amount of time it takes for one degree to pass across the Midheaven.

profection

See annual profections.

progressions

A symbolic timing procedure of directions used in both traditional and modern astrology. In secondary progressions, the positions of the planets and nodes are moved forward from birth at the rate of one day for one year and then compared to the natal positions of the planets and angles. In tertiary progressions, planets and nodes are moved forward at the rate of one day for one month, and then compared to the natal positions of the planets and angles.

progressed lunation cycle

The cycle of the progressed Moon relative to that of the progressed Sun, which has a period of approximately 30 years.

reception

A relationship between two planets in which a planet that occupies a sign it does not rule is received by the planet that is the ruler (or domicile lord) of that sign. For example, Mercury in Scorpio is received by Mars, the traditional ruler of Scorpio. Also see mutual reception.

rejoicing conditions

Conditions that increase the happiness of a planet. When a planet occupies the house of its joy, it takes delight in the matters of that house. There are also several rejoicing conditions according to sect status that contribute to more favorable planetary outcomes: a planet being located in the preferred hemisphere (diurnal hemisphere for diurnal planets and nocturnal hemisphere for nocturnal planets), occupying the preferred sign (diurnal signs for diurnal planets and nocturnal signs for nocturnal planets), and a planet's rising relative to the Sun (diurnal planets rising before the Sun and nocturnal planets rising after the Sun).

relocated return

A solar, lunar, or planetary return chart in which the latitude and longitude coordinates of the geographical location at the time of the return are used to calculate the chart instead of the coordinates of the birth location.

retrograde motion/retrogression

A planet's apparent backward motion along the zodiacal path as seen in the sky. Since retrograde planets move extremely slowly, this was seen by traditional astrologers as a weakening of a planet's energy and hence its significations.

rising sign

See Ascendant.

Sabian symbol

Symbolic images given to each of the 360 degrees of the zodiac. While there is a tradition of planetary rulers for each single degree, the current Sabian symbols originated through psychic insight in 1925, and have been interpreted by Marc Edmond Jones, Dane Rudhyar, Lynda Hill, and others.

secondary progression

See progressions.

sect

A division of planets into two separate groups or factions in traditional astrology. The diurnal sect includes the Sun, Jupiter, and Saturn; the nocturnal sect includes the Moon, Venus, and Mars. Mercury can belong to either sect, depending on whether it rises before or after the Sun. Planets that belong to the favored sect are more likely to act on behalf of the individual's best interests. The Greek term is *hairesis*.

sidereal zodiac
A zodiac based on the fixed stars of the zodiacal constellations.

significator
A planet's association with certain people, things, and events. General significators are associated with fixed topics; particular significators are associated with the topics of the house a planet rules and can vary from one chart to another. For example, Mercury is a general significator of students, books, and business transactions in every chart, as well the particular significator of the topics associated with whatever houses are occupied by the signs Gemini and Virgo.

Solar Return
A chart cast every year around the birthday, when the Sun returns to its natal position that provides a view of the coming year. In traditional astrology, the term Solar Revolution is sometimes used instead.

solar-arc directions
A symbolic timing procedure used in traditional and modern astrology in which all the planets are advanced at the same rate as the Sun's motion, where one day is equated to one year.

solar-phase cycle
Depicts the cycle of a planet relative to the Sun and the critical points in that cycle in terms of a planet's visibility, heliacal rising and setting, speed, and direction of motion. Also called the synodic cycle.

south node
See descending node.

station
The stationary position of a planet that lasts for several days as it changes from direct to retrograde or retrograde to direct motion.

succedent house
The second, fifth, eighth, and eleventh houses. Traditional astrology holds that planets have moderate strength when located in the succedent houses. In Greek, a succedent house is called an *epanaphora*.

synastry
The comparison of the charts of two or more people or events to assess compatibility and outcome.

synodic cycle
See solar-phase cycle.

tertiary progression
See progressions.

time lord
The planet that governs the affairs of the life for a certain period of time, as established by various time-lord procedures. Whatever the planet represents in the natal chart, for better or worse, is more likely to eventuate when it is a time lord.

transit
A timing system that looks at the current zodiacal positions of the planets relative to the natal chart.

trigon/triplicity
A category of zodiacal signs based on triangular relationships. Known as triplicities in Medieval astrology, they were originally associated with the winds from the four cardinal directions rather than the four elements of fire, earth, air, and water. The trigons are composed of the signs Aries, Leo, and Sagittarius; Taurus, Virgo, and Capricorn; Gemini, Libra, and Aquarius; Cancer, Scorpio, and Pisces. In traditional astrology, trigons provide another system of rulerships for planets in which each trigon has a diurnal lord, a nocturnal lord, and a participating lord. There are some variants in the assignment of planetary rulers to trigon groupings.

tropical zodiac
A seasonal zodiac based on the Sun's apparent path north and south of the equator, as demarcated by the equinoxes and solstices, which define the first degrees of the signs Aries, Cancer, Libra, and Capricorn.

under the Sun's beams (USB)
A planet within a standardized distance of 15 degrees either before or after the Sun. In this position, the planet is obscured by the Sun's glare and said to be "under the Sun's beams." In traditional astrology, this was considered to weaken the planet's significations unless the planet was "in its chariot" —in its own domicile, exaltation, or bound. This is similar to the Medieval term "combustion."

void-of-course

A modern term generally used in connection with the Moon. The Moon is said to be void-of-course during the interval between its last aspect in a sign until it enters the next sign. The Hellenistic definition extends this period to the Moon making no applying aspect to a planet for a day and a night, which is 13 degrees; some authors specify 30 degrees. In the traditional definition, the range of the Moon's application extends across sign boundaries, and is a much rarer condition than the modern specification.

Whole Sign house system

The house system of choice in Hellenistic and early Arabic astrology, in which signs are co-incident with houses. Each house contains all 30 degrees of one and only one sign.

zodiacal releasing

A time-lord system generated by a sequence of signs and their planetary rulers that is based on the Lot of Fortune as describing matters connected with the body and material affairs and the Lot of Spirit as describing matters connected with profession.

About the Author

Demetra George, M.A., looks to classical antiquity for inspiration in her pioneering work in mythic archetypal astrology, ancient techniques and history, and translations from Greek of primary source texts. She is the author of *Astrology For Yourself*, *Asteroid Goddesses*, *Mysteries of the Dark Moon*, *Finding Our Way Through the Dark*, and *Astrology and the Authentic Self*. She lives in Oregon, lectures internationally, leads pilgrimages to the sacred sites in the Greece, Italy, Egypt, and India, and has taught at Kepler College and the University of Oregon. She offers personal astrological consultations and mentors individual students in all levels of astrological education.

Demetra can be reached at demetrageorge725@gmail.com.

And please visit:

www.demetrageorge.com

A Word on the Cover

The cover photo shows the Thomas Jefferson Memorial in Washington, D.C. Jefferson (1743–1826) was the primary author of the Declaration of Independence, the third U.S. President, and the founder of the University of Virginia.

The memorial's shape resembles the dome of heaven and has been compared to a celestial observatory. Designed by John Russell Pope in 1925, it is an adaptation of the Neoclassical architectural style favored by Jefferson. The memorial is patterned after the Roman Pantheon, the basis for Jefferson's design for the Rotunda at the University of Virginia.

The Pantheon itself was built on architectural principles inherited from Greece. It is said to have been dedicated to every god and was surrounded by the statues of a variety of deities. It stands on the site of an earlier building commissioned by Marcus Agrippa during the reign of Augustus (27BC–14AD). The present structure was completed by Emperor Hadrian around 126 AD.